THE POETRY OF MARRIAGE

By the same author:

High Wedlock Then Be Honoured—An Anthology of Epithalamia
The Viking Press, Inc.

Grammar As Style
Holt, Rinehart and Winston, Inc.

University of Southern California
Studies in Comparative Literature
VOLUME II

THE POETRY OF MARRIAGE

The Epithalamium in Europe and Its Development in England

Virginia Tufte

Tinnon-Brown, Inc., *Book Publishers*
10835 Santa Monica Boulevard   Los Angeles, California 90025

SBN Number: 87252-012-9
LC Number: 68-28173

European distribution through Feffer and Simons, Inc., 31 Union Square, New York, New York 10003

Acknowledgments

In the notes to each chapter, I have indicated many specific debts to contemporary and earlier scholarship, but I wish to acknowledge here a more general debt to four works: Robert H. Case's volume in the Bodley Anthologies, *English Epithalamies* (A. C. McClurg & Co., Chicago; John Lane, London, 1896); James A. S. McPeek's volume in the Harvard Studies in Comparative Literature, *Catullus in Strange and Distant Britain* (Harvard University Press, Cambridge; Humphrey Milford, Oxford University Press, London, 1939); Cortlandt Van Winkle's edition of *Epithalamion* by Edmund Spenser (F. S. Crofts & Co., New York, 1926), and E. Faye Wilson's unpublished dissertation, "A Study of the Epithalamium in the Middle Ages: An Introduction to the Epithalamium beate Marie virginis of John of Garland" (University of California, Berkeley, 1930).

Chronologically, my first debt is to Professor Ralph Cohen of the University of Virginia, who more than ten years ago suggested that I should write this book. I am grateful also to Professors H. T. Swedenberg, Jr., James E. Phillips, Jr., and John Espey, all of the University of California, Los Angeles, for their comments on an early draft of the manuscript, and to Professors Charles Speroni and Philip Levine, also of UCLA, and Jay Hubert, University of California, Irvine, for suggestions on several chapters. Although these gentlemen are responsible for many improvements in the manuscript, they have not read the final draft and are free of blame for its deficiencies.

For her translation of extracts from Euripides' *The Trojan Women,* I am grateful to my friend, Poet-Professor Ann Stanford of California State College, San Fernando Valley. Talking over some of the poems with her has been greatly to my pleasure and profit. I have welcomed also the chance to discuss some of the poems with Professor Cécile Schreiber of the University of California, Santa Cruz; with Birgitta Wohl and Paola Velli, and with several of my colleagues at the University of Southern California, especially Professor Mary Mahl.

Over the years I have benefited from the gracious attention and interest of the director and the staff of the William Andrews Clark Memorial Library. I wish to thank especially Lawrence Clark Powell, William Conway, Edna Davis, and Elizabeth Angelico. I have appreciated also the help of librarians at the Huntington, Folger, Bodleian, British Museum, and Cambridge University libraries.

For their perceptive editing, my thanks go to Jean Wilkinson and Margaret Flanders, and, for her careful proofreading, to Marla Knutsen.

Permissions to reprint extracts from poems have been granted as follows: Ella Isabel Harris, translation of Seneca's *Medea,* from *An Anthology of Roman Drama,* edited by Philip Harsh. Copyright © by Holt, Rinehart and Winston, Inc. Reprinted by permission of Holt, Rinehart and Winston, Inc. Edith Sitwell, "Prothalamium." Reprinted by permission of the publisher, The Vanguard Press, from *Music and Ceremonies* by Edith Sitwell. Copyright © 1959, 1962, 1963, by Dame Edith Sitwell.

The ornament from Edmund Spenser's *Prothalamion* (1596) is reproduced with permission from the Henry E. Huntington Library.

I wish to acknowledge financial aid from the Clark Library, where I held the Clark Fellowship in 1963–64, from the Bing Fund, and from the Research and Publication Fund, University of Southern California.

V. J. T.

Los Angeles, California
August, 1969

Contents

Wedding is great Juno's crown,
   O blessed bond of board and bed.
'Tis Hymen peoples every town,
   High wedlock, then, be honoured.
Honour, high honour, and renown,
To Hymen, god of every town.

—Shakespeare, *As You Like It*

Introduction

Only one wedding poem has attracted a wide audience, and that is Edmund Spenser's *Epithalamion,* written for his own marriage in 1594. Hundreds of other epithalamia exist but have received little notice, and neither general readers nor literary scholars, for the most part, have given much attention to the long and pervasive tradition of nuptial poetry. The tradition goes back to Biblical and classical times, to the Psalms and the Song of Solomon, to Sappho, Theocritus, and Catullus, and it has been kept alive even in our own time by Edith Sitwell, Robert Graves, and W. H. Auden, by Gertrude Stein, C. S. Lewis, and James Joyce, and by the college students who write poems and songs—tender, grave, sometimes ironic or even bitter—and recite or sing them at the weddings of their friends.

It was in the Renaissance that this literary tradition flowered and brought forth literally thousands of varied works, many by major authors—Sidney, Shakespeare, Jonson, Donne, and Milton among them. It is on these epithalamia of the English Renaissance that this book is centered; however, more than half of the book concerns the roots from which the English genre sprang—classical Greek and Latin, early Hebrew, medieval Latin, and later Italian and French. Epithalamia of those times and places are of interest in the twentieth century, it seems to me, because some of them still give pleasure as works of literary art, or as curiosities, but also because certain basic themes persist and continue to have relevance. Epithalamia are of interest, too, because their themes and conventions play an important metaphorical role in other literature, especially in drama, a role I have tried to point up in this book's critical survey of marriage poetry through the centuries.

After reading hundreds of epithalamia and trying to distill their essence into the pages of this book, I have like many another writer gone to Shakespeare for an epigraph. The epithalamium in the final scene of *As You Like It* celebrates not one but four marriages and characterizes wedlock as a "blessed bond of board and bed." With its blend of solemnity and gentle jesting, and its emphasis on procreation as a principal function of marriage—" 'Tis Hymen peoples every town"—the song epitomizes several of the genre's main themes. Its argument and that of the English nuptial poem generally is that marriage, sanctioned by God and man, is a worthy institution offering fulfillment for womankind in particular, physical comforts for both man and wife, and perpetuation of the family as keystone of an orderly society. Besides coupling four pairs of lovers, the epithalamium in *As You Like It* suggests the prospect of harmony and good fortune in the community, now that the protagonists are "at one together." Confusion has been conquered by orderly union. Such symbolic use of the epithalamium in Renaissance drama and masque is a recurrence of a device seen as early as Aristophanes' comedies, the *Peace* and the *Birds,* both of which conclude with epithalamia.

It is from the Greek that the word *epithalamium* comes, and the earliest surviving poems are Greek—a few fragments from Sappho's works, Aristophanes' two songs, and Theocritus's Eighteenth Idyll. Literally the word means "at the nuptial chamber" (*thalamos*), and initially it probably designated a particular kind of song sung at the door, or at the nuptial couch itself, just before consummation of the union. By the time of Catullus, greatest of the Latin epithalamists, European poets had begun to call almost any kind of wedding song or poem an epithalamium, and before long they applied the term to certain types of poetry and prose which dealt with subjects unrelated to marriage except in a metaphorical way. This book views the nuptial poem as the heart of the genre but touches on a number of works included in the term's broader application.

European poets wrote thousands of epithalamia in a dozen languages and countries before the genre gradually wore itself out in the late seventeenth and early eighteenth centuries and eventually almost disappeared. It is no accident that the form attained its greatest perfection in English in the last quarter of the sixteenth and first half of the seventeenth centuries, for by its very nature the epithalamium lends itself to the synthesis of classical and Christian concepts in which Renaissance authors delighted and excelled. Most epithalamia are shaped in their principal features by literary heredity rather than by social environment; one might even argue that Spenser in his masterpiece owes greater debt to half a hundred literary forebears— Hebrew, Greek, Latin, Italian, French, and Spanish—than to the immediate circumstances of his own wedding.

It was only natural that Spenser's *Epithalamion,* published in 1595, and Sidney's short pastoral epithalamium in the popular *Arcadia,* published in 1593,[1] should help to inspire dozens of other poets, major and minor, to write epithalamia during the next few decades. John Donne, George Chapman, and Ben Jonson each wrote three; Robert Herrick wrote five; and the poets who wrote at least one include Thomas Campion, Francis Beaumont, John Fletcher, Thomas Heywood, Henry Peacham, George Wither, Christopher Brooke, Michael Drayton, Phineas Fletcher,

Francis Quarles, William Cartwright, Thomas Randolph, James
Shirley, Henry Vaughan, Richard Crashaw, Sir William D'aven-
ant, and John Dryden. Even James I once tried his hand; a
fragmentary wedding masque containing an epithalamium, one
of his youthful poetic efforts, survives in two manuscripts.[2]

During this period the epithalamium appears as either
poetry or prose, and as a separate entity or an inserted device
in an assortment of literary genres—drama, epic, erotic epyllion, allegorical mythological poem, psychological treatise, devotional treatise, sermon, emblem book, textbook, and historical-
geographical narrative. Shakespeare includes the form not only in
As You Like It but in *A Midsummer Night's Dream, Romeo
and Juliet,* and *The Tempest;* many other dramatists, some already named, composed epithalamia as parts of tragedies, comedies, and masques. And Spenser and Milton include epithalamia in the two great epics of the age.[3] Among others who use
the device are Chapman in his continuation of *Hero and Leander*
and his *Andromeda Liberata*; Samuel Sheppard in the prose pastoral romance, *The Loves of Amandus and Sophronia*; Robert
Burton in *Anatomy of Melancholy*; Joshua Poole in a textbook
on poetry writing, *The English Parnassus*; Camden in *Britannia*;
and Drayton in *Poly-Olbion*.

Large collections of epithalamia were assembled for English
royal weddings of the seventeenth century, most of them composed in Latin, but some in other languages—Greek, Hebrew,
Italian, French, Spanish, Arabic—and after mid-century a few in
English.[4] Oxford University's 1613 collection honoring the marriage of Princess Elizabeth, daughter of James I, to Frederick,
Count Palatine of the Rhine, included 230 epithalamia, many in
Latin but some in Greek, Italian, and Hebrew. In 1625, for the
marriage of Charles I and Henrietta Maria, Oxford published
129 in Latin and a number in Greek, Hebrew, and French. For
the same occasion Cambridge published ninety-one epithalamia in
Latin, and nine which were all or part in Greek. In 1662, for the
marriage of Charles II and Catherine of Braganza, Cambridge
provided seventy-five poems in Latin, Greek, Italian, and Spanish. The Oxford collection for this occasion numbered more than

a hundred; and along with poems in Latin, Greek, Hebrew, and Arabic, there were sixteen in English, including a tribute to the bride by the printer who had set type for the book.

The celebration of royal weddings has been one of the functions of the literary epithalamium throughout its history. But during the Middle Ages the epithalamium became a device to celebrate "high wedlock" in a special sense, when the Canticle of Solomon and the 45th Psalm, probably written to honor human marriages, were interpreted allegorically by churchmen as representing mystical marriages—Christ and the Church, Christ and the Virgin Mary, or Christ and the human soul. As a result, the epithalamium in the Middle Ages became a Christian devotional poem, retaining many of the conventions of the pagan nuptial poem. Hundreds of Latin hymns called epithalamia were written as tributes to the Virgin Mary or to various saints, or to celebrate such occasions as the birth of a child, the dedication of a church, or the taking of vows by a nun. Many medieval epithalamia became exaltations of virginity rather than marriage. The ascetic epithalamium did not crowd out the pagan nuptial poem, however, and both classical and Christian works exerted their influence in Italy, France, and England. Topographical, patriotic, and historical poems also made their way into the genre.

In Part One of this book I have tried to identify some of the principal streams among the thousands of classical, Christian, neo-Latin, and vernacular forerunners of the English genre, and in Part Two to place some of the more interesting English works against this background. I have commented on a few works which have had no previous attention, but I have also tried to reassess the more important English epithalamia—especially those of Spenser, Chapman, Jonson, and Donne—in relation to the motifs and critical theories displayed in Part One. In addition, I have sought throughout to bring into focus the assorted themes of the epithalamic tradition. What are the concepts that unite certain wedding songs, orations, devotional treatises, hymns to the Virgin, works in praise of virginity, nativity poems, and historical, geographical, and patriotic poems in one genre? What is it that makes a literary work an epithalamium?

No effort is made here to trace sources and conventions poem by poem. A good deal of such work has been done by German scholars studying the English genre, by English and American scholars particularly interested in Catullus and other Latin poets, and by those whose special interest is Spenser.[5] Efforts to identify specific sources tend to break down, however, because almost any epithalamic motif has appeared in various forms in many works. Throughout the book I have concentrated on the literary rather than the social context of the epithalamium, although on occasion I have noted contemporary events, customs, and modes of thought which are pertinent.

The explorer of the epithalamium is fortunate, for a certain grace resides in the subject matter itself, a point noted nearly twenty centuries ago by the literary critic known as Demetrius, writing on the subject of style:

> Grace may reside in the subject matter, if it is the gardens of the Nymphs, marriage-lays, love-stories, or the poetry of Sappho generally. Such themes, even in the mouth of a Hipponax, possess grace, the subject-matter having a winsomeness of its own. No one would think of singing a bridal song in an angry mood; no contortions of style can change Love into a Fury or a Giant, or transmute laughter into tears.[6]

Part One
THE TRADITION

I

The Greeks: Sappho, Aristophanes, Theocritus, and The Beginnings of Pastoral

A few fragments of Sappho's works, along with commentaries, examples, and imitations by rhetoricians and poets who lived a few centuries after her, provide evidence that Sappho was author of a book of epithalamia and that her poems of this kind were widely admired. But it would appear that long before Sappho's time folk songs were commonly associated with the marriage ritual and customs. The *Iliad* mentions bridal songs as part of a wedding celebration in one of the cities pictured on Achilles' shield, and describes the ritual feasting, the leading forth of the brides for the procession, the torches, the choruses of young men and women, and the admiring matrons. George Chapman's translation (1616) was written in a period when similar descriptions had become conventional in English nuptial poetry; indeed some of the customs themselves still prevailed:

> Two cities in the spacious field, he built with
> goodly state
> Of divers-languag'd men: the one did nuptials
> celebrate
> Observing at them, solemne feasts: the Brides from
> forth their bowres
> With torches, ushered through the streetes: a world
> of Paramours
> Excited by them; youths and maides, in lovely
> circles danc't:
> To whom the merry Pipe and Harpe, the spritefull
> Sounds advanc't,
> The matrons standing in their dores admiring. . . .[1]

Also, in the *Iliad* Hera reminds the gods that they had attended the wedding of Peleus and Thetis, parents of Achilles, and that among them was Apollo with his lyre in hand. Pindar knew a version of the tale in which Apollo was present with his lyre but the wedding song was sung by the Muses, the famous "learned sisters" whom Edmund Spenser was later to summon in the opening lines of his *Epithalamion*.[2] Hesiod, father of Greek didactic poetry (probably eighth century B.C.), is credited with an epithalamium on the wedding of Peleus and Thetis; in addition, *The Shield of Heracles,* attributed to Hesiod, describes the hero's shield in much the same fashion as the *Iliad* does, depicting a wedding celebration which suggests that alternate songs may have been sung by several groups.[3] In this procession the bride is riding in a car, a vehicle which became popular with epithalamists to transport not only brides but also the goddess Venus in her journeys to weddings.

Epithalamia may have been written by a number of the very earliest Greek lyric poets. Alcman (*c.* 650 B.C.) was still known for his marriage songs after some three centuries, for he is described in a poem by Leonidas of Tarentum (*c.* 300 B.C.) as "a singer of marriage."[4] The poet known as Stesichorus, born about 632 B.C., whose reputation and influence apparently were very great in his own time, is believed to have written an epithalamium in his *Helen,* from which Theocritus later borrowed in his Idyll 18, the epithalamium for Helen and Menelaus. C. M. Bowra quotes a three-line fragment from Stesichorus which appears to have come from a narrative poem describing the wedding of Helen and Menelaus. The scene was apparently the bridal procession:

> Many Cydonian quinces they cast on the chariot of the prince, and many leaves of myrtle, and crowns of roses, and twisted wreaths of violets.[5]

But the earliest surviving lines which may be identified as coming from epithalamia are the brief fragments from Sappho's poems, probably written near the end of the seventh century B.C., and collected into one book, possibly the ninth, by her Alexandrian editors. About a dozen and a half fragments have been assigned to the epithalamia. Also attributed to Sappho is a fragment on the marriage of Hector and Andromache from a third-century papyrus, which describes a scene as joyous as that on the shields in Homer and Hesiod, with the maidens singing a holy song and the men shouting a hymn of thanksgiving and praising the god-like Hector and Andromache.[6] This fragment begins with a herald announcing the good news of the approaching marriage and praising the bride's beauty and the rich gifts. There follows a description of the procession, with the throng of women, dainty-ankled maidens, and men riding in wheeled cars and chariots. To the heavens rise the clouds of the singing and rejoicing, as the celebrants mix festal bowls and cups, and revel in the fragrance of myrrh, cassia, and frankincense.

The festive mood of such wedding celebrations shines in the bits and pieces of Sapphic epithalamia, and there is evidence, mainly provided by the rhetoricians, that Sappho at times cast herself as a kind of master of ceremonies directing the celebration, a role which many later epithalamists assumed. From the fragments, it seems that Sappho anticipated other epithalamists in the following themes: (1) summoning both human and divine participants; (2) recounting the proceedings, including the wished-for arrival of the evening star; (3) praising bride and bridegroom with similes from nature and comparisons to mythological beings; (4) commenting on the bride's modesty and fears, and urging her to come forth; (5) engaging in good-natured banter directed at the bridegroom and others; (6) describing the preparation of the nuptial chamber and the role of Aphrodite, the Graces, and the Loves; (7) urging the consummation and offering advice to the couple; (8) congratulating the pair on their good fortune and wishing for future blessings; and (9) bidding farewell to the couple and urging the departure of the singers.

In one of the most famous of the Sapphic fragments, the maiden is compared to a sweet apple which cannot be reached by those who would gather it too soon but is permitted in all its blushing beauty to him who waits until the appropriate season. Almost equally popular with later poets is Sappho's comparison of the girl to the trampled flower whose crumpled beauty adorns the earth. Other fragments liken the bridegroom to a slender sapling, and an unidentified person to a vine clinging to a tree. Sappho's comparison of the bridegroom to Ares, god of war, occurs in a fragment made famous by J. D. Salinger's title, "Raise High the Roof-beam, Carpenters." These lines, I believe, not only refer to the bridegroom's height and mien but also suggest that the festive nature of the occasion is so great that the room is simply not large enough to contain the celebration:

> Raise high the roof-beam, carpenters,
> Hymenaeus!
> Like Ares comes the bridegroom,
> Hymenaeus!
> Taller far than a tall man,
> Hymenaeus![7]

Very different in tone are the Sapphic fragments which bespeak the bride's modesty, hesitation, and reluctance to give up her maidenhood. When she is called to come forth to join her bridegroom, her desires for love are acknowledged and her beauty is praised as befitting the goddess of Love. However, not all is praise and elevation. Demetrius remarks on Sappho's artistry in changing from a singing to a prosaic style in lines mocking the bridegroom and the doorkeeper of the wedding chamber.[8] We do not have Sappho's lines teasing the bridegroom, but we may presume that they were good-humored. Certainly intended to be playful were the lines, preserved in Hephaestion's *Handbook of Metre,* about the doorkeeper whose feet were seven fathoms long, and whose sandals took five bull's hides to the pair, and ten shoemakers to make.

A second-century papyrus provides a fragment which may pertain to the chorus of maidens who spend the night at the door of the nuptial chamber, singing of the love between the thrice-happy bridegroom and a bride as sweet as violets. The maidens are told to leave when dawn comes. Hephaestion and other writers quote a line from Sappho which appears to be an exclamation of farewell by the poet, possibly to the bride and bridegroom.[9]

From the fragments it is apparent that Sappho's epithalamia were not limited to songs sung at the door of the nuptial chamber. Bowra emphasizes that we must not press too strongly for the precise implications of the word *epithalamion*, "which strictly stands for songs at one stage only of the proceedings," but that we must give a liberal interpretation to *epithalamia,* as wedding songs in all their range.[10] Bowra describes three stages in Greek wedding rites, which appear to provide background for Sappho's epithalamia. The proceedings began with a feast, usually at the home of the bride's family, and with sacrifices to the gods of marriage. The feast may have been rather formal—"solemne" is the word Chapman used in his translation of the *Iliad*—with the bride veiled and sitting alone until she was called to be presented by her friends and relatives to the bridegroom. Then followed the second stage, a procession to the bride's new home, such as that described by Homer and Hesiod, the *hymeneal* proper being sung at this stage with its refrain to the marriage-god sung or shouted. With torches lighting the way as evening advanced, the couple and guests arrived at the bridal chamber, and at this third stage was sung the song originally designated as the *epithalamion*. Mockery, possibly something like the later *fescennina iocatio* of Roman epithalamia, was mixed with praise for both bride and groom and was followed by congratulation.

Like Bowra, Kurt Wöhrmann has predicated, from the Sapphic fragments, the existence of songs for various stages of the rites, among them songs to greet the evening star, songs arguing the value of virginity, songs developing from a hymeneal shout to a cletic hymn honoring the marriage-god, songs praising the bride, and songs sung in front of the actual *thalamos*.[11]

Aristophanes

John Addington Symonds suggests that "in order to form a remote conception of what a Sapphic marriage chorus might have been" one should study later poems which he believes are imitations of Sappho's style—in particular, Aristophanes' epithalamium in the *Birds,* Theocritus's Idyll 18, and the three marriage poems of Catullus.[12] Whether or not Aristophanes' poem is an imitation of Sappho, it is one of his two important contributions to the epithalamic tradition, both being found at the ends of comedies, one in the *Birds,* and the other in the *Peace.* Instead of the tender comparisons and gentle mockery seen in the Sapphic fragments, these songs offer robust celebration of marriages which symbolize the hope for unity and peace in the nation.

Critics have disagreed, however, on the tone and intent of these songs. Fordyce describes both epithalamia as "burlesque"; Bowra characterizes that of the *Peace* as "frank and even bawdy" and the one in the *Birds* as having "an exalted gaiety as befits Zeus and Hera whom it celebrates"; and J. Hookham Frere believes that the epithalamium in the *Peace* is a rustic one, not very different from the rustic extempore poetry of modern Greece.[13] The poem in the *Birds* he sees as "a Town Epithalamium, such as we may suppose to have been composed and perpetrated in honor of the nuptials of the more noble and wealthy families of Athens." Frere believes that the vulgar town poet is eager to exhibit his education by imitating and borrowing passages from the most approved lyrical poets, but that he reduces their imagery and expressions to the natural level of his own dullness, thus bringing about in the verse a strange balance of the ludicrous and the sublime.

Certainly the poem at the end of the *Birds* is extravagant, but playful rather than ludicrous or burlesque, I think, in its demonstration of epithalamic conventions. In what was probably almost characteristic fashion, it praises the splendor of bridegroom and bride, invokes the heavenly Muse, welcomes and congratulates the couple, compares the wedding to that of Zeus and Hera, summons Hymen in a refrain which was probably already conventional, and ends with joyous praise of the gods.

From the realm of the gods in the *Birds* epithalamium, we descend to barley fields and fig groves in the wedding hymn in the *Peace*—Norwood calls it "jovial"[14]—for the marriage of the countryman Trygaios, and Opora, one of the attendants of the goddess Peace. Messengers are sent to bring out the bride and to get torches; all the people are asked to join in the rejoicing and dancing. Prayers are made to the gods that the people may produce abundant barley, wine, and figs; that there will be no war; that the wives may bear children. The guests are reminded, too, that after the festivity the farm implements must be carried back to the fields. The bride appears; the groom joins her and says he will take her into the fields with him and consummate the marriage. The chorus calls him thrice-happy. Repeatedly the chorus sings the hymeneal refrain, and there is some phallic humor, ending with an invitation by the bridegroom to all to eat their fill of the bridecakes. The nuptial song begins as the chorus send some of their number to fetch the bride (whose name has been translated as "Fruit" and "Harvest-home"), last seen in the play as she was going to her bridal bath.

The most significant conventions to be noted in this poem are the earthy humor stemming perhaps from the fertility rites which gave origin to comedy, and the almost ritualistic use of marriage and the epithalamium as symbols of prosperity, increase, and peace, a convention in which Aristophanes anticipates Renaissance writers of comedies and masques. The rustic setting of the *Peace* epithalamium provides a hint of the pastoral elements to follow in later epithalamia, especially in France and England.

Theocritus

With Idyll 18 of Theocritus begins the association of epithalamia with the pastoral tradition. Theocritus brings into the epithalamium also a variety of humor somewhat more delicate than Sappho's taunts at the big-footed doorkeeper of the nuptial chamber or Aristophanes' elevated extravagance and rustic bawdiness. One of the most popular epithalamia with English translators, it is a narrative poem for the marriage of legendary characters, Helen and Menelaus, and is believed to imitate lost passages from both Stesichorus and Sappho.[15] The argument of Theocritus 18 is briefly expressed by its first English translator, an anonymous poet whose *Sixe Idillia* from Theocritus were published at Oxford in 1588, a time when Theocritus was little known in England:

> Twelve noble Spartan Virgins are brought in singing in the evening, at the chamber door of Menelaus and Helena on their Wedding Day. At first they prettily jest with the Bridegroom, then they praise Helena, last they wish them both joy of their marriage. Therefore, this Idyllion is entitled Helen's *Epithalamion,* that is, "Helen's Wedding Song."[16]

The dozen Spartan virgins are Helen's friends, all from Sparta's first families. Young and fair, their hair adorned with fresh flowers, they dance and sing at the door of the newly-painted wedding chamber in the palace of Menelaus. They tease the bridegroom: "Why do you want to go to bed so early? Are you sleepy because you've had too much wine? If you're so fond of sleep, you should have slept some other time, and alone, and let Helen stay a while longer with her mother and in the company of her friends. After all, for all the years to come, Helen will be yours." The maidens then praise the bridegroom in his happiness and good fortune, teasing him with the suggestion that some good spirit must have sneezed on him to bring such good luck. They tell him how lucky he is to have beneath a coverlet with him the daughter of Zeus, so fair a lady that no other Grecian woman can compare with her. Surely it will be a wonderful child that she bears, if it be like the mother.

In the two epithalamia of Aristophanes, attention is focused on the bridegroom. In Theocritus, although the bridegroom receives attention at the beginning and end of the poem, praise centers in the bride. The chorus of maidens insist they know of Helen's faultless beauty, for they are of like age with her, have run the same race, and have been anointed with her at the baths of Eurotas. Of all the four times sixty girls, Helen is most fair.

The comparisons which illustrate the beauty of Helen are ingenious. She shines among her friends like the rising dawn as it lightens the darkness of sacred night; like the bright spring as winter relaxes its hold; like the crops that spring from the rich plowland; like the cypress tree tall in the garden; like a horse of Thessalian breed which enhances its chariot: even so is rosy-red Helen the glory of Lacedaemon. Helen's skills equal her beauty, the maidens declare. No one matches her in spinning or weaving, or in playing the lyre and rendering hymns to Artemis and Athena. Now that the maid has been made a matron, her friends will miss her, they say, and they use a pastoral comparison to describe the tender affection with which they will remember her, "like youngling lambs that miss the teats of the mother-ewe." In her honor, the girls will gather flowers and will twine a wreath and hang it on a shadowy plane tree. And on the bark of the tree, they will engrave a message that the passerby may read:

WORSHIP ME, I AM THE TREE OF HELEN.

At last the virgins bid farewell to the bride and bridegroom, and ask that Leto bless them with children, that Cypris grant them mutual love, and that Zeus give them prosperity to be handed down to their noble progeny. The maidens conclude their song by urging the couple to sleep, "Breathing love and desire each into the other's breast." But they warn the couple to wake with the dawn, for the chorus plans to return when the earliest cock crows. *Hymen, o Hymenaee,* rings the refrain.[17]

The importance of Theocritus 18 in the tradition lies not so much in its particular conventions as in the fact that it establishes the epithalamium in the pastoral tradition. As this study proceeds, I will advance the epithalamium's claim as a division of the pastoral, along with the elegy, complaint, and singing match. That it has not been generally identified as such may stem from the declarations of the critics who thought certain subjects not appropriate for pastoral. Creech's 1684 translation of Theocritus is preceded by a translation of Rapin's *Discourse of Pastorals,* and one paragraph serves to summarize the attitude of several critics:

> But as for these matters which neither really are, nor are so wrought as to seem the actions of Shepherds, such as in *Moschus's Europa, Theocritus's Epithalamium of Helen,* and *Virgil's Pollio,* to declare my opinion freely, I cannot think them to be fit subjects for Bucolicks: And upon this account I suppose 'tis that Servius in his Comments on Virgil's Bucoliks reckons only seven of Virgil's ten Eclogues, and only ten of Theocritus's thirty to be pure Pastorals, and Salmasius upon Solinus says, that among Theocritus's Poems there are some which you may call what you please Beside Pastorals: and Heinsius in his scholia upon Theocritus will allow but Ten of his Idylliums to be Bucoliks . . . .[18]

Although the subject matter of Theocritus's epithalamium may not seem "the actions of Shepherds," the poem nevertheless embodies several elements of the traditional pastoral, notably the setting, the comparisons to nature, the singing maidens bedecked with garlands, and the reference to the youngling lambs. This Idyll does not, however, introduce the conventional pastoral dialogue which later became a feature of many epithalamia. The earliest example of this I have seen is perhaps contemporary with Theocritus, a poem attributed to Bion but probably the work of one of his imitators.[19] A fragmentary pastoral dialogue relating the tale of Achilles in disguise among the maidens, it was titled by Fawkes, in his translation, "The Epithalamium of Achilles and Deidamia." Two shepherds, Myron and Lycidas, are talking, and Myron encourages his friend to sing of the romance. Lycidas begins his song, but the fragment is brief.

Works of this kind, along with several of Theocritus's Idylls, especially Numbers 18, 7, and 9, appear to have inspired the French pastoral epithalamists of the sixteenth century. (See Chapter VI.) Through adaptations, direct translations, and new poems, the pastoral epithalamium ultimately moved into English, both as an individual poem and as an inserted song in pastoral romances, masques, and plays.

II

Catullus

The most important author in the classical epithalamic tradition, and the most significant to the English genre, is Catullus. Three of his longer carmina—61, 62, and 64—deal with weddings and are called epithalamia in some manuscripts as well as by early editors.[1] The three poems differ greatly, and each is the origin of a stream of conventions which flows through many centuries and countries.

Carmen 61 is a lyric epithalamium of 235 lines written for the marriage of Manlius Torquatus and his bride, called both Junia and Aurunculeia. In it the poet assumes the role of *choragus* or master of ceremonies, directing and commenting on events of the wedding day, somewhat as Sappho appears to have done.[2] The conventions of Carmen 61 are those most frequently imitated by European epithalamists, notably the Pléiade in France and their English successors, but there are relatively few imitations of the poem in its entirety.

Much more frequently imitated or adapted as a unit is the shortest of Catullus's marriage poems, Carmen 62, an amoebaean epithalamium of sixty-six lines, which is a singing contest between a chorus of young men and a chorus of virgins, written in alternate parallel strophes, a form which would seem to be related to the Theocritean singing match between two shepherds.[3] There is no evidence that Carmen 62 was written for a particular wedding.

In contrast with the two lyrics, the third marriage poem is an epyllion of 408 lines. Carmen 64, the longest of all Catullus's works, is often titled in later manuscripts and earlier editions *The Epithalamium of Peleus and Thetis,*[4] and describes the attendance of the gods at the wedding, an event mentioned also in the *Iliad*. Carmen 64 includes a rhetorical epithalamium of fifty-nine lines sung by the Parcae and devoted mainly to the offspring of the marriage, Achilles, and his exploits. But through more than half its length the epyllion is a presentation of a scene embroidered on the coverlet of the nuptial bed of Peleus and Thetis, a scene depicting a union not sanctioned by marriage, the ill-fated affair of Theseus and Ariadne. To conclude the work, an epilogue declares that after the heroic age, men became impious; therefore, the gods no longer appeared in bodily form at the ceremonies of men.

Because of the special importance of these three poems in the tradition, they will be considered here in some detail.

Carmen 61

"Never was there, and never will there be probably, a nuptial song of equal beauty." So wrote Walter Savage Landor of Carmen 61, the epithalamium for Manlius and Junia.[5] Certainly this poem and Spenser's *Epithalamion* are the two greatest works of the epithalamic tradition, and both rank among the lyric masterpieces of all literature.

Like its Greek predecessors, Carmen 61 is a festive poem. It is filled with color and light—the nuptial wreath, the flame-hued wedding veil, the yellow bridal slippers, the golden pine torches, the glossy-leaved myrtle, the hyacinth flower, and the polished door of the wedding chamber. We are told of the radiant eagerness of the bridegroom and the shining countenance of the bride, who is compared to a white daisy and a flame-colored poppy. We feel the day's swift motion as the dancers' feet beat the ground to the rhythm of the wedding song, the boys shake the gleaming torches, and the bride and attendants come forth in procession. We are apprised of the majesty and worth of legal marriage as the poet summons the wedding-god Hymenaeus, son of the Muse Urania, from his home on Mt. Helicon. What god dare match himself with this god? It is Hymen who seizes the tender maid from the arms of her mother and carries her off to the man. It is he who binds the couple in honest love, calls to her home the new mistress of the household, makes possible the joys of nuptial union, and gives children to perpetuate the race and provide guards for the nation's borders. In salute to him, the poet summons the chorus of *integrae virgines*, for whom a like day is coming, and asks them to join in singing the hymn, *O Hymenaee Hymen, o Hymen Hymenaee.*

Virtue is coupled with beauty. The bride is as beautiful as Venus, as delicate as tiny flowering branches of myrtle; and she is good. In her inborn modesty she weeps, and is reluctant, although she feels the promptings of love. The poet urges her to come forth. The bride appears, and the procession moves toward the home where the bridegroom awaits them.

Realistic marital counsel accompanies the ritualistic ribaldry. The poet, refusing to delay any longer, begins the *fescennina iocatio*, the wanton jests believed to ward off the evil to which man is most susceptible in time of good fortune.[6] In one of the Sapphic fragments we noted the taunts directed at the doorkeeper of the nuptial chamber. Here they are directed at the *concubinus* of the bridegroom, and it is the *concubinus* who is told to scatter the nuts customarily thrown during the singing of the *Fescennini*: "da nuces pueris, iners concubine . . . lubet iam servire Talassio, Concubine, nuces da."[7] Addressing the bridegroom, although he is not present, the poet warns that he must now abstain from pursuits which may have been tolerated in a bachelor but are not permitted in a husband. The bride too is counseled on her marital responsibility, being advised not to deny those favors which her husband seeks, lest he go elsewhere to find them. With ceremony proper to the occasion, the *pronubae*, good women who have had but one husband, attend at the placing of the young girl on the *lectus genialis*.[8]

The poet expresses wishes for offspring and the hope that the young child will in appearance resemble his father, in order that the purity of the mother may be attested. The poem concludes with a final injunction to the married couple to live happily and, in the exercise of their marital duty, to employ their vigorous youth.

Carmen 61 is almost a catalogue of scenes, themes, actions, and images for the epithalamic tradition. As Fordyce points out, the poem is clearly not a hymn to be sung on the actual occasion of the marriage, but a fantasy in which the traditional topics of the genre and Hellenistic formulae are combined with the representation of the main features of a Roman wedding.[9] Some of the customary rites of the Roman wedding do not appear and others are altered, but the general pattern of the ceremonies is clear, the poet functioning as *choragus* throughout.[10] The main topics are as follows:

1. *Lines 1–35.* Invocation to Hymen, including descriptions of Hymen and the bride.[11] The poet speaks as if standing before the bride's home, awaiting her coming forth for the procession to the home of the bridegroom. Hymen's costume is like that of a bride. The bride herself is like Venus, a good maiden with a good omen, the latter referring to the taking of auspices as an essential part of a Roman marriage. Here and later in the poem the bride is compared to various flowers and plants.

2. *Lines 36–45.* Exhortation by the *choragus* to the maidens to join in singing praises of Hymen, so that he may come more willingly, the forerunner of honest love.

3. *Lines 46–75.* Hymn in praise of Hymen, with the *choragus* leading the virgins in singing.

4. *Lines 76–120.* Call to the bride to come forth and to dry her tears, letting her inborn modesty not delay her. Come forth and join the procession, she is told, *prodeas nova nupta.* Consolation to the bride by praise of her beauty, praise of the fidelity and virtues of the bridegroom, and praise of the joys of love. Apostrophe to the nuptial couch, "O cubile quod omnibus . . . Candido pede lecti, Quae tuo veniunt ero, Quanta gaudia. . . ."

5. *Lines 120–125.* Coming forth of the bride.

6. *Lines 126–155.* Singing of the fescennine verses on the way to the bridegroom's house, addressed to the former *concubinus* of the bridegroom, to the bridegroom, and the bride. (The bridegroom is not present, however, but is waiting at his home.) The *concubinus* scatters nuts. Marital counsel to the bride and bridegroom.

7. *Lines 156–170.* Arrival at the bridegroom's home and ceremony at the threshold.

8. *Lines 171–180.* The eager bridegroom, reclining at the nuptial feast, awaits his bride.

9. *Lines 181–185.* Escorting of the bride to the wedding chamber.

10. *Lines 186–190.* Placing of the bride on the nuptial couch by the *pronubae.*

11. *Lines 191–205.* Summons to the husband to join the bride. Praise of both. Admonition to avoid delay.

12. *Lines 206–230.* Song before the couch. Number of joys of love compared with the number of grains of sand in Africa and the thousands of twinkling stars. Admonition to consummate the marriage and bring forth children. Description of prospective offspring and wish that they may reflect the noble stock and bring it honor.

13. *Lines 230–235.* Admonition to the virgins to close the door and depart. Final benediction and adjuration of the couple

to live happily and employ their vigorous youth in exercising their marital duty.

In the foregoing summary of topics we see that Catullus has included most of the themes of the Sapphic fragments. For Catullus's successors, Carmen 61 became a handbook of themes and poetic techniques, establishing the characteristic epithalamic point of view—the poet speaking as master of ceremonies. Every strophe in Carmen 61, as Mangelsdorff has noted, is directed at someone—Hymen, the chorus of virgins, the nuptial couch (personified), the youths carrying torches, the *concubinus,* the bridegroom, the bride, the *praetextus,* the *pronubae,* and the bridal couple.[12] The particular sequence of major themes as it appears here became almost a formula: the invocation to Hymen, the appeal for help in singing the nuptial hymn, the hymn itself, and the presentation of the events of the wedding day in chronological order.

The pattern of refrains in Carmen 61 is also of interest for its influence on later works. Catullus repeats a single refrain a number of times, varies it slightly, and introduces additional refrains. Fifteen stanzas end with the ritual cry *Hymen Hymenaee,* which we have seen in the Greek epithalamia, four with a repeated *o* and eleven with *io.* There are three other refrains— *compararier ausit* three times; *concubine, nuces da* twice; and *prodeas, nova nupta* three times. Variations in a single refrain, or use of multiple refrains, came to be characteristic of many English epithalamia, among them poems of Sidney, Spenser, Jonson, Donne, Sir Henry Goodere, Chapman, and Herrick. Catullus's division of his poem into short strophes (each consisting of four glyconics and a pherecratean), the shortness of the lines, and the particular lightness and speed of the rhythm also found many English imitators.[13]

I have already remarked on the poem's images of color, light, and motion. The work is noteworthy too for its nature imagery. Besides comparing the bride and bridegroom to flowers, the poet twice uses the familiar comparison of the couple to the vine entwining the tree. One of the nature comparisons, that of the bride to the branches of myrtle, introduces into the epithalamium the nymphs who are to figure prominently in the genre for many centuries. Here they are wood-nymphs, *hamadryades,* playful creatures who nourish with dewy moisture the tiny flowering branches of myrtle as playthings for themselves. Here too is the nymph Aganippe, personifying the Muses' sacred spring whose water imparts poetic inspiration, ancestor perhaps of the river-nymphs who abound in French epithalamia and also in those of Spenser and many other English poets.[14] Additional mythological figures and geography also contribute to the imagery—Mt. Helicon, Urania, Venus, Paris, the Aonian grottoes of the Thespian rock, Talassius, Telemachus and Penelope.[15]

The prominence of mythological characters and setting is partly responsible in this poem for the fact that the human participants do not emerge strongly as individual personalities. The bride and bridegroom here and in most other epithalamia are almost faceless despite extensive description. The rhetorical and conventional character of the description makes it fit almost any bride and bridegroom; the mythical Hymen is more vivid than the human Manlius and Junia. We do not become as well acquainted with Junia in the epithalamium as we do with the poet's Lesbia in the short lyrics. Thus in Carmen 61 is demonstrated a leading trait of the epithalamium: it is usually not a highly personal poem. Carmen 61 does, nevertheless, come closer to genuine human interest than many of its successors, particularly in its reference to the prospective offspring of the marriage, the infant Torquatus who will stretch forth his tender hands from the lap of his mother and with lips half-open, smile sweetly at his father.

Carmen 62: The Marriage-Versus-Virginity Debate

Carmen 62, the "Vesper adest" or *Chorus of Youths and Virgins,* is second only to Carmen 61 in its influence on succeeding generations of epithalamists. The most characteristic aspects of the poem and the ones most influential on the English tradition are these:

1. The amoebaean form, with a choir of youths and one of maidens engaging in a singing match, responding to each other in alternate symmetrical strophes.

2. The subject matter of the debate: marriage versus virginity.

3. The personification of Hesperus or Vesperus, the evening star, as the patron of marriage, uniter of wedded couples, and enemy of virginity.

4. The pair of nature similes used by the two choruses to describe the unwed virgin: The maidens compare her to a protected flower in an enclosed garden, unknown to cattle, never bruised by the plow, caressed and fostered by gentle breezes as well as by the sun and the rain, desired by everyone until it is deflowered by a sharp fingernail, and then no longer desired by anyone. The young men respond by comparing the unwed virgin to a mateless vine in a vacant field, unable to lift itself up or bring forth fruit, unloved and untended until it is mated with a husband elm in equal marriage, whereupon it is cherished by everyone.

5. The tripartite division of the bride's virginity: The bride is directed not to struggle but to yield to her husband, for her virginity is not all her own—a third belongs to each of her parents. Now that the parents have given her in marriage, they have transferred their rights in her person to their son-in-law, together with the dowry.

Unlike Carmen 61, the poem is not linked to a particular occasion or even a specific locality. Fordyce, Fraenkel, and others see the poem as a fanciful composite picture in which Greek and Roman motifs are combined.[16] The poem announces the time as evening, "vesper adest," the traditional time for weddings in both Greece and Rome. Fordyce suggests that the scene of the opening lines is that of a Greek wedding, with a feast in the bride's father's house, the men and women seated in separate areas. The bride, however, is not present at the feast as she would be at a Greek wedding but, as the poem opens, is expected to arrive. Later she appears, as she would at a Roman wedding, for the *deductio* to her new home.[17]

The young men see the long-awaited evening star, and they rise in expectation of the arrival of the bride (lines 1–4). The girls rise to face them (lines 6–9). The young men say there will be no easy victory for them in the singing match, because their minds have been diverted elsewhere while the young girls have been hard at work preparing for the contest. The singing match begins at line 20, with the girls addressing five lines to the evening star, reproaching him for cruelty: Hesperus, what fire more cruel than yours moves across the sky? For you tear away the daughter from the embrace of the mother and bestow the chaste girl on the ardent young man. What more cruel thing than that do enemies perform when a city is seized?

The young men reply in five lines closely parallel in structure to the preceding lines of the girls: Hesperus, what fire more delightful than yours shines in the sky? For you make firm the marital agreements which have been plighted beforehand but not joined until your flame has presented itself. What god-given thing is there that is more longed-for than the happy hour you bring? A second pair of presumably symmetrical stanzas is marred by the loss of some lines.[18] In a third pair of stanzas, which correspond closely although the girls have nine lines (29–47) and the men ten (49–58), we hear the much-imitated flower and vine similes for the virgin and wife.

The men regard themselves as winners in the match, and they have the last word, addressing a homily to the bride, who apparently has arrived during the singing. They advise her not to strive with her husband but to yield to him in obedience to her parents' wishes. The jestingly exaggerated display of arithmetic in regard to the three shares in the bride's virginity (lines 62–64) seems, in Fraenkel's opinion, "to be in keeping with that peculiar outlook of the Romans which annoyed Horace so much: *Romani pueri longis rationibus assem discunt in partis centus diducere etc.*"[19]

Fordyce remarks on the poem's humor and vivacity, its careful symmetry, calculated repetitions, and formal use of the refrain —*Hymen o Hymenaee, Hymen ades o Hymenaee*.[20] These characteristics, along with its compact unity and the general applicability of its motifs, made Catullus 62 a favorite for imitation and adaptation in Latin, Italian, and French.

It should be emphasized that Carmen 62, like Catullus's other lyric epithalamium, is not highly personal. The two songs are not concerned primarily with the private feelings of the poet or of the characters involved in the action of the poem, but are devoted primarily to the subject of marriage as an institution and to an assertion of the ideal felicity of wedding. Unlike Carmen 61, which stresses benefits to the couple, the family, and the state, Carmen 62 emphasizes the advantage to the maiden and her family. In both poems marriage is contrasted with some other mode of conduct: in Carmen 61, as we have seen, the young man is warned that now that he is to have the joys and responsibilities of marriage, the time of the *concubinus* is past; in Carmen 62 fruitful marriage for the young woman is contrasted with fruitless virginity.

Carmen 64: The Epyllion

Catullus 64 also praises marriage and contrasts it with another mode of behavior. The legal union of Peleus and Thetis, whose wedding is being celebrated, is seen in relation to the illicit affair of Theseus and Ariadne, an unblessed union not attended with proper ceremony. The tale of the unhappy union is introduced into the account of the wedding festivities as a story depicted in the embroidery of the coverlet of the wedding couch.

Unlike the lyric Carmina 61 and 62, this poem is a short epic or epyllion, a narrative based on ancient myths, involving gods and men and concluding with an epithalamium followed by an epilogue. Thus an epithalamium is in this work placed in a broad context. Some critics, viewing the work only as a marriage poem, have seen the epyllion as lacking in unity,[21] and the elaborate Theseus–Ariadne episode as digressive and artistically indefensible. McPeek, although admitting the "tempestuous liveliness" of the episode, believes it inappropriate in that its twofold theme, the perfidy of Theseus and the sorrow and revenge of Ariadne, is "not suited to the epithalamic spirit."[22] Other critics, however, defend the episode and the unity of the epyllion. Clyde Murley argues that the happiness reflected in the legitimate marriage of Peleus and Thetis, and the unhappiness resulting from the ignoble passion evident in the Ariadne episode, swells into a larger, universal theme, a contrast of a "golden age" when gods and men mingled as equals, and a "fallen age."[23]

I agree with Murley and others who view the epyllion as more than a juxtaposition of two contrasting tales, and see it as having a wider range than simple rejoicing over the marriage of Peleus and Thetis. I would point out that the Theseus–Ariadne story is only one of a series of somber and ominous elements in this work, and that they are an integral part of the structure, not at all out of keeping with an aspect of the epithalamic tradition which has received no previous attention, so far as I know. This is the phenomenon which I have labeled the "anti-epithalamium" (see Chapter III). It continues through the centuries, appearing in various forms in epic, epyllion, drama, and romance.

In the present chapter I want to focus on the general scheme of Carmen 64 and define some of the characteristics which appear to have influenced later epic epithalamia. Because of its length, difficulty, and mixed nature, it has rarely been imitated or translated in its entirety,[24] but in a number of ways it is significant in the tradition. The structure of the epyllion is as follows:

1. *Lines 1–30.* The *Argo,* built by Athena, sets forth upon her voyage to Colchis in quest of the golden fleece. Rising in the waves, wondering at the strange new craft, are the nereids, with naked breasts. One of the Argonauts, Peleus, falls in love with the sea-nymph Thetis. Although she is a goddess, Thetis does not disdain the love of a mortal, and Jupiter, perceiving the romance,

yields her to Peleus. The poet salutes this happiest of ages and hails heroes sprung from gods and the progeny of good mothers.

2. *Lines 31–50.* When the wedding day of Peleus and Thetis comes, the palace is thronged with a joyful crowd bearing gifts. Fields and vineyards are deserted as all the people of Thessaly flock to Pharsalus. The guests are amazed at the splendor of the palace, including the marriage-bed fashioned of Indian ivory, and covered with purple.

3. *Lines 51–266.* The coverlet of the marriage-bed is described, with its wondrous embroidery depicting ancient figures including those in the tale of Theseus and Ariadne. This inserted tale follows the version of the myth in which Ariadne falls in love with Theseus, who has come to Crete to slay the Minotaur and free his country from the necessity of making human sacrifices to the monster. Ariadne aids Theseus, flees with him by sea, and is abandoned by him in the Isle of Dia while she is asleep. Ariadne is pictured as she wakes on the shore and distractedly gazes after her lover as he sails away. To develop the tale, the author uses description and narration, as well as direct speech of the characters, the long lament of Ariadne and the charge of Aegeus to his son Theseus being in the first person.

4. *Lines 267–302.* The narrative of the wedding of Peleus and Thetis is resumed, the mortal guests giving place to the gods, who arrive bearing gifts, among them Chiron, the river-god Penios, Prometheus, and Jupiter with his wife and all his children except Phoebus and Diana.

5. *Lines 303–322.* The gods recline on the snowy couches at the wedding feast, and the aged Fates (Parcae), engaged in their unending task of spinning the wool, utter chants foretelling the future.

6. *Lines 323–381.* The Parcae sing the prophetic epithalamium, foretelling the birth of Achilles and describing his exploits.

7. *Lines 382–408.* The epilogue laments that gods no longer attend such ceremonies of men, or permit themselves to be seen in the light of day, now that religion is despised and the earth is dyed with hideous crimes.[25]

The elements of rejoicing in this epyllion are much like those in the lyric epithalamia. The marriage torches are "taedis felicibus"; the guests "dona ferunt prae se, declarant gaudia vultu"; and the abodes of Peleus "fulgenti splendent auro atque argento./candet ebur soliis, collucent pocula mensae,/tota domus gaudet regali splendida gaza."[26] The gods bring woodland gifts —flowers woven into mingled garlands, and lofty trees torn up by the roots and placed far and wide around the house to make a bower of foliage.[27] In the opening stanza of the epithalamium itself the bridegroom is praised for his virtue and valor and for the son to be born to the couple. The motif of the evening star, which we have seen in Catullus 62, also appears. Hesperus brings longed-for gifts to the wedded couple, the joys of love and marriage which come with the arrival of the bride.

> languidulosque paret tecum coniungere somnos,
> levia substernens robusto brachia collo . . .
> nulla domus tales umquam contexit amores,
> nullus amor tali coniunxit foedere amantes,
> qualis adest Thetidi, qualis concordia Peleo.[28]

This is followed by promise that a son will be born, his name Achilles, who will know no fear of his enemies and will often win at the games, outstripping even the flying hind. Achilles' heroic but bloody war-time exploits are then detailed, and it is not until the two final stanzas that the joyful mood is resumed. Then, in the traditional way, the couple are urged to unite:

> quare agite optatos animi coniungite amores.
> accipiat coniunx felici foedere divam,
> dedatur cupido iamdudum nupta marito.

With the wish for descendants the epithalamium ends, and the poet comments that these were the strains of prophesy, promising happiness, which the Fates sang in days of yore.

Such are the elements of rejoicing and happy omen. Interspersed, however, are aspects of tragedy and foreboding. The tale of Ariadne is marked by the madness and despair of Ariadne as she realizes her lover has deserted her; her lament that she has abandoned her own family to follow a lover stained with her brother's blood; her curse on Theseus and her appeal to the Eumenides to punish him by bringing ruin on him and those dear to him; the thoughtlessness of Theseus in failing to hoist, on his homeward approach, the white sail signifying good tidings as instructed by his father; the suicide of Aegeus, who on seeing the black sail presumes his son is dead and throws himself headlong from the cliff; and the grief of Theseus.[29]

It seems significant that the poet chooses the Parcae to sing the epithalamium, rather than the Muses or Phoebus as in some older versions of the legend,[30] or a chorus of youths or virgins as is usual in lyric epithalamia. There is something ominous about the singers themselves, as has been pointed out, their aged bodies swaying and shaking, and bitten ends of wool clinging to their withered lips.[31] We hear the drawn threads and turning spindles, as McPeek has noted,[32] in the onomatopoeic refrain, "Currite ducentes subtegmina, currite, fusi," at the end of each stanza, and the sound seems somehow relentless and faintly ominous.

The song, although ostensibly praising the surpassing achievements and renowned deeds of Achilles, emphasizes the sorrow and bloodshed and death which attend his activities. Mothers beat their breasts at the funerals of sons slain by Achilles; with foeman's steel Achilles fells the sons of Troy like a husbandman mowing down thick grain in the yellow fields; the channel of Scamander is choked with heaps of slain corpses, and the streams are made warm with mingled blood, witnesses of Achilles' great deeds of valour. Witness too of his valour is the sacrifice assigned him in death, the maiden Polyxena. The snowy-limbed maiden is slaughtered on Achilles' tomb, her blood wetting the tomb as on bended knee she falls victim to the two-edged steel and bows her headless trunk.

The cheerful aspects of the epithalamium, which I have noted earlier, occupy the space of six stanzas, four at the beginning and two at the end of the song, and Achilles' bloody achievements fill the intervening six stanzas. It seems possible that these were not designed solely to move the reader to admiration but perhaps to inspire as well some feeling of pity that the human race glorifies each deeds. This interpretation is borne out in the epilogue, in which the poet moralizes on the degeneration of society. Religion has been scorned, men have banished justice from their greedy souls, brothers sprinkle their hands with brothers' blood, fathers and mothers engage in unnatural sexual alliances; so the gods no longer attend the ceremonies of men:

> omnia fanda nefanda malo permixta furore
> iustificam nobis mentem avertere deorum.
> quare nec tales dignantur visere coetus
> nec se contingi patiuntur lumine claro.[33]

The epilogue thus ties the conclusion of the epyllion to a motif introduced very early in the poem—the poet's salute to the happy age when gods did not disdain mortal espousals.[34]

To summarize, among the characteristics of Catullus 64 which make it significant to the epithalamic tradition are these: the use of the epithalamium as part of the intricate plan and cosmic theme of an epyllion; the introduction of ominous elements; the narrative structure of the tale within a tale, accomplished by a description of a work of art;[35] the rhetorical rather than lyrical tone of the epithalamium; the use of mythological characters and mingling of gods and men; the role of the Parcae; the refrain of the whirring spindles; and the concentration of the epithalamium on the prospective offspring of the marriage.

Thomas M. Greene has observed that in the epithalamic tradition "a wedding is an ambiguous enough event to permit many interpretations."[36] It may be primarily a sexual event, but it may be also a social, religious, or political event. It may even in certain poems be related to the macrocosmos and thus become a kind of cosmic event. Greene does not suggest the distinction with reference to these poems, but it seems to me that in the two lyric epithalamia of Catullus, marriage is viewed mainly as a sexual, social, and political event. In the epyllion the two contrasting unions of human beings are woven into a context involving the gods and the future of mankind, and thus marriage is related to the cosmos.

III

The Anti-Epithalamium

The classical epithalamium as seen in the Sapphic fragments and the lyrics of Aristophanes, Theocritus, and Catullus rejoices over a union attended by proper ceremony. It celebrates the glory of marriage as an institution, the beauty and virtues of the participants, the pleasures of love, and the anticipation of offspring. Thus, it is a poem of happiness and good omen, often symbolizing man's harmony with nature and his hope of prosperity, peace, and immortality.

In the classical tradition, however, one also finds a number of works in which epithalamic imagery and conventions are used to dramatize situations and emotions of a directly opposite kind. For convenience in discussing this group, I have coined the term "anti-epithalamium," although it is admittedly not a very satisfactory label. Instead of expressing joy over a proper union, the anti-epithalamium expresses lamentation or foreboding over a union which for some reason is improper or unsanctioned, and thus presages tragedy, death, dissension, revenge, murder, war, or other disruptions of order and nature. Sometimes, but not always, the misfortune is partially resolved on a note of hope or triumph. In general, the anti-epithalamium is a poem or excerpt using epithalamic devices in an expression of unhappiness, disorder, and evil omen associated with an improper union.[1] As in Catullus 64, marriage assumes a relationship to the cosmos. This negative or ironic use of the epithalamium is seen in drama, epic, erotic epyllion, and mythological narrative. In addition, pastoral funeral elegy also occasionally associates epithalamic devices with death, but the epithalamium here usually symbolizes triumph over death by means of rebirth in nature or mystical union in heaven. However, elegies use both normal and negative epithalamic imagery.

These negative uses of the epithalamium tend to fall into recurring patterns, with certain conventions appearing again and again. A single work may utilize only one of the following patterns, or it may combine them:

1.   It remarks on the *absence* of the ritual and order customarily associated with marriage. It asserts that no torches gleam in a wedding procession, no garlands adorn the participants, no wedding veil covers the face of the bride. There are no singers, no fathers and mothers to give blessing. The gods too are absent, in particular Hymen and Juno, and no Graces dance.

2.   It remarks on the presence of the epithalamic trappings, but they are functioning in reverse: Hymen's torch does not gleam but flutters weakly or goes out, his coat is not saffron but sullen, and he drags his torch instead of waving it. Human attendants, along with the Graces and the Loves, weep rather than dance, and the flowers in the nuptial wreath wilt and die.

3.   Instead of seeking to repel the elements and symbols of evil omen as is customary in the wedding ritual and epitha-

lamium, it summons them or remarks on their presence. The Furies prepare the bridal bed, bearing tapers they have stolen from a funeral; a cursed owl sits at the head of the nuptial couch; Darkness and the Shade cover all.

4. It places a conventional epithalamium in a situation already tragic or horrible, or about to become so. In the drama especially, a conventional epithalamium is used in this way for dramatic irony, the reader or audience at times being aware of the impending tragedy or evil when the participants are not. Sometimes the "anti" devices are inserted in a conventional epithalamium; sometimes an opposing song precedes or follows the conventional one.

The earliest use I have seen of the anti-epithalamium falls into the fourth pattern. It is in *The Trojan Women* of Euripides, which was presented at the Great Dionysia in 415 B. C., a play which has been described as a pageant of the miseries of war, especially of defeat.[2] It portrays the fate of the Trojan women when Troy was taken by the Greeks and the princesses of the house of Priam were apportioned by lot to the several chiefs of the victors. Polyxena is doomed to be sacrified on the tomb of Achilles, an event noted several centuries later in Catullus's epithalamium of the Parcae, discussed in the preceding chapter.[3] Hecuba is allotted to Odysseus, Andromache to the son of Achilles; and Cassandra, daughter of Hecuba and Priam, is assigned to be the concubine of King Agamemnon. Gifted with prophetic foreknowledge of the tragic and horrible events to come, Cassandra in the white robes and wreaths of a priestess sings her own epithalamium, waving a blazing torch and dancing in mad exultation:

> Hold it up, show it, bring the torch!
> I worship with flame.
> Look! look!
> I light up this holy place!
> Hymen, Hymenaeus, Lord
> Blessed the bridegroom

Blessed I too
Whose wedding song leads to the bed
Of a king in Argos.

Seeing that you, mother, can only weep
And lament for the death of my father
And cry out over our loved country,
I must light the fire of the torch
For my own wedding.
To the brightness! to the glory!
I offer to you, O wedding god.
And you, O Hecate, give light
For the marriage bed of a maid, as is the custom.

Whirl, feet high in the air.
Lead on the chorus.
Evan! Evoi!
As when my father's fortune
Was most blessed.

Apollo—thou—
Lead the ritual chorus.
I perform your rites
In your temple among the laurels.

Dance, mother, lead on,
Turn your feet here and there with mine
Carry the sweet steps.
Call out the *Hymen, O*
In happy song
And the shout for the bride.
Come, maidens of Phrygia,
Splendidly dressed
Sing for my wedding
And for the husband
Fate sends to lie beside me.[4]

This play of Euripides was presented six years after the *Peace* and one year before the *Birds,* the two comedies of Aristophanes which include epithalamia.[5] Cassandra's epithalamium displays the same kind of almost wild excitement and exuberance as those of Aristophanes, but here it is put to tragically ironic purpose. The exclamatory refrain *Hymen, O Hymenaeus,* first seen in the epithalamium in the *Peace,* also appears here along with the torches, dancing, and invocation to the deities of the sun and the moon. These tokens of celebration are used by the frenzied Cassandra to herald two events, her impending forced union with the hated Agamemnon, and her anticipated reunion in death with her father, Priam, who had been slaughtered in the siege of Troy. After this song, the chorus suggests that the queen restrain the wild Cassandra, and Hecuba, sadly speaking of the piteous flame of Hymen, the marriage-god, takes the torch from Cassandra. But Cassandra will not be silenced, and she asks her mother to adorn her hair with flowers and send her forth, a bloodier bride than Helen, to have her revenge against Agamemnon:

> Mother, crown me with wreaths of victory.
> And be glad for this my marriage to a king.
> Escort me, and if I seem to you unwilling
> Push me away with force. If Apollo lives still
> Helen's marriage was not so troublesome
> As mine will be to the great Agamemnon.

She prophesies at length the coming fate of both Troy and Greece, and laments that the unnecessary war was brought on by the Greeks for the love of one woman. She praises the bravery in death of the heroes of Troy and pledges that she likewise as she goes to her espousal and her death will help to destroy the enemy:

> Mother, there is no need to pity this your land
> Nor weep over my marriage. For by this joining
> I shall destroy those that both of us hate the most.

As she is escorted to the ship by the Greek Talthybius to become the bride of Agamemnon, Cassandra hails the three Furies, declares herself one of them, and then concludes on a triumphantly vengeful note:

Where is the ship of the general? Where must I go to embark?
No longer will you be the first to watch for the wind in the
     sails
Who take me away from this land—one of the three Avengers.
Say goodbye to me, mother, do not cry. Loved place where I
     was born
And brothers down there in the earth and father who begot us
Soon you will welcome me. But I shall come to death victorious
Having destroyed the house of Atreus which has ruined us utterly.

The anti-epithalamium thus dramatizes not only Cassandra's forced union with Agamemnon, her plans for his destruction, and her prospective reunion in death with her father, but symbolizes also the theme of the entire play—the miseries for all mankind of a war brought about by the illicit and unsanctioned union of Paris and Helen.

As used in *The Trojan Women,* the anti-epithalamium consists of a conventional epithalamium interrupted and followed by the "anti" devices. In another play of Euripides, the fragmentary *Phaethon,* a somewhat similar technique appears to have been employed.[6] Here, however, an actual epithalamium is sung by a chorus of virgins and is followed by an anti-epithalamium sung by a chorus of female slaves. Phaethon is the son of an illicit union between Clymene and the Sun-God, but Clymene has deceived her husband, Merops, into believing that Phaethon is his son. Merops arranges for Phaethon's marriage with a goddess, but Phaethon is determined not to marry above his rank and decides to go off on an adventure of his own, driving the chariot of the Sun. Struck down by a thunderbolt of Jove, Phaethon crashes, and his body is brought in, sulphurous smoke surrounding it. Grief-stricken Clymene, fearful that her husband will learn the truth about her affair with the Sun-God, has the body of Phaethon borne into the palace and hidden, just as Merops approaches, leading a chorus of virgins singing an epithalamium for the wedding he has arranged between Phaethon and the goddess. It is a conventional epithalamium, addressed to Hymen, Venus, and Love, asking them to bless the union between a son of earth and a daughter of sky; but as soon as it is over, thick streaks of black smoke pour forth from the body of Phaethon concealed in the palace, and Merops assumes it is from sacrificial rites associated with the coming wedding of his son. He goes to investigate, and the female slaves, who have assisted Clymene in hiding the body of Phaethon, replace the chorus of virgins and sing a song of the illicit union, the tragic results, and the inpending peril:

> Oh misery! oh misery!
> Where shall I stay my flying feet?
> How, where no mortal eye their trace can see,
> In air, or earth's profound obscurity,
>   Find an inscrutable retreat?
>   Alas! alas! the wretched queen,
>   And her dead son, in vain concealed,
>   Her grief, her shame, will now be seen,
>   And all the fearful truth revealed.
> Revealed will be the Sun's illicit love,
> The fire-imprinted wounds, the lightning-brand of
>   Jove.
> Oh wretched with immeasurable grief,
> Daughter of Ocean! to thy Father spread
> Thy hands in prayer, to speed to thy relief,
> And chase the perils which o'erhang thy head.[7]

Much of the play is lost, and the evidence is incomplete as to the total role of the epithalamic devices in the theme and outcome, but here again the anti-epithalamium is associated with an illicit union which appears to accompany and presage disastrous cosmic consequences.

Seneca's *Medea*

A third example of anti-epithalamium in drama is found in
Seneca's *Medea,* which opens with an anti-epithalamium spoken
by Medea, followed by an epithalamium sung by the chorus of
Corinthians for the marriage of Jason and Creusa. In the opening speech Medea addresses the marriage-gods, calling particularly upon Juno Lucina, guardian of the genial bed, and
Pallas Athena, as well as the deities of the sea, the sun, and
the moon:

> Ye gods of marriage;
> Lucina, guardian of the genial bed;
> Pallas, who taught the tamer of the seas
> To steer the Argo; stormy ocean's lord;
> Titan, dividing bright day to the world;
> And thou three-formed Hecate, who dost shed
> Thy conscious splendor on the hidden rites!
> Ye by whom Jason plighted me his troth . . . .[8]

Medea then declares that rather than these gods, she will in-
voke the powers of darkness and evil. She calls on the king
and queen of Hell, and like Ariadne in Catullus 64, summons
the Furies, asking them to grant revenge on her ex-husband
Jason and to bring death to his new bride, to their children, and
to the bride's father, Creon.

> Chaos of night eternal; realm opposed
> To the celestial powers; abandoned souls;
> King of the dusky realm; Persephone,
> By better faith betrayed; you I invoke,
> But with no happy voice. Approach, approach,
> Avenging goddesses with snaky hair,
> Holding in blood-stained hands your sulphurous
>   torch!

> Come now as horrible as when of yore
> Ye stood beside my marriage-bed. Bring death
> To the new bride, and to the royal seed,
> And Creon . . . .

For Jason, Medea asks the gods of darkness to grant, not death, but what is worse, life—that he may suffer as an exile, hated, poor, and homeless. Her vengeful wish that Jason might beget sons like their father and daughters like herself is particularly ironic in that it echoes the conventional epithalamic wish made for the offspring of a happy bridal couple. She threatens to strike the marriage torches from the hands of the bearers and, indeed, to seize the very light from heaven. Outlining her bloody plans, Medea asks for strength to carry them out, foretells the evils to come, and predicts that posterity will have reason to know of her divorce as well as of her nuptials.

> This still remains—for me to carry up
> The marriage torches to the bridal room,
> And, after sacrificial prayers, to slay
> The victims on their altars. Seek, my soul—
> If thou still livest, or if aught endures
> Of ancient vigor—seek to find revenge
> Through thine own bowels; throw off woman's fears . . .
> . . . Evils unknown and wild
> Hideous, frightful both to earth and heaven,
> Disturb my soul,—wounds, and the scattered corpse,
> And murder . . .
> Gird thee with wrath, prepare thine utmost rage,
> That fame of thy divorce may spread as far
> As of thy marriage!

As Medea concludes, a chorus of Corinthian women enters, singing an actual epithalamium, one in several ways parallel to the anti-epithalamium which has just ended. Like Medea, the chorus invokes the marriage-gods in the opening words, and

continues with pledges of nuptial sacrifices. The gods of the
heaven and of the sea, along with Jove, Lucina, and Venus, are
summoned, and then the bearers of light rather than darkness
—Hymen with his happy torch, and Hesperus, the evening star.

> Be present at the royal marriage feast,
> Ye gods who sway the scepter of the deep,
> And ye who hold dominion in the heavens;
> With the glad people come, ye smiling gods!
> First to the scepter-bearing thunderers
> The white-backed bull shall stoop his lofty head;
> The snowy heifer, knowing not the yoke,
> Is due to fair Lucina; and to her
> Who stays the bloody hand of Mars, and gives
> To warring nations peace, who in her horn
> Holds plenty, sacrifice a victim mild.
> Thou who at lawful bridals dost preside,
> Scattering darkness with thy happy torch,
> Come hither with slow step and drunk with wine,
> Binding thy temples with a rosy crown.
> Thou star that bringest in the day and night,
> Slow-rising on the lover, ardently
> For thy clear shining maids and matrons long.

There follows a glowing tribute to the beauty of the bridal
couple, reminiscent of Theocritus 18, and instructions to the
bridegroom to take the bride, in accordance with her father's
wish. The wedding song reaches a peak of rejoicing with an
appeal to Hymen to light the pine torch, and we hear the sounds
of mirth, music, and fescennine jollity. Then, abruptly, the
epithalamium closes with mention of Medea and the darkness
which attends her.

As in Euripides, the anti-epithalamium and epithalamium
here anticipate the tragedy and horror to come in the remainder
of the play, and nuptial imagery recurs at several points. Marking the end of Medea's bloody day, the chorus notes the arrival

of Hesperus, the evening star, who traditionally heralds the approach of nuptial consummation; and near the end of the play, when Medea has slain one of her children and is about to kill the other, she crowns the horror with a triumphant announcement:

> I have recaptured now my crown and throne,
> My brother and my father; Colchians hold
> The golden fleece; my kingdom is won back;
> My lost virginity returns to me!
> O gods at last appeased! Glad nuptial day!

Seneca's *Troas*

Seneca's version of the *Troas* does not include Cassandra or her epithalamium as in Euripides', but Acts IV and V include a series of anti-epithalamic passages. Helen's opening speech in Act IV, as she contemplates the coming sacrifice of Polyxena on the tomb of Achilles, prepares the way for the subsequent epithalamic devices:

> When angry Heav'n with Curses does prepare
> To couple any inauspicious Pair,
> Let after-Ages say, the ominous Helen's there.
> Troy's Nuptial, and its Funeral-Torch once more
> 'Tis I must light: I must betray the poor
> Unhappy bride . . .[9]

Helen tells Polyxena that she is to become the bride of Pyrrhus; it is, of course, Pyrrhus who will slay Polyxena as a sacrifice on the tomb of Achilles. Andromache denounces Helen, and as Troy burns, speaks an ironic epithalamium:

> Go, Let the Bridal-Bed be quickly made,
> Let all the richest Ornaments be laid!
> What need we Flames, the happy Pair to light?
> What need we Torches, when Troy burns so bright?

Nay, Musick too their Nuptial Rites shall grace;
And Sighs, and Hollow Groans shall fill the Place.

And Polyxena as she goes to her death on the tomb of Achilles
is described as a modest and beautiful bride in a wedding procession:

Then through a Lane of Grecians, in a row,
Before the Bride Five Nuptial Torches go . . . .
Her Eyes she turn'd with modest sorrow down,
And in her Face unusual Beauties shone:
So Evening Blushes grace the setting Sun.

Ovid's Tale of Tereus, Progne, and Philomela

In the plays I have cited, conventional epithalamia, or passages which could be excerpts from conventional epithalamia,
have been used in conjunction with the "anti" devices, all of
them associated with an improper or tragic union attended by
death, bloodshed, and horror. The anti-epithalamium in Ovid's
tale of Tereus, Progne, and Philomela takes a different pattern,
but the tragedy it foretells is even bloodier and more horrible.[10]
King Pandion of Athens gives his daughter Progne in marriage
to the tyrant Tereus, but the gods do not give their blessing to
the match. Five years later Tereus rapes his wife's sister
Philomela, cuts out her tongue, and hides her in a remote and
guarded cottage. Philomela weaves a tapestry portraying her
sad story and sends it to Progne. In revenge against her husband,
Progne slays their child Itys, and serves the corpse as a meal to
Tereus. The sisters and Tereus are changed to birds of prey.
Grief brings King Pandion to his death.

The anti-epithalamium which accompanies the union of
Progne and Tereus, giving omen of the atrocities to come, falls
into the first and third of the four patterns I have listed at the

beginning of this chapter, remarking the absence of the marriage-gods and the presence of the powers of evil. Golding's
sixteenth-century translation makes especially plain that the
augury or "hand-sell" of the improper union is not good:

At this match (as after will appeare)
Was neither Juno, President of marriage wont to bee,
Nor Hymen, no nor any one of all the Graces three.
The Furies snatching Tapers up that on some Herce
   did stand
Did light them, and before the Bride did beare them in
   their hand.
The Furies made the Bride-gromes bed, and on the house
   did tucke
A cursed Owle the messenger of ill successe and lucke,
And all the night time while that they were lying in
   their beds
She sate upon the bedsteds top right over both their
   heds.
Such hand-sell Progne had the day that Tereus did her
   wed;
Such hand-sell had they when that she was brought of
   Child abed.[11]

Lucan's *Pharsalia*

In Lucan's unfinished epic or historical chronicle, *Pharsalia,* or *The Civill Warres of Rome, between Pompey the great,
and Julius Caesar,* there is in Book II an anti-epithalamium in
a war-time setting.[12] I shall not attempt to assess the intended
significance of the anti-epithalamium in this unfinished work,
but an idea of the circumstances which surround it can be gained
from a brief summary of the second book up to the point of the

anti-epithalamium. Thomas May's 1635 translation reviews the argument tersely:

> The Author complaines that future fates are knowne,
> The sorrow of affrighted Rome is showne.
> An old man cals to mind the civill crimes
> Of Marius, and Sylla's bloody times.
> Brutus with Cato does conferre; to whom
> Chast Martia come from dead Hortensius Tombe
> Againe is married in a funerall dresse.[13]

The anti-epithalamium concerns the wedding of Martia and Cato, who are being married for the second time. Martia as a virgin had been married to Cato, and three children were born of the marriage. Cato's friend Hortensius desired Martia, however, and wanted children, so Cato had bestowed her upon Hortensius. Hortensius having died, Martia has returned to re-wed Cato, asking that she be permitted to share in his wartime tribulations.

> These speaches mov'd the man; though these times are
> Unfit for Hymen, when fate calls to war,
> Without vaine pompe to tye a nuptiall knot
> In the gods presence, he refuses not.[14]

The union, therefore, has a kind of sanction, but lacks the usual ceremony and rejoicing, and the poet emphasizes the abnormal nature of the event in his description of the stoic bridegroom, a selfless man whose total devotion is to his country:

> His ore-growne haire hee from that sacred face
> Shaves not, nor will in his sad lookes embrace
> One joy (since first that wicked war begun
> He lets his unshorne hoary lockes fall downe
> Ore his rough front, and a sad beard to hide
> His cheekes, for he alone from factions freed,

Or hate, had leasure for mankind to weepe)
Nor in his Bridall bed would Cato sleepe,
Even lawful love could continence reject.
These were his maners, this sowre Cato's sect,
To keepe a meane, hold fast the end, and make
Nature his guide, dye for his Countreys sake.

Father and husband both to Rome was hee,
Servant to Justice, and strict Honestie.

The anti-epithalamic lines describing this unusual wedding assume the pattern I have listed first at the beginning of this chapter—they remark the absence of the customary wedding ritual and trappings. We note especially the absence of the nuptial couch, and the fact that the description of the couch is like that in Catullus 64: it is made of ivory and decked with embroidery.

No garlands on the marriage doores were worne,
Nor linnen fillets did the posts adorne:
No bridall Tapers shone: no bed on high
With Ivory steps, and gold embrodery:
No Matron in a towred crowne, that led
The Bride, forbid her on the threshold tread:
No yellow veile cover'd her face, to hide
The fearefull blushes of a modest Bride:
No precious girdle guirded her loose Gowne:
No Chaine adornd her necke; nor linnen downe
From off her shoulders her nak'd armes orespred;
So as she was, funerall habited,
Even like her Sonnes, her Husband she embrac'd,
A funerall Robe above her purple plac'd.
The usual Jests were spar'd: the husband wants,
After the Sabine use, his marriage tants.
None of their kindred met; the knot they tye
Silent: content with Brutus auspicie.

Musaeus's *Hero and Leander*

The *Hero and Leander* of Musaeus, sixth-century Greek grammarian, contains an anti-epithalamium as prelude to the drowning of Leander, the suicide of Hero, and their reunion in death. During the Renaissance, Musaeus was thought to be the earliest of the Greek poets, a contemporary of Orpheus, and his work inspired imitations and translations by many poets of the time—among them Bernardo Tasso, Baldi, Marot, and Boscan. In English, Marlowe's fragmentary *Hero and Leander* and Chapman's continuation are much altered and expanded from the original.[15]

In the original compact epic (about 340 lines) the anti-epithalamium dramatizes the central theme and highlights the poem's recurring symbol, the nuptial torch. Hero, virgin priestess of Venus, displays the torch as a guide to Leander, swimming through the darkness to her. The union of the lovers is not attended with proper cermony, and an anti-epithalamium marks the fact. Subsequently, the torch goes out, Leander drowns, and Hero, seeing his body borne to shore on the waves, casts herself from the tower.[16]

Musaeus begins with an invocation and sums up the story he is about to tell. This is Stapylton's 1647 translation:

> Speak Goddess, of the Torch (Love's witness made
> At Nuptials stealing through the gloomy shade,
> Ne're seen by th' incorrupted morning-light)
> Of Sestos and Abydos: here by night
> Leander swimming, Hero marry'd there.
> Heark, the Torch ruffled by the wind I heare,
> The steering Torch that did to Venus guide,
> The flaming Signall of the cloweded Bride,
> The Torch that for night-service aiery Jove
> Should make a Star, the star of wandring Love,
> The Marriage-star, because it still gave ayme,
> And watcht the Marriage-houres with sleepless flame

Till by the rude wind th' envious Gust was blown;
And then (aye me) change Hymen's softer tone,
And let our Verse with one sad Close be crown'd,
The Torch extinguisht, and Leander drown'd.[17]

The anti-epithalamium near the end of the poem, giving
omen of the impending tragedy, is somewhat like that we have
seen in Lucan:

They had a wedding, but no Dancing there
A Bride-bed, but they did no singing heare;
Their sacred Nuptials no Poet prais'd,
About their private bed no Torches blaz'd,
No Dancer in a nimble caper sprung,
No Hymnes the Father or grave Mother sung.
But Darkness at Love's houres the Bride-bed made,
Drest up the Room: the Bride's Veyle was the shade.
Farre from Epithalamions were they matcht;
Night only at their Ceremonies watcht;
Aurora never did Leander view
A Bride-groome, in that bed he so well knew.
Who swam back to Abydos, breathing still
Those Hymeneall Sweetes that never fill.
But long-veyl'd Hero mock't her Parents sight,
A virgin all the day, a Wife by night;
Both often chid the Morning to the West,
And thus the fury of their loves supprest,
Enjoying secret, but short-liv'd delights,
For short time dates their strange stoln marriage-rites.[18]

The poem ends with the extinguishing of "Hymen's torch,"
and the lovers' death and reunion:

And now upon the lofty Turret rear'd
Fate's brand, no longer Hymen's torch appear'd . . . .

And the false torch out as the sharp wind tost,
His Love and Life bemourn'd Leander lost . . . .
For her lost Husband she her self destroy'd,
And ev'n in death each other they enjoy'd.

Bion's *Epitaph for Adonis*

Imagery and trappings of the epithalamium are on occasion moved from the nuptial bed to the death bed. Epithalamic imagery in the elegy, although associated with death, does not usually have the implication of disaster which is present in the other genres discussed here. Instead, the epithalamium seems to signify an anticipated triumph over death through rebirth or spiritual union.[19] In an early example, Bion's *Epitaph for Adonis,* Hymen's torch has gone out and the wedding garment has been cast away; Hymen joins Venus, the Loves, and the Graces in hovering over the dead Adonis, as if preparing the ceremonial placing of a bride on the nuptial couch. The poem ends with the forecast of seasonal death and rebirth. The opening lines of the following exerpt from Thomas Stanley's translation (1651) refer to the little Loves who customarily attend Venus and flutter about the bride in the nuptial chamber:

One sits behind, and fans him with his wings:
Loves weep for Cytherea's sufferings.
The wedding garment Hymen in the porch
Cast quite away, and quencht the genial torch:
To elegies our hymeneals turn,
We for Adonis, we for Hymen mourn:
The Graces (griev'd for Cynara's fair son)
Adonis, to each other say, is gone:
Louder than thine, Dione, are their cries;
Adonis, in their songs the destinies
Call back Adonis, but their lure disdain'd,
He never minds, by Proserpine detain'd.

Dry thy eyes, Venus, for to-day and keep
Some tears in store, for thou next year must weep.[20]

In this chapter I have presented from classical works a few examples of epithalamic devices used in a way which I think no writer on the epithalamium has previously noted. I am not sure that these examples should all be classified under the name "anti-epithalamium" or, indeed, any other single label. However, inasmuch as English poets of the Renaissance make use of these devices in similar ways, the designation will be useful in citing later parallels.

IV

The Rhetorical
Epithalamium: Statius,
Claudian, and Their Followers

Catullus's rhetorical panegyric of Achilles in Carmen 64 anticipates a trend in the development of the Latin epithalamium in
the hands of Statius, Claudian, and their followers. Statius's
Epithalamium in Stellam et Violentillam (277 lines), written
about A.D. 90, is one of the first of many long rhetorical and epic
epithalamia in Latin hexameters,[1] the form appearing at its best
in his work and in the two epithalamia of Claudian (A.D. 398
and 399), *Epithalamium de Nuptiis Honorii Augusti* and *Epithalamium dictum Palladio V. C. tribuno et notario et Celerinae*,[2]
In late antiquity, interest in this type of poem apparently was
stimulated by the works of such rhetoricians as the pseudo-
Dionysius, Menander, Choricius of Gaza, and Himerius, who

wrote rules for the writing of wedding orations called epithalamia, and constructed examples.³ Much of our knowledge of
Sappho's epithalamia, as I have said earlier, comes from these
writers. Van Winkle believes that at the beginning the epic
epithalamium writers derived their conventions from the descriptions of weddings in Homer and Hesiod.⁴ Morelli argues
that the conventions came from both Catullus 64 and from
Sappho, and thus he divides the epic epithalamium into two types:

> Due tipi di epitalamio epico stavano a fronte: l'esiodeo–catulliano,
> che fa convenire alle nozze eroiche—specialmente cantate dovet-
> tero essere quelle di Teti e Peleo—tutti gli dei; e il neo-saffico,
> dove un dio primeggia, Venere.⁵

Unquestionably Venus becomes the central figure, with Hymen
and other gods taking minor roles. In Statius it is Venus who
unites the couple, sanctions the passion which brought them together, and increases their amorous desires.⁶ Her companions
are her son Cupid, with his crew of playful brothers, the little
Loves, along with the Muses and Graces. To the chariot of
Venus, Cupid harnesses a pair of white swans; then he takes the
reins and drives her chariot through the clouds to the scene of
the wedding. Venus adorns the bride, prepares the bridal bed,
and persuades the virgins of the joys and glory of wedlock. Thus
Venus Pronuba replaces Juno Pronuba and the human *pronubae*
of earlier poems.⁷

Statius's epithalamium, apparently written for a bridegroom who was a fellow poet,⁸ opens with the hills of Rome
echoing the music of the nuptial, as the Muses journey from
Helicon, their torches blazing forth the ritual flame for the joining of the bridal, and their songs ringing in the air. Venus arrives, and the poet announces that now he knows what day it is
—it is the day for which the Fates (as in Catullus 64) have set
up a snow-white skein, the day for the nuptials of Stella and
Violentilla. The gods bring chaplets of flowers, and the Loves
and Graces pelt the embracing couple with roses, lilies, and
violets. The couple are encouraged to unite.

At this point the epithalamium is interrupted in order that the poet may tell how the marriage was made in heaven, and we hear the details in a dialogue between Cupid and Venus. Cupid argues the merits of the bridegroom, relating that Lucius Arruntius Stella is a youth of famous patrician family, who because of his beauty received his name from the sky. In the fire of his love Stella surpasses all the lovers of old, and thus as a poet Stella will write of love rather than wars. Cupid pleads that Venus will grant Stella the bride he desires. Venus replies with praise of the bride Violentilla, using the same themes with variations—the renown of the bride's family, her beauty, riches, and accomplishments. Venus says that she has cherished the bride and helped her to become a beauty like herself, worthy to have been born from the blue waters and to sit in a car of pearl. The bride's riches are great, Venus declares, but her mind is even greater.[9]

The Cupid–Venus dialogue here is reminiscent of the alternating choruses in Catullus 62 and in the pastoral singing match; the dialogue or *lis* becomes of increasing importance in the rhetorical epithalamium. The goal of this contest in panegyric, as E. Faye Wilson has pointed out,[10] is to prove the bride and bridegroom equal in merit: "Like twin roses in one meadow," in the words of Himerius.[11]

Returning to the scene of the nuptials, the poet presents Venus in a long monologue addressed to the bride, praising marriage, relating it to the cosmos, and promulgating the doctrine of increase. Birds and flocks and tribes of savage beasts are coupled by Venus; the sky itself weds earth; thus it is that the life of the world and all things after their kind are renewed. The pleas of Venus, and the virgin's remembrances of her lover's pleas, win the hard heart of this pre-Petrarchan maiden. The hills and woods echo with triumphant song. The poet-gods bring gifts to the poet-bridegroom: a lyre, the tawny skin of a spotted deer, wands, a quill to strike the lyre, a wreath of bay, and Ariadne's crown of stars. The gates are decorated with leaves and there is the stir of preparation. As the crowd gathers, Hymen stands in the gateway composing a new nuptial song. Juno blesses the knot that binds the couple; Concord with twin torches hallows the union. Such was the day, says the officiating poet. Of the night, let the bridegroom-poet himself sing.

The writer calls upon his fellow poets to join in singing a song worthy of the bridal couple, declaring that his own poem is motivated by friendship: he and the bridegroom are kindred spirits, and "my own Parthenope" cuddled the bride at her birth and knew her as a toddling child.[12] The closing lines of Statius's poem, which in part echo a theme of Catullus 61, inspired succeeding poets through the centuries, and later we shall see their expression in English in the conclusion of Ben Jonson's best epithalamium. D. A. Slater's translation of the final lines of the epithalamium effectively enumerates its motifs:

> Soon let a noble offspring be born of ye to Latium, to govern camp and courts and make merry songs. Let Cynthia be kind and bless the tenth month with early fruit. Only may the birth-goddess be merciful and the pledge wound not the parent tree! Spare, child, that delicate frame, those swelling breasts; and when Nature has moulded thy brow in secret, may'st thou be born much like thy father, like thy mother more. But for thee, fairest of all the daughters of Italy, at last thou hast a worthy master and lord: cherish the bond he sought so long to knit; so may thy beauty never diminish; so may thy young brows keep the bloom of youth for many a year, and that loveliness be slow to fade into decay.[13]

Claudian

Claudian, panegyrist of the Emperor Honorius, in 398 wrote a 341-line epic epithalamium for the marriage of Honorius and Maria, daughter of Stilicho, and accompanied the epithalamium by four fescennine verses, twelve to forty-five lines in length. His second epithalamium, that for Palladius and Celerina, is 145 lines and probably belongs to the following year.[14] Both epithalamia feature the goddess Venus, with Hymen and Cupid in minor roles. The longer epic opens with a description of the Emperor Honorius, wounded by Love and no longer interested in hunting, riding, or javelin-throwing. A long soliloquy by the tormented lover is followed by the laughter of Cupid, who hurries proudly to break the news to his mother. There follows a detailed description of the Paradise of Venus, an enclosure rich in untended flowers, shady groves with birds chosen for the beauty of their songs, and trees which unite in love—palm mating with palm, poplar sighing with passion for poplar, plane tree whispering to plane tree, and alder to alder.[15] Here are found two fountains, one of honey and one of poison, in which Cupid dips his arrows. A thousand of his brother Loves frolic on the banks; nearby are the nymphs, their mothers. We are told that Cupid, child of Venus, subdues the stars, the gods, and heaven, and that his brothers prey upon the common people. Also peopling the grove are other deities, among them License, Anger, Tears, Pallor, Boldness, Happy Fears, Pleasure, and Lovers' Oaths. Wanton Youth bars Age from the grove. In the background gleams the jewel-studded palace of Venus.[16]

Cupid flies into the Paradise, to find Venus seated on her throne, with the three Graces occupied in dressing her hair. One pours nectar upon it, one parts her tresses with an ivory comb, and a third arranges the ringlets, carefully making one portion seem untended, for such seeming negligence is most becoming.[17] Venus admires her reflection, greets her son, and is informed of the wound Cupid has inflicted on Honorius. Cupid asks Venus to seal the royal union.

Venus sends her crew of Loves to find Triton, who will bear her over the ocean on his back. Luxuriously mounted on scarlet coverlets, she begins her sea voyage to the city of the bridal couple, the winged Loves escorting her and smoothing the surface of the ocean. The sea-gods join the entourage, among them Leucothoe, frolicking in the water; Palaemon, driving a dolphin with a a bridle of roses; Nereus, strewing violets among the seaweed; and Glaucus, adorning his own hair with undying flowers. A crowd of nude sea-nymphs throngs around Venus, mounted on various beasts—a sea-tiger, a ram, a sea-lion, a sea-calf. They sing praises of the bride Maria, and ask Venus to bear their gifts to her; Cymothoe presents a girdle, Galatea a precious necklace, Psamathe a diadem encrusted with pearls gathered from the Red Sea, Doto a coral plant. They ask Venus to tell the bride that Ocean is her slave, and that it was they who bore up the fleet of her father, the warrior Stilicho.[18] Arriving at the shore, Venus flies to Milan, and at her coming, the clouds retire, the standards of war bloom with flowers, and the spears sprout with living leaves. Venus tells her comrades to banish war, so that on this occasion joy may be unrestrained. With bustling efficiency, she summons Hymen to prepare the festal torches, the Graces to gather flowers, Concord to weave garlands, the Loves to busy themselves as needed—hanging lamps, entwining the doorposts with myrtle, sprinkling the palace with nectar and incense, spreading tapestries on the ground, and employing all their arts in decorating the marriage-bed. She orders that jewels and the gathered wealth of the family be heaped on the nuptial canopy.

Meanwhile, as Maria the bride is being tutored by her mother in learning and chastity, Venus bursts in upon them and exclaims at the beauty of the pair, like two roses upon one stalk. The goddess hails Maria as the future mother of kings and praises her beauty—her lips like roses, her neck whiter than hoar-frost, her hair like flowers, her eyes like flames. She commends the bride's delicate eyebrows, her blush, her pink fingers, her firm shoulders. Venus urges the bride to go forth, to mate with this bridegroom who is worthy of her, and to share with him an empire which covers all the world. Acting as *pronuba,* Venus adorns the bride with the gifts of the nereids, parts the bride's hair with a spear's point,[19] and arranges the wedding veil. The procession halts at the door, bringing the chariot in which the bride is to sit. The ardent prince is compared to a noble steed, his passions stirred, shaking his mane and coursing over Pharsalia's plains to the mares, who take pleasure in their handsome mate.[20]

The army has laid aside its swords, and the soldiers, dressed in white, gather around their general—the bride's father Stilicho

—scattering flowers like rain and singing a song in praise of Stilicho. They profess even firmer allegiance to the Emperor Honorius now that Stilicho's daughter is becoming the emperor's bride. They wish that Stilicho's other children may be equally blessed, and that Maria's womb may grow big and a little Honorius may soon rest in his grandfather's lap.[21]

The *Fescennina*

Accompanying this epic epithalamium of Claudian are four *Fescennina* in various meters, for the most part lyrical in tone, only the fourth having any hint of the bawdiness associated with the fescennine jests. The first one glorifies the bridegroom Honorius, who in his beauty and skill as a hunter surpasses the very gods and would cause Venus to scorn Adonis, and Cynthia to disapprove of Hippolytus. As a ruler he vanquishes all people; blessed is the bride who calls him husband.[22]

The second, which is most important to the English tradition, is an invitation to Nature to unfold all her splendor at the marriage of the ruler.[23] The poet enjoins Earth to honor the marriage feast; the woods, rivers, and ocean to sing; the plains and hills to give their blessing; the mountains to clothe themselves with roses and the fields of ice to grow red; the rivers to echo the choral songs; and Rome to crown her seven hills with flowers. Let the rejoicing be heard in Spain, for that country cradled ancestors of both bride and bridegroom, and the two branches are now, like twin streams, reunited. Let peace and joy fill the earth, let the storms be still, and let Zephyrus have sole rule over the year.[24] This brief lyric, perhaps the most succinct and graceful expression of the participation of Nature in wedding festivity, has been much imitated, notably in the opening lines of Gil Polo's Spanish epithalamium, a poem which assumes importance early in the English tradition.[25]

The theme of the third fescennine verse, and one which echoes through many centuries of royal marriages—a theme we have seen earlier in Aristophanes—is the wish that the marriage may bring peace through union of the two families. Let the trumpets of war cease and the propitious torch of marriage banish savage Mars.[26]

The fourth fescennine is more clearly in the tradition of the *fescennina iocatio*. As Hesperus, the evening star, appears, and the modest bride is in tears, the young lover is urged to seize the bride, even though she oppose him savagely with cruel fingernail, for none can enjoy the honey from Hybla if he fears that thorns may scratch his face. Thorns arm the rose, the poet advises, and bees find a defense for their honey, but sweeter is the kiss snatched through tears, and such victory is better than that in war. The poem continues with an *allocutio sponsalis*[27] urging the couple to enjoy love and harmony, and comparing their clasped hands to the familiar ivy and tree, their kisses to those of doves. The poet asks that when lips have mingled souls, the couple may sleep, and that the coverlet of the wedding couch may give evidence of victory in the night's encounter.[28] Soldiers, youths, and virgins are urged to make merry all night long and to indulge in the permitted jests. The shout re-echoes: Fair Honorius weds Maria.[29]

Claudian's Second Epithalamium

The second epithalamium of Claudian is prefaced by a note from the poet explaining why he has written the poem. "I find," he says, "that I cannot refuse the bridegroom Palladius because he is my friend and comrade-in-arms, or the bride's father Celerinus because he is my general, and in rank and dignity far above me; the love I bear the one demands my good offices as a poet; the awe in which I hold the other requires a soldier's obedience." As the poem opens, Venus, her hair in pleasing disorder and her breasts undraped, is discovered asleep in her leafy Paradise, surrounded by nymphs, Graces, and Cupids, the latter with their bows unstrung and quivers hanging from the branches of trees. Some of the Loves wake and frolic through the thickets in search of birds' nests, or they pick apples and grapes, or climb to the tree tops. Others keep guard, driving off the wanton dryads and amorous fauns. Sounds of merriment, music, and dancing rise as all the hills of Italy repeat the name of Celerina, and every field re-echoes that of her husband Palladius.[30]

Aroused by the pleasant sounds, Venus searches out Hymen, son of one of the Muses; Venus has made him the patron god of marriage. She finds him lying beneath a tall plane tree, playing pastoral tunes on his pipe. As he sees Venus, he stops, and his pipe falls from his fingers to the ground.[31] She asks the reason for the music and celebration, and Hymen tells of the wedding, describing the brilliance of the bridegroom, the bride, and their families, especially the military glory of the bride's father. Hymen urges Venus and her entourage to attend the wedding, and expresses his own eagerness to participate and to answer with his pipe the choirs' songs.

Venus bathes in the cool stream, decks herself for the occasion, and sets out in her flower-garlanded chariot. From all sides the birds flock together. The playful Loves catch and harness the birds and ride them through the clouds, engaging in mock battles, and tumbling from the backs of the birds. The Cupids fall but are unhurt, and using their own wings they overtake the birds in flight. Then the Loves empty baskets of roses and violets in the nuptial chamber. Venus takes the tearful bride from her mother, joins the hands of the bridal couple, blesses the union, and incites them to a thousand kisses, that lips may join and souls may meet.[32] She gives counsel to bridegroom and bride, urging the youth to entreaty rather than rude love-making or threats, and the bride to submission. From her winged attendants, Venus chooses the two best marksmen and instructs them to dip their shafts in pure honey, and to implant their arrows at equal depths in the hearts of the couple.[33]

The epithalamia of Statius and Claudian are important for the appearance of or increased emphasis on the following motifs: (1) Venus as principal deity, with her crew of attendants—Muses, Graces, Cupid and the other little Loves, nymphs, sea-deities, birds—and her car drawn by swans; (2) the pastoral Paradise of Venus, with its flowers, trees, grottoes, and streams; (3) Nature's participation in the rites, with music echoing in the woods and hills, and trees and streams uniting; (4) Hymen as a subordinate of Venus in the role of a pipe-playing shepherd; (5) water-nymphs and sea-deities, catalogued by name, active in the festivities; (6) marriage as a bringer of peace to the state and harmony to the cosmos; (7) love-making as a battle; (8) Platonic relationship of lips to souls, and mind to beauty; (9) incarnation of abstract ideas—Concord, Anger, Youth, Age— and elements of allegory; (10) panegyric of both families; and (11) attention to personality traits and individuality of both gods and human participants.

Many imitations of both Statius and Claudian became long, tedious, and formula-like, and this tendency may account for the inclination of some critics to discount the merit of the originals, or to ignore them. One critic has called the epithalamium of Statius a "rather wooden mythological narrative centering on Venus and Cupid" and remarked that after Statius the only interesting nuptial poetry is found in Claudian's lyric fescennines.[34] Some of Statius's motifs do not seem to me "wooden"; for example, the persuasive advice of Venus to the reluctant bride, and the tender concern that the child shall not injure the mother-to-be as he makes his entrance into the world. There is humor as well as insight in Claudian's portrayal of Venus, with her calculated "sweet disorder" of dress and coiffure, her frank admiration of her own beauty, and her efficient delegation to her subordinates of the details of the wedding preparations. Unfortunately, such human elements as these were less susceptible of imitation than the more conventional aspects of theme and structure. Many of the successors of Statius and Claudian, and the rhetoricians who wrote the rules for epithalamium-writing tended to perpetuate the form rather than the spirit of these two poets.

Ausonius

An example of an epithalamium written by rule is the rhetorical tour de force, *Cento Nuptialis,* of Ausonius, Roman poet and grammarian, contemporary with Claudian.[35] In remarks preceding the poem, Ausonius explains that a cento is a patchwork composition built of lines borrowed from another poet or poets, and that in it a writer may borrow half a line, a whole line, or a line and a half, but never two whole lines in a row. Thus, says Ausonius, a cento is like the puzzle which the Greeks called *ostomachia,* in which fragments of bone are pieced together to form pictures of countless objects—a monstrous elephant, a brutal boar, a goose in flight, even a tower, or a tankard. Ausonius reports that his *Cento Nuptialis* was written at the command of the Emperor Valentinian, who had once described a wedding in a *jeu d'esprit* of this kind and had challenged Ausonius to compile a similar poem. Centos were common in later antiquity, but Ausonius is somewhat apologetic about having degraded the majestic verse of Virgil by picking from it fragments for his rhetorical game.

The *Cento* is of interest from the standpoint of epithalamic rhetoric in that it is divided into eight sections: (1) Praefatio; (2) Cena Nuptialis; (3) Descriptio Egredientis Sponsae; (4) Descriptio Egredientis Sponsi; (5) Oblatio Munerum; (6) Epithalamium Utrique; (7) Ingressus in Cubiculum, and (8) Imminutio. The Imminutio is preceded by a Parecbasis; the latter is a technical form used in oratory, and, according to Quintilian, has as its purpose to soften by anticipation the bad effect which something following may produce.[36] Here in the Parecbasis, Ausonius apologizes for the freedom of speech to come in the Imminutio but justifies it on the basis that the crowd at a wedding loves fescennine songs, and that there is long-established precedent. The poet declares that he blushes twice-over, however, in making Virgil immodest in the subsequent discussion of the secrets of bedchamber and couch. The Imminutio is followed by further apology from the poet and the declaration, quoted from Martial, "Lasciva est nobis pagina, vita proba," along with citations of precedent in Pliny, Sulpicia, Apuleius, Cicero's letters to Caerellia, Plato's *Symposium,* and the erotic verse of various other poets.[37]

Except for the Imminutio, the sections of this work express many of the usual commonplaces. The preface is somewhat like that of Claudian; later sections mention the bride's white foot, her flowing tresses, her robe like that of Helen, her beauty like that of Venus. Included also are the scattering of nuts, the prediction of the Parcae, the invocation of Venus and Juno as patrons of marriage, and the presentation of love-making as a battle. Unusual among the gifts for the bride, however, is a slave-girl with twin children at her breast, and for the bridegroom, four youths and four maids with shorn heads and gold necklets.

Sidonius

Two later narrative epithalamia are those of the Gaul, Apollinaris Sidonius (*c.* 430–483), which introduce Christian elements, although the poems abound in deities and mythological references. His *Epithalamium Ruricio et Hiberiae*[38] is marked by emphasis on the sea-deities we have seen in Claudian, the preface describing the wedding feast of the sea-maiden Thetis, daughter of Nereus, whose wedding to Peleus had by this time become a favorite subject of epithalamists. At the feast are assorted gods exhibiting their special talents—Jupiter hurling harmless thunderbolts, Hercules frolicking with his club, Mars brandishing his spear. Orpheus introduces the Muses and their instruments; Hymen is there, and Apollo with his lyre. Again Venus is portrayed on Triton's cushioned back, accompanied by Galatea and the sportive Loves, one riding a dolphin, and another a sea-calf, disdaining the bridle and clinging fearlessly to the calf's horns. The familiar Cupid–Venus dialogue appears, after which Venus sails off into the blue in her chariot drawn by swans, attended by the Graces, Plenty, Flora, Osiris, Ceres,

Pomona, and others. They arrive at the bridal chamber; here are incense, nard, balm, and myrrh, from the Psalms, and here too, the Phoenix—a new actor in our genre—amid the spice of his living pyre.[39] Venus joins the right hands of man and maid and wishes them not only children and grandchildren but great-grandchildren, too, who will envy the bliss of their great-grand-parents.

Written for a scholar and his bride, Sidonius's epithalamium addressed to *Polemio et Araneola*[40] is marked by its lengthy description of two adjoining temples consecrated to Pallas Athena, goddess of wisdom and of arts and crafts. The first temple is a home of philosophy, where the bridegroom Polemius learns all the doctrines of the sages, and the second is devoted to the textile arts. There the bride Araneola sits, doing wonderful embroidery, her subjects mostly from the love stories of mythology. Pallas indicates to Araneola that she prefers the subjects which are cultivated in the philosophical temple, and Araneola playfully begins to embroider a philosopher, Diogenes the Cynic, in a ridiculous situation. The goddess laughs and advises the bride-to-be not to mock the philosophers, because she is about to marry one. Pallas tells the bride to put on the bridal veil, summons the bridegroom, and orders him to put away his Stoic frown, to imitate the Cynic lovers, and shortly to bring her a second little Plato. The Fates with one accord unite the golden threads of the lovers.[41]

Martianus Capella

The textbook quality of the second epithalamium of Sidonius with its catalogue of philosophers and philosophies is not unique. Another work of about the same time, or possibly earlier, actually used as a textbook, is the curious encyclopaedic allegory in nine books by the Carthaginian Martianus Capella, the elaborate mixture of prose and poetry entitled *Satira* or *Satyricon*.[42] The first two books form a separate work, *De*

Nuptiis Philologiae et Mercurii, and treat of the apotheosis of the nymph Philology and her marriage with Mercury; the remaining seven books contain expositions of the seven liberal arts and the educational system. In the *De Nuptiis,* Mercury (Eloquence), seeking a bride, consults Apollo, who praises Philology (Learning). Jove decides to permit the marriage, and a council of the gods gives consent, throwing out Discord and Sedition, and raising Philology to the level of a deity. Juno as *pronuba* invites the gods to the wedding feast. Philology, dressed as a bride, is attended by the four cardinal virtues as bridesmaids; Mercury presents his gifts to her. The seven maids who will serve Philology are the seven liberal arts. The hymeneal for the occasion is sung by the Muses and is largely concerned with Philology's exaltation to the skies rather than with nuptial joys.[43]

Because of its use as a school book, this work exercised an influence in the Middle Ages out of all proportion to its intellectual and aesthetic deserts.[44] E. Faye Wilson sees the allegorical interpretations of this work, and possibly of other pagan rhetorical epithalamia, as a decisive factor in the creation of the Christian ascetic epic epithalamium.[45] Mercury and Philology—even Peleus and Thetis—become the bride and bridegroom in the mystical marriage of the Church and Christ, as in the Canticle of Solomon.

V

The Medieval Epithalamium and the Christian Tradition

The notion of a human marriage allegorized as a spiritual marriage runs through all Christian poetry and was widespread in the Middle Ages. The most influential works in this period were two Biblical epithalamia, the Canticle attributed to Solomon and the 44th Psalm of the Vulgate, the "Eructavit cor meum," which is the forty-fifth in the Authorized Version. As a result of the medieval interest in these two poems, the epithalamium of the period became a devotional as well as nuptial poem.[1] Hundreds of hymns and prose treatises called epithalamia, and a smaller number of rhetorical epic poems, were written for religious purposes, many of them uniting pagan and Christian conventions. Among the main themes were (1) celebration of mystical union with Christ; (2) praise of virginity as a mode of life; (3) tribute to a saint or celebration of a saint's day or other occasion such as the dedication of a church, birth of a child, or taking of vows by a nun; and (4) tribute to the Virgin Mary. The medieval devotion to allegory resulted ultimately in interpretations of epithalamia as chronicles of the whole progress of the race.[2]

Early in the Middle Ages the rhetorical epithalamium became a mixed and varied species, with some Biblical influences appearing, as we have noted in Sidonius.[3] Paradoxically, at about this time several Christian poets reinforced pagan and fescennine elements in the rhetorical genre. Although in Claudian's epithalamium for Palladius and Celerina the cruder rural deities had been banned from the Paradise of Venus,[4] a few years later they appear in full force in the epithalamia of Dracontius, a Christian living in the Vandal court of Africa in the late fifth century. Pan, Bacchus, and others of the retinue of Venus dance at the wedding and sing fescennine verses. Silenus, riding an ass, nods drunkenly as the Loves, nymphs, dryads, nereids, and others engage in sexual revelry.[5] Pagan deities and pastoral surroundings also appear in the rhetorical epithalamia of two other Christian epithalamists and hymn writers, Ennodius (b. 474) and Fortunatus (b. 430), although the pastoral environment is not the heavenly Paradise of Venus as in Statius and Claudian but an earthly setting for a mortal wedding.[6]

The Bacchic revelers and the fescennine songs disappear in the *Laurentian epithalamium,* sometimes attributed to Claudian but now generally agreed to be post-Claudian.[7] It is a de-paganized rhetorical epithalamium, perhaps influenced by the hostility of the church toward pagan practices at weddings, which was officially expressed in the canons of the Council of Laodicea in the fourth century forbidding Christians to sing or dance at weddings. Reproducing the praise of the bride and bridegroom, and the *allocutio sponsalis* of the Greek form, it stresses both the physical beauty of the bride and her mental gifts—she engages in intellectual activities, she reads and writes well, and she cultivates the Muses. The rites are Christian, although some are those adopted by Christians from pagan ceremony: the *iunctio dextrarum,* the veiling of the bride, and the use of the ring. Instead of fescennine revelry, we have the musical instruments of the Christian Psalms.

The rhetorical epithalamium takes its place in the background as the great Christian lyrics emerge—the Biblical Canticle ascribed to Solomon by Christian commentators, and the other Hebrew epithalamium, the 44th Psalm. In the view of Biblical commentators, it was Solomon who composed the first epithalamium, often referred to as "the sacred pastoral," but David also knew the art. Christian commentators explained that the Hebrews passed the art to the Greeks, who, failing to comprehend Solomon's mysteries, nevertheless adopted the form. Interpretations of the Hebrew epithalamia as celebrations of mystical marriage appear in Christian literature as early as Origen (*c.* 185–254). According to E. Faye Wilson:

> . . . the Canticle was considered to be an epithalamium in the form of a drama celebrating the Incarnation: the wedding of Christ, the bridegroom, to the flesh, the bride, in the marriage chamber of the Virgin Mary. Or to put it in other ways, the marriage of Christ and the Church, of the human soul and the Logos, of Christ and the human soul, or later of Christ and the Virgin Mary, the mystical type of both. Origen thought of the dialogue as between four participants: the bride and bridegroom; and two choruses, one composed of companions of the bridegroom, angels and saints, and the other of companions of the bride, the faithful of the church on earth. The *44th Psalm,* beginning at least with St. Augustine, was subjected to the same sort of interpretation. He clearly identifies it with the sort of epithalamia being composed and recited at weddings by rhetoricians of his day.[8]

Looking at the 44th Psalm as an epithalamium for a human union, one sees in it praise of the bride, the bridegroom, and their marriage. The reader is reminded of Claudian's preface by the brief prologue in which the writer tells of his eagerness to sing a tribute to the king who is the bridegroom:

> My heart overfloweth with a good matter;
> I speak the things which I have made concerning the king;
> My tongue is the pen of a ready writer . . . .[9]

The bridegroom is praised for his fair appearance, his prowess in war, and his love of righteousness. His sweet-scented garments smell of myrrh, aloes, and cassia. The bride is praised for her beauty, both inward and outward, and her rich raiment. The poet pictures the virgins who attend her, and the rich gifts of the daughters of Tyre and others. She is urged to forget her own people, for the king desires her, and to worship the king as her lord. The poet remarks on the gladness and rejoicing, promises offspring who will become princes, and pledges to the king that his name shall be remembered by succeeding generations and praised forever. The role of the poet himself is significant in that the poem appears to be a spontaneous expression of the poet's rejoicing not only in the good fortune of his king but in the poet's own craft, culminating in his pledge that as a poet he will make immortal the name of his king.[10]

St. Augustine in his commentary on the 44th Psalm in *De Civitate Dei* begins by explaining the allegorical and metaphorical method which he construes the Psalmist to have used:

> For although there be some manifest prophecies, yet are they mixed with figures; putting the learned into a great deale of labour, in making the ignorant understand them, yet some shew *Christ* and his *Church* at first sight . . . as for example, *Psal. 45* . . . . Who is so dull that he discerneth not *Christ* our *God,* in whom we beleeve, by this place? . . . And then behold his Church, that spirituall spouse of his, and that divine wed-locke of theirs . . . .

> Seeing therefore that the Prophet so long agoe said that of this citty which now we behold come to effect: *Insteed of fathers thou shal have children, to make them Princes over all the earth*

(for so hath shee when whole nations and their rulers, come freely
to confesse & professe Christ his truth for ever and ever) then
without all doubt, there is no trope herein, how ever understood,
but hath direct reference unto these manifestations.[11]

The Spanish scholar Juan Luis Vives, who at the instance of his
friend Erasmus in 1522 published an elaborate commentary on
Augustine's *De Civitate Dei,* in his elucidation of this passage
reinforces Augustine's view of the Psalm as an allegory by citing
other examples of poems diverted from their original purpose to
a new one.[12] His main examples are the centones:

> Like parcells Centones are peeces of cloath of diverse colours;
> used anyway, on the back or on the bedde . . . . Metaphorically it
> is a poeme patched out of other poems by ends of verses . . . .

Vives then elaborates on how a poet may pick verses out of "some
greater workes concerning another purpose," and apply them to
his own purpose "as some Centonists did, turning Virgils and
Homers words of the Greekes and Troyan warres, unto Christ
and divine matters: And Ausonius turneth them unto an Epithalamion."[13]

Augustine views the Canticle also as a metaphorical poem
of rejoicing over the mystical marriage of Christ and the Church:

> Now for the Canticles it is a certaine spirituall and holy delight
> in the mariage of the King and Queene of this citty, that is,
> Christ and the Church. But this is all in mysticall figures, to in-
> flame us the more to search the truth and to delight the more in
> finding the appearance of that bridegrome to whom it is sayd
> there: *truth* hath *loved thee,* and of that bride, that receiveth this
> word, *love is in thy delights.*[14]

The Catholic allegorical view of the Canticle was adhered to on
the whole by the reformed church, and one need only consult the
chapter headings in the Authorized King James Version to see
reiterated the view of the union as that of Christ and the Church.

Modern scholars tend to see both the Canticle and the 44th Psalm as poems associated at their origin with human love and marriage.[15] Schonfield says the Canticle was probably written in the first quarter of the fourth century B.C. when Palestine was still under Persian rule, and he and other commentators suggest that, like the pagan epithalamium, the Canticle may owe something of its language and structure to the old fertility cult rituals. The fertility rites fit in with the wedding-feast customs and those of betrothal, Schonfield remarks,

> . . . for they celebrate in some sense like the allegory theory the mystical union of Heaven and Earth, and the sowing of seed which enables the Earth embraced by the rains to yield its produce . . . . The love passages and *wasfs* of the liturgies equally have natural affinities with many an ancient love song.[16]

The details of the many modern interpretations of the Canticle— for example, the drama theory and the wedding-feast theory— are of little concern to us here. There is little question that the poem concerns a wedding or union of lovers, that its pastoral nature is sophisticated and literary rather than of folk origin, that the poem is erotic, and that it displays many parallels with other wedding literature. E. Faye Wilson's view of the poem as an epithalamium of a comparatively slender structure is as defensible, I think, as any other interpretation. In her view, the poem begins with a dialogue between bride and bridegroom (chapters 1–3). A description of the beauty of the bride is followed by praise of the bridegroom. The remainder of the epithalamium is addressed to the bride by the bridegroom.[17]

In relation to the epithalamic tradition, the extensive commentaries on the Canticle through the centuries are almost as important as the poem itself. The informal structure, as Miss Wilson observes, was a great advantage to the commentators, for it enabled them to see in it any sort of wedding ceremony they wished, pagan Greek or Christian Roman. Origen could identify it with the most elaborate type of Greek nuptial poetry, a part of a drama such as those forbidden to clerks by the Council of Laodicea. St. Jerome could see in it a Roman marriage ceremony, with the attendants of the bride and bridegroom singing alternately. Their allegorical interpretations of the poem as celebration of a mystical marriage between Christ and the Church could even be pushed by St. Augustine to the point of using the song as a criterion for settling controversies within the church.[18]

The commentaries themselves became a part of the epithalamic tradition when many authors, among them Innocent III, applied the title *epithalamium* to their bulky allegorical treatises. Such treatises, sermons, and homilies on the Canticle were produced by the hundreds, the most prolific author being St. Bernard of Clairvaux (d. 1153), who wrote eighty-six homilies of about 170,000 words but died before he got beyond the first verse of the third chapter.[19] The Canticle commentaries played another role in the epithalamic tradition in that they helped to preserve through several centuries the theory of the epithalamium as rhetoric. Although the Canticle itself is lyric and dramatic, some critics made rhetorical exercises of their commentaries. Cassiodorus, for example, divides his remarks into *divisio, expositio,* and *conclusio,* and asserts that in keeping with the style among orators, the bridegroom and bride are each described in four ways, which he elaborates at length.[20] Thus, the superimposing of rhetorical conventions upon the Canticle helped to keep the concept of the rhetorical epithalamium alive.

The Ascetic Epithalamium

Glorification of mystical marriage as allegorized in the Canticle and 44th Psalm was concomitant with the disparagement of earthly marriage. The medieval rage for virginity is demonstrated in the ascetic epithalamium, which frequently utilizes pagan nuptial conventions in celebrations of virginity as a mode of life. Miss Wilson's investigations indicate that the earliest ascetic epithalamia are lyric. Among the first is that of Methodius of Olympus in 311, modeled upon the Greek marriage song and honoring the mystical marriage of virgins dedicated to the bridegroom Christ. In it are two choruses of virgins engaged in the exaltation of virginity in contrast to the exaltation of marriage. We have seen the marriage-versus-virginity debates in the classical epithalamium, with the palm going to the defenders of marriage. In the ascetic epithalamium we find the same debate, but virginity wins. Another example of the theme is found in the *In laudem virginitatis* of Gregory Nazianzen (*c.* 355), a student of Himerius at Athens. His epithalamium is a debate similar to that of Catullus 62, with Christ giving the decision to the champions of virginity. The same poet's *Exhortatio ad virgines* is an epithalamium written after the model of Himerius, in praise of the virgin as the mystical bride of Christ. A prose epithalamium, the letter of St. Jerome to Demetrias, a virgin of noble birth who dedicated herself to Christ, urges the young lady to hold fast to her decision but describes the way she would be adorned if she were a bride. As a virgin she will have only "rosae virginitatis et lilia castitatis" and the white robe of virginity.[21]

In the epithalamium of Paulinus of Nola for Julian and Titia we recognize a familiar vehicle. The chariot of Venus drawn by swans or doves has been taken over by Christ, and the heathen attendants are replaced by Christian personifications, *Pax, Pudor,* and *Pietas.* A car of some kind, as we have seen, had long been a feature of pagan epithalamia as a conveyance for the bride in procession or for Venus en route to weddings. Brides of the Church in the sacred epithalamium were accommodated with similar transportation, Radbert Paschasius, monk of Corbei, having found justification for the vehicle in the chariot of Aminadab in the Canticle. In the later Middle Ages Venus's chariot became the chariot of the Evangelists or even the chariot of the Church. In the work of Paulinus, instead of Love animating Chaos as in the pagan mythology, it is God himself who sanctions marriage in the creation of Eve. Christ replaces Hymen as speaker and serves as *pronuba,* adorning the maiden with virtues.[22]

Parts of the *Laurentian epithalamium* are used by St. Aldhelm, one of the earliest writers in England whose name we know and one of the first proponents of the classics, to exalt virginity rather than marriage in his long prose *De virginitate*. Both Paulinus and Aldhelm use a device of antithesis or negation reminiscent of some of the poems I have cited as anti-epithalamia in the classical tradition.[23] In this spiritual marriage there are no noisy wedding processions, no dancing in the streets, no wedding gifts, no golden ornaments, no rustling silks, no false beauty, no perfuming of garments, no building of lofty turrets on the head. The poets glorify virginity and the hardships of the ascetic mode of life by citing the absence of pagan nuptial adjuncts.

The pagan epithalamium thus exerts its influence in a variety of ways, and combines, in Miss Wilson's words,

> . . . with the sensuous Hebrew epithalamium as its confederate . . . to glorify the mystical marriage of Christ and the church in Origen, Augustine, and Cassiodorus and all the commentators after them; and asceticism in St. Jerome, Paulinus of Nola and Aldhelm—a few examples among many.[24]

The Epithalamium as Tribute to a Saint or Celebration of a Religious Event

In the development of the medieval epithalamium as a tribute to a saint, the name of Radbert Paschasius, monk and later abbot of Corbei in the ninth century, is significant. Author of a long commentary in three books on the 44th Psalm, in which he includes excerpts from the Canticle, he was well versed in the Hebrew epithalamia and their multitude of interpretations. Influences from the two epithalamia and the second book of Cicero's *De inventione* are combined with biographical data in Radbert's history of a saint's life, the *Vita Adalhardi*, written to honor a one-time abbot of Corbei. Miss Wilson describes the *Vita* as "an unusual combination of epithalamium and eclogue devoted to the uses of panegyric."[25] Two centuries later another monk was persuaded by Gerard of Corbei to rewrite the *Vita* in order to have "the flowers gathered from the over-verdant mead," Gerard arguing that the original work was so full of the amorous langour of the Canticle that it was indeed an epithalamium rather than a biography. Gerard regarded as particularly offensive the closing eclogue, in which two nuns, Galathea and Phyllis, compete in praising and mourning the saint; the erotic symbolism of the Canticle pervades the saint's apparel, his abbey, and his mind, the latter being the "garden enclosed" of the Song. But the new version was also very like an epithalamium.

Radbert also wrote a commentary-epithalamium as a kind of love-note to the nuns of Notre Dame de Soissons in 846, feeling that he was thus "scattering flowers before the couches of the virgins of God."[26] The bride is the Church, and the nuns are the virgins dedicated to the Church. In commenting on the history of the epithalamium, he refers to the 44th Psalm as a trope of the kind designated by the grammarians as *antomasia*, in which the significance of the thing is drawn out by the question and answer method. Trope books in celebration of saints' days thus become associated with the epithalamium; in fact, some became collections of poems called "epithalamia."

The need of the early church for appropriate literature for celebration of saints' days and other special occasions is important as a motive in the writing of epithalamia. In the Mozarabic liturgy[27] is presented a collection of hymns dating from the eighth century, which includes a lyric epithalamium connected with an actual marriage ceremony. It is one of a group of hymns appropriate for various "calamities" of life, and is to be sung by the people of Christ in the church during the wedding ceremony. Adam and Eve are substituted for the pagan gods and goddesses, there is decoration of the couch and wedding chambers, the musical instruments are those of the Psalms and of the commentaries on the 44th Psalm, and the conclusion expresses the hope of a large posterity. As Miss Wilson remarks, the skeleton is that of the pagan epithalamium with the flesh of Genesis and the Psalms.

In Bede's *Ecclesiastical History* there is inserted a hymn for St. Edilthrida, praising her as a bride of Christ and saluting her as "nupta Deo" rather than as the "nova nupta" of Catullus. We see the coming of the *sponsus,* the wedding torches, the gifts, songs, and exultation over heavenly joys. Also, one finds the dedication of a church in the eighth century treated in the same way—the church as the bride of God, a description of its beauty, and praise of the Bridegroom.[28]

Theodolf of Orleans, a scholar at the Carolingian court, is author of some epithalamium-like verses written to accompany his gift of a magnificent psalter to one Gisla on the occasion of her marriage to Suavericus. It includes several of the characteristic themes of the classical epithalamium—the musical instruments of the Psalms, the reference to wool and advice about household duties, and the promise of offspring. In the seventeenth century Richard Crashaw wrote such an ascetic epithalamium to accompany his gift of a prayer-book to a young woman.[29]

Although it may not have been written for any particular saint or occasion, a related practical example of the epithalamium appears in a ninth-century versified commentary on the Canticle by one Sigfred. It is in the form of an abcedarius.[30]

Epithalamia to the Virgin Mary

The tendency to make all sacred literature contribute to the praise of the Virgin is illustrated in the development of the epithalamium. In the twelfth century it becomes customary for the Virgin Mary to appear as a substitute for the Church and the human soul as the mystical bride of Christ. Much earlier, in some of the commentaries and in the poem of Gregory Nazianzen, she had been a bride of Christ along with the virgins of God, but she assumes a special role in the twelfth century, best defined by Alan of Lille.[31] According to him, the Canticle in a particular and spiritual sense refers to the Virgin Mary, and he compares the Church to Mary in a great many different ways. The Church of God is the mother of Christ by means of grace; so the Virgin is the mother of Christ by means of the Incarnation. Just as the Church is without spot or wrinkle, so is the glorious Virgin. Just as the Church possesses all gifts in different persons, so the Virgin Mary in herself is the whole of virtue.

A great number of psalters dedicated to the Virgin and called *epithalamia* appear in the late twelfth and early thirteenth centuries.[32] They always contain panegyric, and usually several stanzas portray the mystical marriage, and present an epithalamium. Sometimes a lyric epithalamium precedes the psalter as an introduction. There is frequently extensive description of the Bride, often utilizing imagery from the Canticle. The Virgin has golden hair bound with laurel; her eyebrows are faultless and unpencilled; and her eyes, ears, nose, cheeks, head, arms and hands are described in detail:

> O quam praeclara lumine
>   Sunt oculi micantes,
> Ut stellae de cacumine
>   Caelorum illustrantes.
> Sunt nares aequalissimi,
>   Sunt labia rubentes,
> Ut ebur candidissimi
>   Resplendent, ecce dentes.[33]

In the marriage chamber are flowers from the Canticle, with additions from Pliny and the herbals. The Paradise offers flowers, trees, and music, including the instruments from the Canticle and the Psalms. In one romantic epithalamium by Conrad of Hirschau, we see the strewing of flowers and fragrant herbs, the attendant maidens bearing palms of victory, the Virgin Bride wearing garlands of flowers, the bridal couch decked with roses and lilies.[34] The poet's theme is the triumph of the Virgin of God and of virginity in general, in a setting of a paradise of divine love, just as the rhetorical epithalamia of Statius and Claudian displayed the triumph of the goddess Venus and love in a pagan paradise. The Virgin ascends to heaven in a chariot like that of Venus; she is attended by a court of the Virtues in place of the Loves, Graces, and Muses. There is a suggestion of the personification which produced the fantastic bird courts of the medieval love paradise. In Conrad's work the Virtues are pictured as doves beside abounding streams, flowing from two sources, the evangelists and the fathers.

The thirteenth-century *Epithalamium beate Marie Virginis* of John of Garland in ten books of hexameters is a Mary epic, a panegyric written in honor of the Virgin in whom the Church and the soul of man are also represented.[35] But in a sense, according to Miss Wilson, it is also a cloak for the paganism of the classical epithalamium. The author viewed it as a revival of the epic epithalamium of ancient times, with the Virgin Mary replacing Venus as heroine. He also viewed it as a kind of Mary psalter, and as a textbook in the form of an epithalamium. As an epic, it reflects the rhetorical epithalamia of Claudian and Sidonius, along with the Christian interpretations placed upon Martianus Capella. Miss Wilson situates it in the context of two other works of the time also associated with the epithalamic tradition, the sacred, didactic epithalamium of Alan of Lille, and the pagan and secular *Phyllis and Flora*.[36] In the epithalamium of John of Garland, secular and sacred combine.

The point should be emphasized here that throughout the Middle Ages secular and sacred forms mingled. The Canticle, treatises, and hymns influenced secular love poetry; classical and medieval love poetry influenced the sacred works. Some of the epithalamia of the Mary psalters could be read equally well as secular love poems. The few Latin and Greek secular nuptial lyrics of this period are of relatively little consequence in the development of the genre.[37]

The Epithalamium as the Chronicle of Man

Medieval epithalamia came to include hymns expressing mystical longing of the soul for union with God, tributes to saints, songs for dedication of churches or commemoration of saints' days, textbooks, Mary psalters and epics. They also include hymns and eclogues on the Nativity and the Incarnation, and these came to be associated with the fourth eclogue of Virgil, which the Middle Ages considered the "Messianic eclogue," foretelling the birth of Christ and portraying the golden age which would follow.[38]

Revived interest in the classics and the desire to reconcile pagan wisdom with Christian revelation produced new commentaries on the major classics, including Virgil's *Eclogues, Georgics,* and *Aeneid,* as well as Plato's *Timaeus* and Ovid's *Metamorphoses.* Writers applied to them the same sort of allegorical interpretation they had given the Scriptures, and also wrote original allegorical epic poems concerned with the nature and fate of man. One aspect of this humanistic revival was renewed attention to the *De Nuptiis Philologiae et Mercurii* of Martianus Capella, as well as to other rhetorical epithalamia.[39] A commentary attempting to reconcile the *De Nuptiis* with the Christian Scriptures was written by Alexander Nequam. He interpreted the nuptials celebrated in this book in three ways: (1) earthly harmony, which is the union of the four elements; (2) mellic harmony, the union of eloquence and wisdom; and (3) human harmony, the union of the soul and body which is man. Further, he allegorized the bridegroom Peleus as representing earth; Thetis, water; and Jupiter, who joined the two in marriage, fire. Of this union was born Achilles, the perfect man. Peleus is then flesh; Thetis, humor; and Jupiter, soul.[40]

Biblical commentators also viewed the Canticle as a complete epic of mankind, beginning with the Creation and concluding with the marriage feast of the Lamb. Epithalamia, or marriages, thus became chronicles of the whole progress of the individual man, and the human race. As Miss Wilson points out, by means of the historical epithalamium (the marriage of Adam and Eve) man is born; by means of the philosophical epithalamium (the *De Nuptiis* of Capella), he is educated in the knowledge of God; by means of the theological epithalamium (the Canticle), the marriage of the spiritual Bride and Bridegroom, he is saved.[41]

The multiple modes of development of the medieval epithalamium and the interweaving of classical and Christian strands were part of an intricate and lengthy process. Most writers on the epithalamium have given little attention to this phase of the tradition, partly, I am sure, because Miss Wilson's study has not been readily available. One writer has remarked: "In the Middle Ages Latin devotional poems entitled *Epithalamium* were written, but they had virtually nothing in common with the classical genre."[42] One purpose of this chapter has been to demonstrate that these devotional poems had, indeed, a great deal in common with the classical genre. In subsequent chapters, their importance as background for the English tradition will become clear. The summary here is greatly indebted to Miss Wilson and necessarily sketchy, but the bounds of the present study demand that, like St. Augustine in his comments on the Canticle, "I omit many things with silence, to draw the work towards an end."

VI

Neo-Latin and Continental Vernacular Epithalamia of the Renaissance

Prose orations, rhetorical works in hexameters, and lyric poems in a variety of meters all appear among the hundreds of neo-Latin epithalamia of the fifteenth and sixteenth centuries. At the same time, the lyric predominates among the vernacular epithalamia in Italian, French, and Spanish.[1] Van Winkle observes that the many neo-Latin epithalamia between the fall of Constantinople and the time of Spenser were "tedious for the most part, sadly lacking in inspiration, novelty of thought or expression."[2] There are exceptions, however, and in some of the better neo-Latin poems I note three trends which seem to be of consequence to the English tradition: increased emphasis on political, topographical, and historical description and narrative, as in Ariosto and Buchanan; concentration on erotic description of conjugal union, as in Pontanus and Secundus; and use of the epithalamium as vehicle for philosophy, social commentary, and moral instruction, as in Erasmus.[3] The vernacular poems, especially those of the Pléiade but also a few poems in Italian and Spanish, were important to the English genre in that they transmitted classical and later-Latin motifs, in particular from Theocritus, Catullus, Statius, and Claudian. In addition, they reinforced the role of the epithalamium as a pastoral poem, and they provided metrical patterns suitable for imitation in English —subtleties in refrain, varied line length, linking rhymes, the sonnet form, and the nine-line stanza. And certain of the vernacular poems were chosen for direct translation or adaptation into English.

Neo-Latin Epithalamia

Among the collected Latin epithalamia are those of German, Italian, French, Dutch, Scottish, Belgian, Hungarian, and Danish poets.[4] The largest single collection of such works, the *Delitiae Poetarum Germanorum* (1612), contains more than two hundred poems, "quite uninspired," to use Van Winkle's words, and of little influence on the English tradition. Apparently some of these poets increased their incomes by dedicating such verses to newly-married persons.[5] Peleus–Thetis narratives are interspersed with praise of bride and bridegroom, and long Teutonic family names are incorporated into the verse. Many poems are modeled on Statius and Claudian, but a few are patterned on the Catullan lyrics and on classical eclogues. Christ and the angels sometimes replace the heathen deities or join them, as in some of the thirty *Nuptialia* of Georgius Bersmannus (1536–1611).[6]

Among the Italian Latinists are Francesco Filelfo (1398–1481), Gabriel Altilius (late fifteenth century), Joannes Jovianus Pontanus (1426–1503), the elder Flaminio (*c.* 1464–1536), and

Lodovico Ariosto (1474–1533). Filelfo's epithalamia are prose orations which follow the precepts of the rhetoricians but include Christian argument. The oration for the marriage of Beatrice d' Este and Tristano Sforza in 1455, for example, discusses the origin of wedlock, declaring that God in Paradise designed it, and that Christ was born in wedlock, and at the nuptials at Cana showed his approval of it.[7] The long poem of Altilius for the marriage of Isabella of Aragon and the Duke of Milan is partly modeled upon Theocritus but is mainly descriptive.[8] An epithalamium by the elder Flaminio is almost a cento, a re-arrangement of the phrases of Statius.[9] The epithalamia of Pontanus, some of them written for the weddings of his daughters, are more original. His bold treatment of the joys of conjugal love anticipates that of Tasso and Marino, and of the Dutch Secundus, the French Bonefonius, and a few English poets, among them Ben Jonson. J. A. Symonds says that Pontanus in these poems is "bent upon expressing the facts of modern life, the actualities of personal emotion, in a style of accurate Latinity."[10] Several are in elegiacs but some of the brief lyrics are in hendecasyllablics, among them his "Nuptiis Joan. Branchati et Maritellae," with the central motif of love as a battle in the nuptial chamber.[11] Another work written about the same time, Ariosto's epithalamium (1501) for the marriage of Lucrezia Borgia and Alphonso d'Este, son of the Duke of Ferrara, includes many original features, although it is basically an adaptation of the amoebaean Catullus 62. The exchanges between the youths of Rome and the youths of Ferrara, with details of local politics, topography, and history, foreshadow some later poems in England.[12]

The most remarkable neo-Latin contributions are those of the Dutch poets, among them Erasmus, whose *Colloquies* include an epithalamium; Johannes Secundus (1511–1536); Hadrianus Junius Hornanus (mid-sixteenth century); Joachimus Axonius Gravianus (d. 1605); Daniel Heinsius (1580–1665); Hugo Grotius (1583–1645); and Caspar Barlaeus (1584–1648). Erasmus's witty dialogue between Alipius and Balbinus pokes good-humored fun at the mythological trappings common in epithalamia but manages also to praise patrons of liberal studies, philosophize on the obtuseness of the schoolmen, and give advice on marriage. It identifies as patron of marriage, not a lustful Venus, but a heavenly one who unites beautiful souls and minds in beautiful bodies. The work ends with a brief song, each of the Muses in turn asking a blessing and comparing the bride or bridegroom to historical figures noted for marital devotion. The introductory dialogue presents Alipius in the role of a discerning man chatting with the Muses and Graces, who have come to sing an epithalamium for Petrus Aegidius and his bride Cornelia. Contrasted with Alipius is Balbinus, a disciple of Duns Scotus, who is unable to see or hear the Muses and Graces, even after Alipius has taken a laurel bough and splashed him with water from a clear spring.

The mixed playful-serious style of the exchanges between Alipius and the Muses allows a considerable amount of instruction about proper marriages to be carried easily on the flow of conversation.[13] It may be said that the infinite variety of the epithalamium is never better illustrated than in the works of this whole group of Dutch neo-Latin poets. In contrast to the easy wit and sweet reasonableness of Erasmus, we find, for example, the stiff formality of Hadrianus Junius Hornanus, who in 1554, in 770 hexameters, paid tribute to the marriage of Philip of Spain and Queen Mary of England, borrowing heavily from Virgil.[14] Joachimus Axonius Gravianus devoted more than eight hundred lines to an epithalamium, which he preferred to call a "gamelion," and in it included a Christian priest and the Christian marriage ceremony, along with Juno, Hymen, and Apollo. Much more in keeping with the tone of Erasmus are the epithalamia of two other scholars, Daniel Heinsius, from whom Jonson admits borrowing in his epithalamium written in 1608, and Hugo Grotius, whose third book of *Sylvae* is devoted to nuptialia, including narratives, an amoebaean song, a translation of Theocritus's Idyll 18, and his "epithal. Pottei," which has been described as "a noteworthy essay of the frank, erotic school."[15]

Foremost among the Dutch epithalamia, of course, is an earlier poem of "the frank, erotic school," the work of Johannes Secundus (Jan Everaerts). Its influence on English poetry may have been enhanced by the praise it received from Puttenham in his chapter on the epithalamium in *The Arte of English Poesie:*

> Catullus hath made of them (epithalamia) one or two very artificiall and civil: but none more excellent then of late yeares a young noble man of Germanie as I take it *Johannes Secundus* who in that and in his poem *de basiis,* passeth any of the auncient or moderne Poetes in my judgment.[16]

Like Pontanus in the "Nuptiis Joan. Branchati et Maritellae," Secundus uses the hendecasyllabic metre favored by Catullus in his shorter poems.[17] The 145 lines of Secundus's poem are divided into eleven strophes ranging in length from ten to eighteen lines, and marked by a refrain with novel variations. In the first five stanzas the same refrain is repeated and concerns the happy man and happy maid, "O felix iuvenis, puella felix." The consummation of the union is marked by a change in the refrain of the next five stanzas, the new refrain commenting on the blissful night, with variations indicating an increase in the degree of bliss, moving from the conventional thrice-happy to four times, and beyond measure:

> O noctem ter et amplius beatam!
> O noctem quater et quater beatam.
> O noctem quater, o quater beatam!
> O noctem nimis et nimis beatam!

The final stanza returns exultantly to

> O felix iuvenis, puella felix![18]

Secundus borrows from Catullus's Carmina 61 and 62 and also utilizes the kissing motif of Carmen 5, source also of the theme of his *Basia.*[19] The amorous struggle in Secundus's epithalamium is reminiscent too of Claudian's fourth fescennine verse. Secundus at times attains some of the grace of Catullus, but as McPeek remarks, "the difference between his manner in his *Epithalamium,* sensuous and pleasantly wanton as compared with the fine delicacy of Catullus, is as the difference between Rubens and Giorgione."[20] Another difference, significant in relation to the general trend of the epithalamium as a genre, is that in the classical epithalamium any description of the bridal night is part of the large tapestry of events, but in Pontanus and in Secundus such description becomes the central concern.

A disciple of Secundus among the French Latinists is Joannes Bonefonius (1554–1614), whose "Pervigilium Veneris" Ben Jonson praised to Drummond and said he had imitated.[21] Adrien Turnebus (1512–1565) and the French chancellor Michel de l'Hospital (1504–1573) were among those to write Latin epithalamia for the marriage of Mary Queen of Scots and Francis II of France, poems which Case describes as "tedious." A more original epithalamium of the French Latinists is that by Areodatus Seba (*c.* 1550), "In nuptias Jani Garneri et Margaretae Uraniae," in which the poet assails the bride for stealing from him his friend, the bridegroom.[22] The poet pleads with Margareta to "give me back my Janus" and describes the virtues of his friend. The poet proposes a compact: Instead of demanding the time of her new husband night and day, will Margareta permit him to join his friends half of the time? When his request is denied, the poet demands that the bride, in return for her husband, must each year give another Janus to his friends.[23] McPeek points to the influence of Catullus 62 on Seba's poem as well as on other epithalamia of the French neo-Latinists.[24]

Ideas from Catullus and Statius blend with Scottish history in the most important epithalamium of the English neo-Latinists, that of the Scot George Buchanan for the marriage of Mary Queen of Scots and Francis II, one of the best

Latin epithalamia after Claudian.[25] It opens with the woods
of Parnassus ringing, the streams rejoicing, Apollo and the
Muses singing—sounds that may be heard now that war has
ended. Throngs of people on the streets of Paris join in the
exultation and shout *Hymen, Hymenaeus adest* as the wedding
day arrives. The poet praises and exhorts the bridegroom,
then comments on the bridegroom's good fortune in being
able to woo his bride in person instead of having to rely on a
painting which might have lent her charms she did not have.
His love is praised as virtuous and prudent rather than lustful, and the people of France are said to regard the bridegroom's joys as their own. Elaborate praise of the bride includes her physical beauty and mental powers. The next part
of the poem is significant in indicating a trend in the tradition: about one-third of the epithalamium is an account of the
history of Scotland and the race of kings which sired the
bride, the account concluding with the declaration that this
glorious history is the dowry which the virgin brings. The poet
cites the firm treaties which have joined Scotland and France
in the past, expresses the usual appeal for offspring, and prays
for the continued unity of Scotland and France.[26]

Italian Vernacular Epithalamia

The increasing use of the epithalamium as panegyric for
members of royal or wealthy families, as in the Latin poems
of Claudian, Ariosto, and Buchanan, brought with it inclusion of more and more biographical, historical, and geographical data. The trend is best demonstrated in the Italian
vernacular epithalamium, which had its beginning in the early
sixteenth-century "raccolte"—collections of verse, sometimes
in several languages, dedicated to some special person or occasion.[27] The "per nozze raccolte" came into being after the ad-
vent of printing, taking the place of the Latin wedding orations
and eulogies customary in the fifteenth century among patrician

families. Torquato Tasso writes that his father Bernardo in 1537 composed the first epithalamium in Italian.[28] Whether or not this is correct, others had appeared by mid-century, but it was not until the later years of the century, according to C. Hagberg Wright's study of the London Library's collection of over 2,500 *nozze,* that there came into vogue anthologies of verse—"per nozze raccolte"—printed for private circulation at the marriage of nobles, and "more or less appropriate to the occasion."[29] Editions of from fifty to one hundred copies were printed for distribution among the families of the bride and bridegroom.[30]

Over the years such poems gradually came to have less and less personal application, Wright observes, and eventually "historical essays, accounts of voyages, and biographical sketches took the place of the old extravagant eulogies and fulsome tributes to the bride's perfections."[31] The later *nozze* frequently dealt with a noteworthy event or personage of preceding centuries, only the title page having any reference to the bride and bridegroom. Sometimes even the dedication was addressed to someone other than the bridal couple, as in a 1611 work: although the poem was written to honor the wedding of an Austrian noble to a countess living in Vicenza, the dedication was addressed to the Venetian ambassador.[32] The complete transformation of the *nozze* took about two centuries, but the trend away from the older epithalamic conventions and toward emphasis on topographical, historical, and patriotic motifs is evident in the sixteenth century.[33]

The works of the two most important writers of nuptial poetry in Italian during this period—Torquato Tasso and Giambattista Marino—are highly individual, although both poets borrow from the traditions. Students of the English epithalamium have for the most part ignored Tasso's thirteen nuptial poems,[34] perhaps because he did not title them *epithalamia* but "Nelle nozzi di ..." or "Per le nozze di ...." All are short lyrics, most of them sonnets, and they reveal his familiarity with the marriage poems of Catullus and the *fescennina* of Claudian, although they do not dwell on the usual motifs. Marino also wrote nuptial sonnets, but his main works in the genre are much longer than Tasso's, the ten *Epitalami del Cavalier Marino,* published in 1616,[35] ranging from three pages to thirty-three pages and differing greatly among themselves. Marino's familiarity with classical and neo-Latin epithalamia is apparent, but his works are even more unconventional in theme than Tasso's. Of consequence to the English tradition are a few traits the two poets have in common—extravagant conceits, bold expression (found occasionally in Tasso but regularly in Marino), and use of the sonnet and *canzone* metrical patterns. Metrical characteristics include stanzas of varying numbers of lines—nine, ten, eleven, thirteen, fourteen, sixteen, are typical; use of a *tornata;* lines of varying length in accordance with a regular pattern; and interlacing rhymes. There is some preference for the nine-line stanza, and this is seen also in French, Spanish, and English epithalamia.[36]

Tasso's poems are not conventional descriptions of the events of the wedding day, narrative accounts of mythological marriages, singing contests, praise of marriage as an institution, or conventional panegyric. In several of them Tasso makes a brief nod in the direction of a classical epithalamium, as if he were setting out to imitate it, but he soon abandons the model. For example, in the "Celebra le nozze del signor Principe d'Urbino e di madama Lucrezia d'Este lodando l'una casa e l'altra"[37] written in 1570, the opening line summons Hymen in the manner of Catullus 61, "Lascia, Imeneo, Parnaso, e qui discendi," and the third and fourth stanzas likewise summon him, "Vieni, Imeneo." The entire poem is a hymn to Hymen, but it bears little additional resemblance to Catullus 61. In like manner, Tasso's "Celebra le nozze del signor don Alfonso (d'Este) il giovine e de la signora donna Marfisa d'Este"[38] appears to have been inspired by Catullus 62. The poem opens and closes with the motif of Hesperus, the evening star, and it makes brief reference to the Catullan motifs of the ivy embracing the tree, and the untouched rose which is plucked, but most of its 120 lines are original.[39] Thetis and Peleus of Catullus 64 are mentioned in one of Tasso's 1581 nuptial sonnets, but except for the names there is no resemblance to Catullus. Here and there in Tasso's *nozze* there are evidences that he has read Claudian, but the references are little more than hints of the original.[40]

It is difficult to describe these poems of Tasso as a group. The stylistic artifice is such that the appeal is more often to the intellect than to the senses, in spite of extensive use of vocabulary normally considered sensuous, a phenomenon later to be observed in a number of English epithalamia.[41] The theme of love-making as a battle, which in Pontanus and Secundus is an erotic demonstration, in Tasso loses some of its eroticism, partly because the reader's attention is diverted by unusual metaphors, word-play, repetition of sound patterns, novel twists on conventions—a general exhibition of virtuosity. A few excerpts from Tasso's epithalamium of 1578, and from one of the nuptial sonnets, will illustrate. The passage in the longer poem is introduced with an address to Hymen:

> Santo Dio, che congiungi
>   A l'opre de la vita
>   Sotto giogo di fé concordi amanti;
>   Che molle pungi, ed ungi
>   Di mêl poi la ferita
>   Sí che stilla per gli occhi in dolci pianti;
>   Tu, che d'unir ti vanti
>   Entro il voler d'un petto
>   Pensier casti e lascivi,
>   E vezzosi atti e schivi
>   Tempri, mirabil fabbro, in un aspetto;
>   Tu, Dio, tu pungi il core
>   In cui spuntò le sue quadrella Amore.[42]

In the space of a few lines the bride is referred to as a beautiful warrior, a conqueress, a phoenix, a small deer, a "verginella," a cruel beauty, an untouched rose, and the sacred, happy trophy of the bridegroom.[43] The bridegroom is compared in slightly more conventional fashion to an eager war horse awaiting the trumpet's sweet invitation to battle.[44]

This poem's closing stanzas, among the most conventional to be found in any of Tasso's nuptial poetry, echo Catullus 62 and Claudian, but Tasso has made the conventions very much his own:

> Si coglie intatta rosa
> Fra le pungenti spine
> E fra gli aghi de l'api il dolce mêle.
> Lascia pur ch'ella cele
> Sue voglie e ti contrasti;
> Rapisci: piú graditi
> Sono i baci rapiti
> E piú soavi son quanto piú casti:
> Non cessar fin che 'l sangue
> Non versa e vinta a te sospira e langue.

> Sacra lieto trofeo
>   Del bel cinto disciolto
>   E de le spoglie sue di sangue sparte,
>   E i giochi d' Imeneo
>   Rinnova in nodi accolto
>   Piú bei di quei ch' unîr Ciprigna a Marte.
>   Se Febo a me comparte
>   Suo spirto e 'l ver mi scopre,
>   Dal bel grembo fecondo
>   Verranno Alfonsi al mondo,
>   I quai rinnoveranno i nomi e l' opre
>   Famose in pace e'n guerra
>   Di quei ch'ornano il ciel, ornàr la terra.

Ma ecco in orïente
   Appare Espero amica;
   Espero no, ché luce annunzia e porta.
   Facciasi a questa ardente
   Lusinghiera fatica
   Tregua ch' a pugna invita e riconforta;
   E la fanciulla accorta
   Gli occhi tremanti abbassi,
   E su l'amato fianco
   Appoggi il capo stanco.
   Versi fiori Imeneo su' membri lassi,
   E lor temprin gli ardori
   Col ventilar de l'ale i vaghi Amori.

Desta, canzone, i cigni
   Cui dolce il Po dà l'ombra e l'esca e l'onda,
   Ché debil canto gran voce seconda.[45]

The motif of love as a battle is treated very differently
in one of Tasso's nuptial sonnets. Here the sensuousness of
the vocabulary, especially in the repetition of words which
refer to sweetness, is almost nullified by the reader's con-
sciousness of the device itself. In its total effect in this sonnet, the motif of love as a battle has been removed from
the merely erotic:

Tessano aurea catena Amore e Lite,
   Che quella fabbricaro onde conteste
   Son le cose mortai, per cui sian queste
   Alme belle e leggiadre insieme unite.
Le dolci guerre dolcemente ardite
   E le repulse dolcemente oneste,
   Da vezzi e paci dolci a seguir preste
   Sian spesso dolcemente anco seguite.
Lite i divisi cor spesso rintegri
   Con soave unïone; e stabil Fede
   Tra mille sdegni se medesma avanze.

> E di brevi timori e di doglianze
> Non lunghe sian poi certa ampia mercede
> Candide e liete notti e giorni allegri.[46]

A few themes and images occur repeatedly in Tasso's nuptial poems, and some of these seem of possible consequence to the English tradition. Like Catullus in Carmen 61, Tasso often uses images of light and brilliance—suns, stars, lightning, torches. Rivers constitute another favorite topic, along with other aspects of topography—seas, mountains, torrents, hills, lakes, valleys, and beaches. Aspects of nature are prominent—trees, flowers, clouds, birds of several kinds, animals. An interest in antiquity, and a love of country, also are evident. One unusual reference, appearing several times, is to the swans on the river Po. An instance appears in the opening lines of the epithalamium written in 1570, combining the swan theme with the summons to Hymen:

> Lascia, Imeneo, Parnaso, e qui discendi
> Ove fra liete pompe il regal fiume
> Col canto de' suoi cigni a sé t'appela.
> Ben sai ch' a' tuoi ritorni ognor piú rendi,
> Come prescritto è da fatal costume
> D'inusitata gioia adorna e bella
> Questa non pur famosa riva e quella
> Che di trofei piú che di piante abbonda . . . .[47]

The poem of Tasso which best illustrates the general trend of Italian epithalamia toward topography and antiquity is his "Ne le nozze di Vincenzo Gonzaga, principe di Mantova, con Leonora de' Medici, principessa di Toscana," written in 1584. The fact that the bride and bridegroom came from opposite sides of the Apennine mountain range gave the poet excuse for his topographical motif: What nature had divided, love unites. The opening stanza indicates the tone of the poem:

> Italia mia, che l' Apennin disgiunge
> E da mille suoi fonti
> Mille fiumi in duo mari infonde e versa
> Quel che partí Natura Amor congiunge,
> Tal che non ponno i monti
> E i gran torrenti ond' è la terra aspersa
> Far l' una a l' altra avversa:
> Amor le tue divise e sparse voglie
> Or unisce e raccoglie,
> E spiana l' alte vie nel giogo alpestro
> Dal tuo sinistro lato al lato destro.[48]

A protracted conceit running through several stanzas treats the bridal couple as two suns; we shall see later imitations of it.[49] One stanza will illustrate:

> Duo soli di valor e di bellezza
> Ambo ne l'oriente
> Rotano i raggi incontra o stanno a paro;
> L' un per l' altro fiammeggia e per vaghezza
> De l' altrui foco ardente,
> E l'un per l' altro è piú sereno e chiaro:
> Né mai destino avaro
> Ce li asconde o sommerge, e 'n giro alterno
> Non fanno state e verno,
> E sempre sono eguali i raggi e i passi
> Perché un mai l' altro non oscuri o lassi.[50]

Succeeding stanzas relate the two suns to various aspects of Italian history. One other legacy of the Italian epithalamium to the English may also be demonstrated by this poem —the function of the *tornata*. In it the poet addresses himself to his song and expresses something of his purpose in writing it:

> Canzon, di raggio in raggio.
>   Segui la nova e glorïosa luce
>   Ch' al pensier mio riluce;
>   Ma perché non t' accenda e non avvampi,
>   Per sua pietà candida man ti scampi.[51]

Both the form of the *tornata*—it is normally shorter than the preceding stanzas—and its conventional content are to be seen in some of the later English epithalamia.

Fortunately the character of the epithalamium in English had been fairly well established by the time of the publication of Marino's ten epithalamia in 1616. Traces of his influence do occur, however, so I shall indicate briefly the nature of his *Epitalami*. Their diversity of theme is revealed in a list of the titles: *La Francia Consolata, Il Balletto Delle Muse, Venere Pronuba, L'Anello, La Cena, Il Torneo, Il Letto, Le Fatiche d'hercole, Urania,* and *Himeneo.*[52] Souchay attacks Marino for his choice of unconventional themes and for spoiling even the themes he borrows from Claudian or Sidonius by his indecency, and by his sterile abundance of description. In *La Francia Consolata,* for example, a poem of more than a thousand lines written for the marriage of Louis the Just and Anne of Austria, the main theme is lost, Souchay argues, and the mind repelled by the protracted description and the inclusion of inappropriate matter. France, personified in this poem, is torn by internal wars, and mounts to the skies to implore the protection of Venus. The goddess, seated on her throne, is embroidering a blindfold for Love, who lies sleeping on a bed of roses. Moved by the tears of France, Venus leaves her work, puts on a magnificent dress, and flies to Aquitaine, where she finds the god of war and appeases his fury. Then the two get into the same car and fly to Paris, capital of the realm, followed by Love. At journey's end, Love throws his arrows on the Louvre, which at that time was the palace of the royal family. Fiction such as this might have some merit, Souchay concedes, if it were not obscured by description:

> Le Poëte ne laisse rien à décrire, ni le trône de Venus, ni le lit de l'Amour, ne le bandeau qui luy est destiné, ni le char de la Déesse, ni les tributs que les divers Elements luy apportent sur son passage; ni sa robe, dont le tissu est de pierres précieuses, & dont la couleur est changeante.... Ce n'est pas que les riches descriptions qui n'entrent point dans une matiére lugubre ne puissent convenir à l'Epithalame; mais lorsque'elles sont & si Longues & si fréquentes, elles rebutent l'esprit, & sont disparoître le sujet principal.[53]

Souchay also condemns *Le Fatiche d'hercole* (written for the wedding of Conte Hercole Pepoli) because it is "une indécente & froide allusion aux travaux du Dieu fabuleux"; *La Cena,* because "il introduit un Pêcheur qui chante des choses très-communes, quoyque, s'il faut l'en croire sur son propre témoignage, les oiseaux & les ventes même fassent silence pour les écouter," and *Himeneo* because in it the drunken Silenus sings "sans aucune allégorie" the epithalamium of the shepherd Amyntas.[54]

Early in his career Marino wrote his *Baci,* an imitation of the *Basia* of Secundus.[55] One of Marino's favorite motifs in the epithalamia—love as a battle—appears to have been inspired partially by Secundus, as well as Pontanus, and the fourth fescennine verse of Claudian. Examples of the extensive elaboration which Marino worked on this motif are his *Venere Pronuba* and *Il Letto. Venere Pronuba* for about half of its 648 lines is a translation of Claudian's 145-line *Epithalamium of Palladius and Celerina.* But Marino departs from his model for three hundred lines or more of detailed description of love as a battle in the nuptial chamber. The blunt boldness of Pontanus is replaced by the lavish embroidery characteristic of "marinism," as may be seen in the lines below. Hymen, with rose-colored feathers, has come from Helicon to the nuptial chamber. The timid young girl has entered the *thalamos,* and the poet advises the bridegroom:

> Ella, appoggiata il capo
> sovra molli guanciali
> t'attenderá tremante;
> di lagrime dolenti
> spargerá forse stille,
> di sospiretti ardenti
> essalerá faville.
> Ma te nulla ritardi
> lagrimentta o sospiro;
> anzi con le tue labra
> quelle e queste in un punto
> dagli occhi e da la bocca
> canaletti amorosi
> asciugherai bevendo,
> ammorzerai suggendo;
> e, qual nocchiero accorto
> de le sirene al canto,
> serra l'orecchie al pianto,
> che dal corso felice
> il tuo legno desvia . . . .
> Quivi, fervido e caldo
> di dolce foco il seno,
> tacito t'apparecchia
> a la pugna beata.[56]

Urging the bridegroom to vigor in the combat, the poet offers some practical counsel:

> Combatti, abbatti, opprimi,
> impugna, espugna, atterra,
> finché, mancando il moto
> a le languide membra,
> rilassandosi i nodi

de le molli catene,
con flebili sussurri
la voce infievolisca,
travolti e vacillanti
si socchiudano i lumi,
stupefatte ed immote
agghiaccino le lingue,
e 'n tepide rugiade,
sudando a stilla a stilla,
l 'anima si destempri.
Io spero che non deggia
ne l' alta scaramuzza
la lena abbandonarti,
però che sei sul verde
de l'etá tua fiorita . . . .
Cerere, ti ricordo,
per te sia lieve e parca:
suol dar la lauta mensa
piú peso che sostanza.

Later in English we shall see echoes of the concluding lines:

Passò di fibra in fibra
ne le midolle interne
dolcissimo veleno;
gîr serpendo per l'ossa
favillete soavi;
s'appigliâro nell'alme
di scambievole affetto
sviscerati desiri;
e, transformando l'un ne l'altro core,
ne fêro innesto e v'allignâro Amore.[57]

Elaborate description of the nuptial bed appears in *Il Letto,* written in 1608 "per le nozze di Francesco Gonzaga, principe di Mantova, e di Margherita, infanta di Savoia,"[58] but the principal role of *il letto* is as a field for the traditional love combat. For the bridal bed the little Loves make pillows of rose petals and of their own feathers.[59] The imagery of the final stanza is less gracious, but "il primo sangue" is a topic frequent in Marino, and it makes an occasional appearance in English. The stanza may have been inspired by a nuptial custom mentioned in Claudian's fourth fescennine verse and common in various cultures.[60] Here, instead of the coverlet of the wedding couch, it is Cupid's blindfold that will provide the evidence of consummation:

> Amor, poscia che strinse
> l'uno a pugnar con l'altro,
> giudice accorto e scaltro
> de la pugna dubbiosa, il vel si scinse;
> e di sua man s'accinse
> ne la benda a raccôrre,
> quando vedesse alfin l'armi deporre
> la bella coppia essangue,
> de la prima ferita il primo sangue.[61]

French Vernacular Epithalamia

French poets, prolific authors of epithalamia more than half a century before the genre became popular in English, wrote mostly lyric epithalamia, many of them pastorals. The amoebaean song appears frequently, along with lyrics modeled on the Italian *canzone,* eclogues, odes, sonnets, and a few long rhetorical narratives. Popular motifs from Catullus and Theocritus fuse with a few favorites from Statius, Claudian, and the neo-Latin poets. Echoes of the Canticle and Psalms appear in both nuptial and devotional epithalamia. Pagan, Christian, Petrarchan, Neo-Platonic, allegorical, mystical, panegyrical, erotic, and personal motifs all have their place in the French genre.

Among the French epithalamists of the sixteenth century—
and this list is by no means complete—are Clément Marot, Remy
Belleau, Joachim Du Bellay, Marc-Claude de Buttet, Jacques
Bereau, Pierre de Ronsard, Antoine de Baïf, Guillaume de
Sallust Du Bartas, Philippe Desportes, Jean Dorat, Jacques
Grévin, Estienne Jodelle, François Malherbe, Olivier de Magny,
Louis Des Masures, Jacques Peletier, Pierre Poupo, A. de Ver-
meil, and Jaques Yver. The stream of vernacular epithalamia
begins in France early in the century—Marot's highly original
adaption of Catullus 62 was written in 1528—and continues
through the time when Sidney and Spenser were writing in
English. Among the finest examples are those of the Pléiade, all
of whom wrote epithalamia, except Pontus de Tyard.[62] Those
of Belleau, Du Bellay, Ronsard, and Baïf are of particular interest
in relation to the English tradition, as are the works of two
little-known poets, Buttet and Poupo.

In the French vernacular epithalamium comes the culmina-
tion of several developments noted in the genre in preceding centuries. We have observed the growth of allegory in the epithalamium, not only in the medieval treatment of the Biblical
poems, but also in the gradual transmutation of the pagan gods.
C. S. Lewis in his general discussion of the allegory of love emphasizes the significance of this development in the epithalamia
of Claudian, Sidonius, Ennodius, and Fortunatus.[63] In Claudian,
Lewis notes the pastoral Paradise of Venus in which songbirds
are chosen for their music and

> Each happy tree
> Woos and is wooed. Palms nodding from above
> Exchange their vows and poplar sighs for love
> Of poplar, plane for plane, and whispers low
> Of love along the alder thickets go.[64]

The trappings of the pagan Paradise are adapted for the Christian
Paradise, and later for an earthly one, as we have seen. Lewis
quotes the epithalamium of the Christian bishop Ennodius, who
strikes "the genuine May morning note of the later poets":

When young blades shoot and Nature in her bower,
Sits at her work, the world grows warm the while,
And when the sun paints earth with many a flower,
Love, beauty, bravery, all are in his smile.[65]

In the works of this Christian poet, Venus and Cupid of the pagan Paradise have "died into allegory," in Lewis's words, and have become decorative mouthpieces for the epithalamist. The poet thus "stumbles upon freedom" and acquires, in addition to the actual world and the world of his own religion, a third world of myth and fancy. Thus, "we see the beginnings of that free creation of the marvellous which first slips in under the cloak of allegory."[66] The poet is "free to wander in fairyland."[67] Related aspects of the medieval growth of allegory which concern us here are the development of floral symbolism, and the continued celebration of Nature as representative of concord and order.

The "May morning note" is apparent in the French pastoral epithalamia of the sixteenth century. Nature assumes new importance as both setting and symbol, and marriage becomes an aspect of the harmony and bliss of a new golden age. In this spacious world the landscapes are filled with happy clear rivers; rhythmic streams; bubbling springs; silvery waves; echoing rocks; mossy grottoes; flower-covered islands; fecund pastures, swelling hillocks, and fertile valleys. Skies spill fragrance; the Earth becomes pregnant with Spring. The outdoors and the nuptial chambers abound in lilies, roses, violets, buttercups, marguerites, carnations, poppies, mint, thyme, marjoram, sweet basil, and lavender. Ivy and other vines entwine innumerable trees. There are cypresses, pines, elms, greening willows, reeds, myrtle, laurel, crimson raspberries, grapes, and pink mushrooms. Among the boughs, little winds whistle sweet songlets, and zephyrs gently sigh. Nightingales, larks, crickets, and frogs sing; bees buzz around dainty beehives; doves kiss; wild geese, swans, and peacocks ornament the earth and sky; lambs, goats, fawns, bullocks, a dog or two, and a tiny garden snake frolic among abundant flocks.

Most frequent inhabitants of this fairyland are the river-nymphs. McPeek observes that it is a "well established convention in French epithalamia that the nymphs of local rivers attend nuptial celebrations."[68] Also attending on occasion are nymphs of forests, mountains, and meadows; nymphs with blonde or golden tresses; nymphs with green eyes and sugared mouths; nymphs with beautiful heels and musical voices who sing and dance with doll-like movements. Thousands of little Loves frequent the nuptial chambers, adorning the couch with flowers, fanning the bride with their wings, and officiating at the placing of the bride on the *lectus genialis*. Deities of the sea and of the forests often appear, among them Triton and Pan. The Muses, crowned with chaplets of flowers, sing and play, as the Graces dance, their hands filled with blossoms. Although somewhat subordinate to the swarms of singers, dancers, and busy little Loves, the conventional individual gods are still at hand—Venus cuts the air in her chariot of ivory and gold drawn by doves or swans with bridles made of roses; Hymen comes from Parnassus, wearing his traditional chaplet of flowers and yellow slippers; Cupid descends on wings enameled with scales of delicate blue; Juno Lucina is summoned to provide the blessing of offspring.

The epithalamium may be sung by alternating choruses of river-nymphs, by the Muses, by virgins, by a chorus of French princesses, or by shepherds, whose names are sometimes pseudonyms for the poet himself and his friends and fellow poets. Musical instruments are those of the pagan shepherd and the Christian Psalmist. Descriptions of bride and bridegroom consist often of comparisons to deities and to the moon and the sun. The blazon of the bride is characteristic of the period in that it is reminiscent of both Petrarch and the Canticle—the bride's tender breasts are like flowers, her lips like roses, hands like ivory, teeth like little pearls, eyes like twin stars where a thousand little Loves dip their arrows in honey, and the crescent of her eyebrow like an arch of ebony.[69] Sometimes the bride's hair is like the conventional golden wire of the Renaissance beauty, but a few French brides are admittedly brunette, although the poet may be somewhat apologetic about the fact: "Brunette elle est," writes Marot, "mais pourtant elle est belle."[70] The motif of love as a battle in the nuptial chamber is modified in most of the French epithalamia, the nuptial chamber often being depicted as the scene of playful toying rather than the vigorous combat of the Italian poems.[71] Flowers, perfumes, and Cupids mingle as symbols of the consummation. The marriage itself is offered at times as symbolic of national concord, world peace, or aspirations of immortality.

In making these generalizations, I do not mean to imply that all French epithalamia are alike, for they are not. The features I have described appear over and over, but in a great variety of contexts, and I shall here briefly describe a few, beginning with Belleau's two epithalamia, both delicate pastoral lyrics using many motifs from Catullus 61 and 62. The opening stanza of his *Epithalame de Monseigneur le duc de Lorraine et de Madame Claude, fille du tres-chrestien roy Henry II* written in 1558, invokes the nymphs of the Seine:

> Nymphes qui vos tresses blondes
> Mignotez dessus les bors,
> Des claires & belles ondes
> De la Seine aux plis retors,
> Si quelque flamme amoureuse
> Vous eschauffe sous les eaux,
> Chantex les chastes flambeaux
> De ceste Nuit bien-heureuse.[72]

Devoting a stanza to each, the poet then invokes the river-nymphs of the Meuse, as well as Venus, Cupid, Hymen, and the Muses, the Sky, and the Evening Star. Belleau concludes the opening section with a stanza returning to the role of the nymphs. The poem continues with the nymphs of the Meuse and the nymphs of the Seine singing alternate symmetrical stanzas, the first chorus praising the bridegroom and comparing him to the sun, the second group praising the bride and likening her to the moon.[73] Belleau's second epithalamium is quite similar, except that it is not an amoebaean; in it the poet again functions as master of ceremonies summoning the usual participants.[74] Both poems were included in *La Bergerie de Remy Belleau divisee en une premiere et seconde journee,* published in 1565 and in a revised edition in 1572; in *La Bergerie* the lyrics are loosely connected by pastoral narrative.[75]

A number of poets wrote pastoral epithalamia for the marriage in 1559 of the popular French princess, Marguerite, and Emmanuel-Philibert, Duke of Savoy.[76] Du Bellay's *Epithalame* in its short lines imitates the glyconics of Catullus,[77] but is not strongly Catullan in theme. It is in form a dialogue, with stanzas being sung by the poet; three young virgins named Camille, Lucrece, and Diane; their mother; and the god Mercury. Its principal theme—the desire for peace, world power, and the perpetuation of the Christian faith through union of the two countries—is expressed in the opening stanza and in a long series of stanzas sung by Mercury near the end of the poem. Praise of the bride's learning and the bridegroom's virility is expressed in somewhat novel fashion:

> C'est la Pallas nouvelle,
>   Fille de la cervelle
>   De ce grand Roy François:
>   Des Muses la dixieme,
>   Des Graces la quatrieme,
>   S'il en est plus de trois
>   Adieu soeurs, adieu belles,
>   Adieu doctes pucelles.[78]

> . . . .

> Sa virile jeunesse
>   N'a suivy la mollesse
>   Des lascifz courtisans:
>   Il n'a parmy les Dames,

> Les plaisirs, et les flammes,
> Perdu ses jeunes ans.
>   Io, ïo, victoire,
>   Io, triomphe et gloire.[79]

The poem lacks shepherds and many of the typical pastoral conventions, although it has the usual pastoral deities and setting. It concludes with a reference to Peleus and Thetis, declaring that no discord is sowed here, however, to lead to a Trojan war. In an epilogue, the poet expresses his own inability to do justice to so happy a marriage.[80]

A lesser-known poet, Buttet, was moved to write three poems in celebration of the marriage of the Princess Marguerite—a twenty-six-page epic epithalamium, a sixteen-page marriage ode, and a six-page ode "pour immortaliser la vertu de Madame Marguerite," the last entitled "Aux Muses."[81] In the epic, the usual themes are present, with some emphasis (as in Du Bellay) on the importance of the wedding in maintaining peace. The setting of the wedding, the guests, and the appurtenances of the feast are described in leisurely detail in more than six hundred lines. McPeek sees this epic as strongly influential on Spenser's *Epithalamion,* and I shall cite some of the parallels in a later chapter.[82] The role of the Muses and Pallas in the education of the learned princess is presented with some originality:

> Les neuf Muses, ses soeurs, toutes à sa naissance,
> Laissant leur mont Olympe, accoururent en France
> L'allaiter au berceau, dansant à l'environ;
> Et, se faisant plus grande, en son vierge giron,
> Pallas ouvrit le livre, et par experience
> Lui feit en peu de temps cognoistre la science;
> Puis, lui meit en la main, d'un doux soing diligent,
> L'âpre dé ivoirin et l'éguille d'argent,
> Le fil d'or, et la gaze, et soie cramosie,
> Dont elle feroit honte aux nymphes de l'Asie . . . .[83]

Buttet's "Aux Muses" is a flower-filled tribute to a virgin, but this poem is secular instead of devotional, with the Muses being called upon to gather flowers, and to entwine lilies, roses—and marguerites—for a crown to adorn the learned virgin princess, Marguerite. This poem, or others of its general kind, doubtless influenced Spenser and other English epithalamists, as McPeek has suggested.[84] A brief quotation will illustrate its nature:

> Reveillés-vous, divine race
>   Qui Parnasse
> Habités, ou les fresches eaux
> D'Eurote, ou les beaux bords humides
>   Libetrides,
> Ou les pindiens arbrisseaux.
>
> . . . .
>
> Au nom de la Nymphe roiale,
> Je pren ces trois fleurons divers,
> Le lis, la rose matinale,
> La marguerite virginale
> Ornement de mes petits vers;
>
> Et veus que sa deüe coronne
>   En fleuronne,
> Repeinte en cent mille façons.
> Or est tens qu'on en face offrande;
>   Belle bande,
> Frappés donq' l'air de voz chansons.
>
> Puis dessus l'herbette feconde
> Prenés-vous, et allés dansant,
> Menant des bras une douce onde,
> Virottant toutes à la ronde
> Parmi ce beau pré verdissant.[85]

The Muses figure importantly also in one of Baïf's epithalamia.[86] Apollo and Hymen, son of the Muse Calliope, lead the nine *doctes pucelles* in singing to honor the wedding. Apollo begins, each Muse takes her turn in singing a stanza (reminiscent of Erasmus's neo-Latin poem), and Hymen concludes the song. The poet remarks that it is not often that these *Musiciennes* come to the wedding of mortals as they used to do in the days of Peleus and Thetis.[87] Here the blessing of God is bespoken for this couple whose love is faithful and holy, and the prospective offspring is described in the manner of Catullus 61. As is customary in many French epithalamia, the poet prays that the couple may live. to a happy old age, a device we recall from Statius.[88] Baïf's other epithalamium, a lyric but not a pastoral, is undistinguished except for a few striking lines. His warning to discord, envy, jealousy, bitterness, care, and fear to stay away echoes through the centuries:

> Ce qui trouble le doux desir
> Soit loing d'icy, loing la discorde,
> La jalouzie & la rancueur,
> Loing tout soucy, loing toute peur.[89]

A much more elaborate work is Ronsard's *Chant pastoral sur LES NOPCES DE MONSEIGNEUR CHARLES DUC de Lorraine, & Madame Claude Fille II. du Roy,* written in 1559. After introductory matter, there is a dialogue between Bellot (representing Joachim Du Bellay) and Perot (representing Ronsard himself), followed by a singing match with Michau (Michel de l'Hospital) as judge.[90] Ronsard's *Chant pastoral* imitates not only portions of Theocritus's epithalamium, Number 18, but also other Theocritean idylls, notably Numbers 7 and 9, as well as several of the *Bucolics* of Virgil, and the lyric epithalamia of Catullus. Besides close imitations of specific passages, Ronsard's poem reflects something of the general technique of the Theocritean epithalamium. We see, for example, his use of nature similes in describing the bridegroom, and the resemblance to the passage in Idyll 18 describing the inimitable Helen:

> Il s'eleve en beauté sur tous les pastoureaux
> Comme un jeune toreau sur les menus troupeaux,
> Ou comme un grande cyprés sur un menu bocage,
> Ou comme un gresle jonc sur l'herbe du rivage . . . .

> Comme l'herbe est l'honneur d'une verte prerie,
> Des herbettes les fleurs, & d'une bergerie
> Un toreau qui du pied pousse l'arene au vent,
> D'une fresche ramée un ombrage mouvant,
> Les roses d'un bouquet, les liz d'une girlande,
> Ainsi tu es l'honeur de toute nostre bande.[91]

A more closely imitative passage, and one frequently echoed in English, is Ronsard's description of the bride:

> Comme une belle rose est l'honneur du jardin
> Qui aux rais du Soleil s'est esclose au matin,
> Ainsi Claudine l'est de toutes les bergeres,
> Et les passe d'autant qu'un pin fait les fougeres.
> Nulle ne l'a gangnée à sçavoir façonner
> Un chapelet de fleurs pour son chef couronner,
> Nulle ne sçait mieux joindre au lis la fresche rose,
> Nulle mieux sur la gaze un dessain ne compose
> De fil d'or & de soye, & nulle ne sçait mieux
> L'aiguille demener d'un pouce ingenieux.[92]

Ronsard's feeling for genuine nature mingles with his fondness for pretty artificiality in his detailed description of the stakes for the singing match. Here also the poet finds excuse for inserting a description of a work of art—a device which has turned up in epithalamia (as elsewhere) on various pretexts from the time of Catullus 64. Perot wagers a birdcage he has made, in which he has imprisoned a young lark that sings beautifully; Bellot offers a basket he has woven and decorated with mythological figures:

Il fault pour le vainqueur que nous metions un gage:
Quaint à moy, pour le prix je te mets une cage
Que je fis l'autre jour voyant paistre mes beufs,
En parlant à Thony [Baïf], qui s'egalle à nous deux:
Les barreaux sont de til & la perchette blanche
Qui traverse la cage est d'une coudre franche:
De pellures de jonc j'ay tissu tout le bas:
A l'un des quatre coings la coque d'un limas
A un crin de cheval se pend de telle sorte,
Qu'on diroit à la voir qu'elle mesme se porte . . . .

. . . .

Pour la cage & l'oyseau, je veux mettre un panier,
Gentement enlassé de vergettes d'ozier,
Fort large par le haut, qui tousjours diminue
En tirant vers le bas d'une pointe menue:
L'anse est faicte d'un houx qu'à force j'ay courbé:
En voulant l'atenuir le doigt je me coupé
Avecque ma serpette: encores de la playe
Je me deuls, quand du doigt mon flageolet j'essaye.
Tout ce gentil panier est pourtraict par dessus,
De Mercure, & d'Iö, & des cent yeux d'Argus:
Iö est peinte en vache, & Argus en vacher,
Mercure est tout aupres, qui du haut d'un rocher
Roulle à bas cet Argus, apres avoir coupée
Sa teste cautement du fil de son espée:
De son sang naist un paon, qui ses aisles ouvrant
Va deçà & delà tout le panier couvrant.[93]

Throughout his five hundred-line poem, Ronsard's ingenuity in use of conventions and imagery from the tradition is matched by his dexterity in manipulating the alexandrine couplets. Thus, his *Chant pastoral* becomes one of the most attractive models for later writers of pastoral epithalamia.

Of considerably less felicity is an equally long poem of the same year, Jacques Grévin's *Pastorale* for two marriages, those of Marguerite, sister of Henry II, and Emmanuel-Philibert, Duke of Savoy; and Elisabeth, daughter of Henry II, and Philippe II of Spain. Grévin's shepherds are Collin, Jaquet, and Tenot, representing Nicholas Denisot, Grévin, and Estienne Jodelle, respectively. The poem is worthy of attention for its possible influence on Spenser's *The Shepheardes Calender* as well as its role in the epithalamic tradition. Like Ronsard's *Chant pastoral,* it is a dialogue, followed by a singing match with symmetrical stanzas, and a concluding epithalamium.[94]

The inserted description of a work of art which has been noted in Ronsard's long pastoral epithalamium is somewhat like another convention seen occasionally in French epithalamia —the dream-vision, a form which also has done service in many other genres.[95] Hints of the dream-vision technique appear in Ronsard's short *Epithalame de Monseigneur de Joyeuse, Admiral de France,* written in 1581, one of the shortest and least tedious of French epithalamia using the form. Here the poet speaks in the first person, describing events he visualizes as woven into the skein of life by one of the Parcae on the day the bridegroom, Joyeuse, was born. The poem is skillfully constructed around a series of incidents imagined by the poet, each introduced by "je voy":

> Je te voy, ce me semble, au milieu des tournois
> Un Astre sur la teste, & au dos le harnois . . . .
>
> Je voy dessous l'acier de ton fort coutelas
> Tomber & morions & pennaches à bas:
> Je te voy foudroyant combatre à la barriere
> Et poudroyant le camp d'une viste carriere . . . .
>
> Je te voy preparer pour un plus doux assaut
> Non moins aspre au mestier de Cyprine la belle,
> Que vaillant aux combas quand la guerre t'appelle.
>
> Je voy desia le soir des amans attendu,
> Je voy desia le lict par les Graces tendu,

Qui dansent à l'entour, & versent à mains pleines
Myrtes, Roses & Lis, Oeillets & Marjolaines.
Venus pour honorer ce soir tant desiré,
Dedans son char portée a deux Cygnes tiré
Fendra l'air pour venir, & sur la couuerture
De ta couche nopciere estendra sa ceinture,
A fin que son Ceston d'union composé
Serre à jamais l'espouse auecques l'espousé.

Les Amours t'éuentant à petits branles d'ailes
T'allumeront le coeur de cent flames nouuelles
Je les voy, ce me semble, un desia destacher
Ta robe, & doucement dans le lict te coucher
Te parfumer d'odeurs, & de la mariée
L'autre qui la ceinture a desia desliée,
Et luy verser aux yeux mille Graces, à fin
Qu'une si sainte amour ne prenne jamais fin:
Mais d'âge en âge croisse autant ferme enlacée
Que la vigne tient l'orme en ses plis embrassée . . . .

Je voy, ce semble, Hymen protecteur des humains,
Le brodequin és pieds, le flambeau dans les mains,
Hymen, conseruateur des noms & des familles,
Separer en dux rangs les garçons & les filles,
Et les faire chanter à l'entour de ton lit,
Esclairez de son feu qui ta nopce embellit.

J'oy desia de leurs pas la cadance ordonée,
J'oy toute la maison ne sonner qu'Hymenée . . . .

La Concorde à jamais en ta maison seiourne:
Y seiourne la Foy, & que l'an ne retourne
Sans un petit Joyeaux, qui resemble à tous
deux . . . .[96]

Ronsard's poem demonstrates that even in a brief lyric, an imaginative craftsman is able to work a great many variations on time-hallowed conventions.

Ronsard and his fellow members of the Pléiade were not the only authors able to endow with new vigor a variety of elements from the tradition. A disciple of the Pléiade and poet of nature whose name is little known, Pierre Poupo (*c.* 1552–1591), was likewise skillful. Poupo's work exists in only one complete copy,[97] but he should be ranked among the most important French epithalamists for the originality, versatility, and volume of his work in this tradition. He is the outstanding continental representative of the synthesis of classical and Christian epithalamia, and in this synthesis he anticipated by a very few years the work of the foremost English epithalamist. Poupo and Spenser may have been born the same year, 1552;[98] Poupo died, probably in Geneva, about 1591. A provincial poet and lawyer from Champagne, a convert to Protestantism, Poupo left only one extant work, a collection in three books bound together in a single volume entitled *La Muse chrestienne.*[99]

Poupo fled to Geneva in 1585 from Catholic persecution. When he arrived there, he was welcomed by Simon Goulart, who introduced him to other leaders in the Calvinist capital; thus Poupo became a friend of many illustrious Huguenots. It was Simon Goulart who arranged the publication of Poupo's poems and gave them the title *La Muse chrestienne.* The book first appeared in 1588 without indicating place of publication, and in addition to Poupo's work includes several poems by Goulart on the "vanité du monde." Included in this edition was his *Epithalame* for Sebastien Bruneau and Nicole Le Bey. The second edition, appearing in 1590, consisted of two books and included a series of nine sonnets on his own marriage. In 1592 the third book appeared, and this edition forms the complete *La Muse chrestienne,* of which the only known copy is in the Bibliotheque de l'Arsenal.[100] Besides the sonnets on his own marriage and the epithalamium already mentioned, Poupo's works in the epithalamic tradition include a poetic paraphrase of the Canticle, several nuptial sonnets for weddings of friends, and an *Epi-*

thalame Pastoral of some four hundred lines for the marriage of Jean de Laussoirrois and Elizabeth de Sainct-Amour. Also related to the tradition is another pastoral eclogue, published in 1592 but apparently written much earlier, addressed to his betrothed, Phyllis, in which the poet casts himself as Daphnis in a mystic dialogue of divine love, apparently inspired by his own translation of the Canticle and a familiarity with the medieval epithalamic tradition. The poet argues that worldly images must represent spiritual things, as Christ is joined to his church on earth, and as marriage is a holy union.[101]

In a different way, the idea that worldly images are representative of spiritual things underlies the Laussoirrois epithalamium.[102] The "May morning note" observed by C. S. Lewis in the epithalamium of the Christian bishop Ennodius[103] is never more evident than in this pastoral in which the glory of nature is a reflection of the glory of God. The format is that of the pastoral dialogue with three shepherds, Rozin, Pinsonnet, and Aiglantin—the last-named representing Poupo—composing songs to honor the wedding, and exchanging remarks and songs with three nymphs, Framboisine, Sucrine, and Perline. The praises of the honored couple are accomplished, as Ralph M. Hester, Jr., notes, "only through their association with the glorious landscape about them,"[104] and the poem becomes a hymn to nature. Although Hymen is mentioned, he has "died into allegory," and it is a Biblical angel who brings tidings to the shepherds that the wedding song will be sung. It seems to be the Christian God who is referred to:

> Les oiseaux, gringotans, par ce taillis ramé,
> Du matin jusqu'au soir n'ont eu le bec fermé;
> Les ruisseaux murmurans plus doux que de coustume,
> Le soleil mesmement qui plus clair nous allume,
> Et les vents soupirans d'un gosier adouci,
> Ce sont de bons tesmoins que Dieu arrive ici.[105]

Poupo is important as a Christian poet—at first Catholic and later Calvinist—who utilized epithalamic devices of several traditions in an effective and original manner. His happy mixture of his own variations on Theocritus, Catullus, Claudian, Ronsard, and the Bible may be seen in the space of a few stanzas of the Laussoirrois pastoral. The first excerpt is reminiscent of Theocritus's epithalamium for Helen and of Ronsard's modification of the convention; the second echoes motifs of Catullus 61, Claudian, and countless subsequent poets; the third mixes medieval, Biblical, and Greek devices:

> Comme le doux printemps est l'honneur de l'année,
> Et l'honneur du printemps la rose boutonnée,
> Le gravier sautelant l'honneur d'un ruisselet,
> Et l'honneur de la biche un jeune fan de laict,
> Un jeune fan de laict pendant à la mammelle,
> Et la chaste rougeur l'honneur d'une pucelle,
> Et comme un sainct desir est l'honneur d'un amant,
> Ainsi Dafnis te sert de fleur et d'ornement.[106]

. . . .

> Framboisine:
> Il n'y a pas aux bord tant d'areine menüe,
> Tant d'ombrage aux forests quand le fueille est venüe,
> Tant d'astres reluisants ne logent dans les cieux,
> Qu'ell' a dans ses propos de douceur et de grace,
> De vertus en l'esprit, de beautez en la face,
> Et d'honnestes amours voletans par ses yeux.[107]

. . . .

> Framboisine:
> Ce phenix de beauté, espris d'un feu loüable,
> A choisi pour son nid ta demeure agreable:
> C'est ceste Elizabeth, perle unique en valeur,
> Qui pour ton Laussoirrois a Troye abandonnée,
> Et vient en ton pourpris celebrer l'hymenée,
> Aimant mieux esloigner son pays que son coeur.[108]

Poupo's other long epithalamium is more explicit in its statement of Christian doctrine and also in its sensuous description of the bride's physical beauty. It is a pastoral lyric of thirty-two six-line stanzas, written for the marriage of Sebastien Bruneau and Nicole Le Bey, the young woman who had converted Poupo to Protestantism.[109] The poet speaks in the first person as master of ceremonies and commentator, describing the beauty of the day—it is a genuine May day, "un jour du mois de may, bouquetier de l'annee"—and summoning the breezes, birds, flowers, shepherds, nymphs, and the bride and bridegroom to the wedding. Many passages have a Biblical ring, and although there are no pagan gods, we hear echoes of pagan authors, especially Ovid and the "kisses" carmina of Catullus.[110] The poet's summons to the couple owes some debt to Genesis xxix.20:

> Espoux, vien t'en coucher sur la moussee frizée,
> Au giron pucelet de ta chere espouzée.
> Tu as souffert long temps un ennui bien cruel;
> Mais un si beau loyer valoit un long service.
> Il faut gagner le bien premier qu'on en jouisse:
> Jacob servit sept ans pour la belle Rachel.[111]

More than one-third of the poem is devoted to a sensuous blazon of the bride in which Poupo introduces variations on the Canticle and Ovid. The passage culminates in a stanza in which the bride is likened to Salmacis,[112] and immediately thereafter to the enclosed garden of the Canticle:

> Son col me represente un beau pilier d'ivoire,
> Qu'un roi fait eslever pour marque de sa gloire:
> La base est d'argent fin, d'or le couronnement;
> Et son menton fourchu, une de ces cerises
> Qui ont forme de coeurs sur les branches assises,
> Ornant tout le verger de leur bigarrement.

. . . .

> De cent mille beautez elle est encor pourveüe.
> Je la vi l'an passé se baigner toute nue,
> Mais je n'en diray mot de peur de trop jaser.
> C'est un jardin fermé du'une closture forte,
> Dont un tant seulement a la clef de la porte,
> Et une source vierge où un seul doit puiser.[113]

Abruptly the poet announces that he must change his tone and describe the bride's spiritual beauty, and he then denounces feminine physical charms which are not accompanied by virtue, using a series of metaphors which, although repugnant, have a proverbial and formula-like ring:

> La beauté sans vertu n'est qu'un lustre volage,
> Un arbre infructeux paré d'un beau fueillage,
> Un empois et un fard qui se salit bien tost.
>
> Beauté trop excellent en fille mal nourrie
> Est une bague d'or sur le groin d'une truye,
> Un nid de rossignol où habite un serpent,
> Une plaisante fleur au milieu d'une ordure,
> Un fruit beau par dehors, mais plein de pourriture,
> Et un pommier d'angoisse au mari qui la prend.[114]

Having made this pronouncement, the poet returns to several stanzas praising the beauty *and* virtue of the bride, echoes of the Canticle and Catullus mingling with conceits which anticipate those of the English metaphysical epithalamists.

> Telles sont les vertus de cette nimphe belle,
> Du pays champenois l'ornement et la perle,
> Le fenix, le mirouër, l'honneur et le thresor:
> Perline sans pareille, en beauté tant extrême,
> Qu' on la peut seulement comparer à soi-mesme,
> Comme une grande mer qui n'a ni fond ni bord.

.   .   .   .

> Quand je serois mille ans à dire, dire, dire,
> A ses perfections je ne pourrois suffire,
> Les estoiles du ciel ne les égalent pas;
> Et les vouloir conter en une matinée,
> C'est un fleuve de laict qu'une mouche obstinée
> S'efforceroit de boire en un petit repas.[115]

The poet continues with conventional advice to the couple on their conjugal responsibilities, repeating injunctions from the Bible and the marriage service: the wife must submit herself to the husband, for the husband is the head of the wife; she must forsake father and mother, brother and sister, to live and die with her spouse; the husband is enjoined also to love his wife and treat her with gentleness. The poet concludes with the wish that God may bless the marriage and provide children who will walk in fear of Him. The final lines have the familiar ring of benediction: May the spirit of God bless you and rest upon you, and your souls be gently received in the arms of Christ, their legitimate spouse.

Even stronger in their declaration of Christine doctrine are Poupo's nuptial sonnets, which are almost free of even allegorical pagan gods and of nature as allegory or decoration. One exception is his "Epithalame de I. Lect, C. de G., et de Esther-Chrestienne Guilliaud, dame de Tramayes," in which rivers are cast in the role long familiar in Latin and continental vernacular epithalamia:

> Le Rosne Genevois, comme un ardent espoux,
> Embrassant nostre Saosne au front paisible et doux,
> Presageoit dés long temps ceste heureuse alliance.[116]

His "Epithalame de Nicolas Le Clerc et de S. de Courcelles" is a prayer for blessing by the Christian God, patron of eternal wedlock who made the conjunction of our first ancestors.[117] Most of the sonnets on his own marriage are prayers to the Christian God, although some are addressed to Phyllis, the poet's bride, and the opening sonnet of the group[118] is addressed to the poet's brother, attempting to convert him from Catholicism to Calvinism. The fervor of the poet's love, both divine and human, is revealed in the two following sonnets, the first addressed to God, the second addressed to Phyllis:

Si jamais j'esperay de ta benigne grace,
Si onc je te requis de quelque excellent don,
Et si tu es mon Dieu et mon Pere tres bon,
Fai n'en sentir, Seigneur, à ce coup l'efficace.
    Serre, estrein, colle, noüe, incorpore et enlace
Phyllis avec mon coeur d'un si ferme cordon
Que mesme le ciseau de la Mort sans pardon,
Ni tout autre accident, jamais ne le deffasse.
    Et, comme par nature un pere à son enfant
Qui lui demande un oeuf ne tend pas un serpent,
Ottrey-noi mon desir, bon pere, et mieux encore,
    Faisant que le dedans excelle le dehors,
Que l'esprit fasse honneur à la beauté du corps,
Et la pierre loyale à l'anneau qui la dore.[119]

.   .   .   .

Puisque vous desirez tout ce que je desire,
Vostre desir sans plus soit de me bien aimer;
Autre esprit que le mien ne vous puisse animer,
Et mon coeur seulement par vos levres souspire.
    Un triste repentir plein d'un sombre martyre
Jamais, au grand jamais, ne vous vienne limer,
Et nul vent de courroux ne tourmente le mer.
La mer de vos beaux yeux, où mon plaisir se mire.
    Contentez-vous de moi, comme je fay de vous;
Soyez-moy douce autant que je vous seray doux;
Vivons, mourons ensemble en amitié parfaicte.

> Et prions le Seigneur que nos heureux esprits
> Se tiennent main à main entrant en Paradis:
> Car c'est, chere Phyllis, tout ce que je souhaitte.[120]

In the sonnets on his own marriage the poet has completely fused the nuptial epithalamium and the devotional epithalamium. Thus the contribution of the obscure Pierre Poupo to the epithalamic tradition is substantial. Many of the tendencies which he exemplifies are shortly to be seen in the work of English epithalamists.

The English epithalamic tradition is indebted in a very specific way to another little-known French poet, Jaques Yver, whose work antedates that of Poupo by a few years. The first classical lyric epithalamium in English is a translation of Yver's adaption of Catullus 62, Yver's work having been first published in 1572, the year of his death. It is an inserted lyric in the collection of tales, *Le Printemps d'Yver, contenant plusieurs histoires discourues en cinq journees;*[121] the collection was translated into English in 1578 by a little-known English poet named Henrie Wotton. Yver's poem shows evidence that the author may have known continental adaptations of Catullus 62, as well as the original. There were many such adaptations, but I have found that three of them already referred to in this chapter have a special relationship to each other, although they are in three languages: they were written for three generations of the same family, the Italian house of Ferrara. The Latin adaptation by Ariosto was written in 1501 for the marriage of Alfonso I, later Duke of Ferrara, and Lucrezia Borgia; the French poem of Marot was written in 1528 for the marriage of Ercole, son of Alfonso I and Lucrezia, to Renée, daughter of Louis XII of France; the Italian poem of Tasso was written in 1578 for the marriage of Alfonso II, son of Ercole and Renée, to Marfisa d'Este.[122] Each of the three poems, as well as Yver's, is in a number of ways original, although each carries basic motifs of Catullus 62. Thus we see demonstrated in the continental epithalamium the continuity of the tradition.

Gil Polo's Spanish Epithalamium

Another vernacular epithalamium of importance to English is a Spanish lyric by Gaspar Gil Polo—the song sung by the shepherd Arsileus for the marriage of Syrenus and Diana in Gil Polo's continuation of Montemayor's pastoral romance *Diana Enamorada,* published in 1564.[123] The early translation of this poem into English by Bartholomew Yong, and its relationship to the epithalamium of Sidney, will be discussed in Chapter VIII.

VII

Critical Theory

Repetition through the centuries of the same motifs and techniques in the epithalamium came about by means of imitation of earlier works and attention to precepts established for the genre by rhetoricians. Greek and Roman philosophers and teachers of rhetoric in the second century of the Roman Empire and through the next three or four centuries contrived rules for writing wedding poems and orations, taking as models the lyric epithalamia of Sappho and other early Greek poets, and the three marriage poems of Catullus.[1] The rhetoricians—among them the pseudo-Dionysius, Menander, Himerius, and Choricius—noted the recurrent features of the early wedding poetry, established them as recognized topics for wedding literature, and developed a new variety of wedding composition, the prose oration. It is in the prose orations and pedagogical discussions that much of the evidence concerning Sappho's epithalamia is preserved.

The dicta of the rhetoricians were reflected in the epithalamia of Statius, Claudian, Ausonius, and other later Latin and medieval poets, among them Gregory Nazianzen, whose epithalamium to the Virgin was modeled on an oration of his mentor, Himerius.[2] Helping to preserve the theory of the epithalamium as rhetoric were Cassiodorus and other medieval critics whose commentaries on the Canticle and 44th Psalm were rhetorical treatises. The allegorical and metaphorical method of criticism was applied to both pagan and Christian epithalamia, and this criticism, along with the use of such works for didactic purposes, helped to perpetuate certain conventions and techniques.

For poets of the Renaissance an elaborate restatement of the principles of the Greek and Roman rhetoricians was made by Julius Caesar Scaliger (1484–1558) in the long section on the epithalamium in his *Poetices libri septem*, published posthumously in 1561.[3] In English the most important early rhetorical treatise was Thomas Wilson's *The Arte of Rhetorike*, first published in 1553, which does not deal with the epithalamium as such but contains two sections of significance to the epithalamic tradition: its instructions on techniques suitable for praise of noble persons, and its example of "exhortation"—Erasmus's twenty-four-page "An Epistle to perswade a yong Gentleman to marriage . . . ."[4] One of the many examples offered by Wilson "to make precepts plain," Erasmus's epistle is in the general tradition of the marriage-versus-virginity debate. Unlike the medieval Christian poems and treatises which praise virginity, this epistle is a magnificent argument for marriage, an argument which echoes in English epithalamia and other poetry for a century.[5]

A work more specifically concerned with literary form is the chapter on the epithalamium or "bedding ballad" in *The Arte of English Poesie*, attributed to George Puttenham, published in 1589,[6] which views the epithalamium as one of the kinds of "poeticall rejoysings ... but in a certain misticall sense...." A few years later, although Spenser's *Epithalamion* had appeared in the meantime, Ben Jonson still felt called upon to append an explanatory comment to the epithalamium in his *Masque of Hymen*, describing the poem as intended "both in form and matter to emulate that kind of poem which was called *Epithalamium*, and by the ancients used to be sung when the bride was led into her chamber." For the poem and the masque of which it is a part Jonson provides copious notes, constituting almost a list of sources for any poet interested in epithalamium-writing.[7] Similar detailed notes are provided by Sir Edward Sherburne for the epithalamium in his translation of Seneca's *Medea*, published in 1648.[8] The concern of Jonson and Sherburne that readers should have an understanding of the tradition points up a characteristic of the epithalamium which I mentioned in the Introduction: it is by nature traditional, usually influenced more by books than by life. Wheeler observes that although early poems were rooted in current wedding customs, the nuptial poet soon began to derive inspiration as much from literary works as from the particular situation; thus Roman poets used a surprising number of traditional Greek elements even when dealing with the wedding of a Roman friend. Greene elaborates on the functioning of tradition in the genre:

> As the body of Renaissance epithalamia increased, the influence of any single poem decreased; in place of the poem, the epithalamist drew upon a stockpile of *topoi,* commonplaces, similes, epithets, traditional good wishes, common strategies and techniques. The epithalamist seems to have been aware of the genre, not so much as a number of individual poems among which he could choose his own "source," but rather as a body of poetic material which was itself intricately entangled with borrowings and derivation, a body from which he could draw without necessarily incurring a debt to a given poem.[9]

Greene emphasizes the futility of trying to link Spenser's, or any other epithalamium, to a specific source, because any given *topos* can be found in a number of earlier epithalamia.

I shall summarize first the main precepts advanced by the Greek and Roman rhetoricians and then give some details from the Renaissance treatises I have mentioned. The chief topic of the epithalamium, according to the rhetoricians, should be the gods of marriage and generation. In one of his nuptial orations, Menander recommends that the main topic should be *Gamos,* the marriage-god, and the details concerning the god coincide with the description of Hymen in Catullus 61.[10] *Gamos* is to be described as the first god who came into being after chaos; he is the cause of everything; it is he who brings by means of children the salvation of home, property, and family. Dionysius, whose precepts were available to Renaissance poets in an edition published in 1499, says that the poet must begin with the gods who invented marriage and made it known to men. Since Jupiter and Juno were the first to join and couple, uniting female and male, they are the parents of all and should be so honored. Closely associated with praises of the marriage-gods is the broader topic of the advantages and blessings of legal marriage—for the couple, the fatherland, and the race. Men are urged to abandon irregular love in favor of marriage and family.[11] One of the main points of the epithalamium, according to Menander, should be the family.

Besides praising the gods and the institution of marriage, the poet should praise bride and bridegroom, comparing them to gods and describing their physical beauty, mental endowments, lineage, and accomplishments. Menander also advises the poet to take care to give equal attention to families of both bride and groom.[12] Harmonious love (*concordia*) should be stressed. Dionysius argues that marriage brings peace, prosperity, and companionship; that it helps a person overcome sorrow and trouble; and that it makes joyful situations even more delightful. Checked by marriage, men collect the rewards of temperance, and enjoy the beauty of virtue. In addition, an exhortation to the couple to unite in love is essential, Dionysius recommending that the orator must say that such union is in accord with Nature, that the process of generation and conception is common to plants, animals, and all of Nature. Although other creatures may unite unwisely and at random, mankind has found a certain order and law in the institution of marriage, for Nature has not allowed man to couple in flocks as do the beasts. Through marriage, men have been liberated from a wild and rambling life, and have acquired a gentle and modest mode of existence. Further, although the human race is mortal, it becomes immortal through union and the common bond of matrimony because by the birth of children a light is kindled for posterity. Inasmuch as mankind will continue to propagate, it is a light never to be extinguished. A prayer or wish that the couple may have children usually follows the exhortation to unite. Menander advises the poet to express the wish that the couple may have children like themselves. Catullus's wish that a son may be born who shall be like the father and so attest the mother's purity is traditional. Dionysius speaks at length of the pleasure a man may find in his offspring: he may once again become young with his children. If someone sees his own picture and is entranced by a lifeless object, how much more must he be charmed when he observes an animate reflection of himself—his own child.[13]

Among other topics suggested as appropriate are the season of the year and the hour of the day. Menander recommends details for spring, winter, and summer—beauties of Nature, birds, trees, and flowers. Since weddings in Greece and Rome were usually held at night, poets are encouraged to describe the beauty of the night and of the stars. The singing, music, dancing, and general revelry of the wedding day are likewise proposed as appropriate subjects.

The rhetoricians' advice on the content of the nuptial poem or oration can hardly be separated from that on techniques. General recommendations are made about meter, use of refrains, figures, and various comparisons. Mythological parallels based

on love and marriage are advocated, especially the marriage
of Peleus and Thetis. Marriage is to be compared to other
unions in the world of animal and plant life, Menander suggesting
that if the season is spring, the orator may remind the couple
that trees are now forming unions with trees. He also suggests
myths about the love of trees. The rhetoricians recommend
comparisons of the bride to a flower or fruit, and the groom to
a tree. Other nature comparisons, especially from Sappho, are
suggested.

Division of the epithalamium into four parts is proposed
by Himerius and Menander.[14] The *prooímion* should state the
occasion for the poem as ornately and pleasingly as possible.
The *perì gámou* should glorify the love of the elements which
brought order out of chaos, the latter theme to be particularly
represented by the marriage of Peleus and Thetis; the poet is
encouraged to display his erudition as well as to give pleasure.
The *enkōmion tōn gamountōn*, which praises the couple, should
be concise in order that the author may concentrate on the last
section, the *ekfrasis tēs nýmfēs*, which is devoted to counsel
and comfort to the bride. Here the poet should make use of
all the flowers of poetry at his command, Himerius advising
that a poetic style should be used even in the prose epithalamium.
Dionysius, although he recommends a moderate prose style, like
that of Xenophon and Nicostratus, suggests that at all times
the diction should be elevated and poetic, and like his fellow
rhetoricians, encourages imitation of Sappho and Homer. The
role of the poet as *choragus* or master of ceremonies, best
illustrated in Catullus 61, apparently existed in Sappho, according
to the description of her epithalamia given by Himerius; this highly stylized role with its invocations, apostrophes, and commands
was to become one of the most distinctive conventions of the
Renaissance epithalamium.

During the Renaissance, Julius Caesar Scaliger's admiration
of Catullus as "the greatest and best of poets"[15] and his respect
for the theories of the rhetoricians gave fresh impetus to the conventional themes and techniques in the epithalamium. Although

Scaliger regarded the poet as a creator, he considered poetry as an imitation or recreation of nature according to certain fixed rules observed in earlier great art, every artist, in Scaliger's view, being essentially somewhat of an echo. Scaliger believed that standards for every genre could be arrived at and defined by reason and that it was the duty of the critic to formulate the standards and the poet to follow them. Scaliger's *Poetices,* first published at Lyons, later at Heidelberg and Leyden, was widely influential. Puttenham is indebted to him, Sidney cites Scaliger four or five times in the *Defense,* Jonson and Sherburne refer to him in their notes, and Henry Peacham in 1622 describes him as the "prince of all learning and the judge of judgments, the divine Julius Caesar Scaliger."[16] The fact that so respected a critic chose to devote one of his longest chapters, something like five thousand words, to the epithalamium contributed to the popularity of the genre. Scaliger's chapter is more than a reiteration of conventional content and techniques. Although he divides the nuptial poem into six sections, and four varieties, and describes each one, the author rambles freely into digressive detail and comment. He stresses the great number of subjects which the poet may introduce into the epithalamium, and in order to suggest variations devotes a large part of the chapter to a description of wedding customs of the ancient Romans and of foreigners—among them Greeks, Macedonians, Thracians, Spartans, and the residents of the Island of Cos. The treatise is enlivened by the author's expression of personal opinion: We must not forget to mention, he writes, that the nobler brides of the Greeks rode to the groom in a carriage. The axle of this carriage was burned in front of the doors as assurance that the bride would be steadfast and that no thought of another union or a new marriage might occupy her fluctuating mind, nor an impulse to wander around overtake her—a fault, says Scaliger, that is very common in women.[17]

For the opening of the epithalamium, according to Scaliger, proper subjects are the desires of the bride and groom, their eagerness and concern, or the wedding solemnities and songs. The influence of Petrarch is evident in Scaliger's recommended description of the bridegroom: he should be described as languishing. The poet should refer to the bridegroom's virtues in order to provide an excuse for the lady to relent, or he may pretend that she is forced by the might of Venus and Cupid. In Part 2 the couple should be praised; in Part 3 good fortune should be predicted; in Part 4 gentle jests may be offered; but Scaliger recommends here, and elsewhere, that the poet should exercise modesty, especially in referring to the bride, although he may speak of the coming battle and victory. Part 5 should present promises of offspring, and Part 6 an exhortation to sleep, but sleep for others, not the bridal couple. Scaliger offers additional appropriate topics—praise or description of the nuptial chamber, the bride's dress, and the coverlet of the wedding couch—but does not assign them to any particular section. Impudent jokes and fescennine songs may be offered, their purpose being to drive away evil spirits and bad omens. Also for this purpose, the author notes, doorposts are adorned with woolen bands and anointed with oil. The usual mythological comparisons are urged—Peleus and Thetis, Bacchus and Ariadne, Hercules and Hebe—and description of the role of the various gods at such weddings is suggested.

The comparisons to be made with nature and the universe, concepts familiar from the rhetoricians and late Latin and medieval epithalamia, are set out. The epithalamist, so says Scaliger, should relate that Love and Friendship were derived from the first beginnings of the universe. At the beginnings of the world the nuptials of Heaven and Earth were celebrated, and by this union all living things were brought forth. These living things, imitating Heaven and Earth, propagated themselves by generation, to the end that immortality, which is denied by the nature of matter, may be attained by the ordered succession of forms. The poet may take his praises of Love from Plato's *Symposium*, but Scaliger urges the poet to exercise some art, lest every writer following these precepts should say one and the same thing.

The *Poetices* recommends exclamations to Hymenaeus, and invocation of him repeatedly in inserted verses. Scaliger offers a physiological explanation of the Greek god's name, and a historical one for the Roman Talassio. Wedding rites and lore of many sorts are described at length, including the taking of auspices, the offering of nuptial sacrifices, and the history of pine torches. He repeats the lore concerning the Herculean knot with which the bride's girdle is tied: the knot is a symbol of fruitfulness, for Hercules reputedly begat fifty children in seven days from fifty virgins. He goes on to explain the rites of scattering nuts and fruits, the wearing of garments of the opposite sex by members of the wedding party, the ritualistic bath for the bride, and a multitude of other customs. Repeatedly, he reminds prospective poets that a great assortment of topics is available. He encourages variety in techniques also, and reiterates the rhetoricians' injunction to the epithalamist to display his erudition.

The four kinds of nuptial poems described by Scaliger are (1) the *scolia*, sung at the feast; (2) the *epithalamium*, sung as the bride is led to the nuptial chamber; (3) the narrative poem, such as those of Musaeus on Leander, Ovid on Orpheus, Statius on Stella, and Claudian on Honorius and Maria; and (4) the mixed narrative-lyric of which Catullus 64 is an example. Like other poets and critics, Scaliger uses the term *epithalamium* to mean both the specific song at the couch, and nuptial poems generally.

Concluding his chapter he urges wedding poets to follow in the tracks of Catullus. He points out the three different kinds of beginnings used by Catullus, and gives quotations also to illustrate other characteristic elements. Regarding the brief fescennine passage of Carmen 61, he suggests that poets should know of this element but should not imitate it, for the poet who speaks impudently endangers his reputation and his life. Scaliger concludes the treatise with additional references to the epithalamia of Catullus, Claudian, and Aristophanes, and a discussion of metrics.

The relationship of marriage to nature and the universe, the doctrine of increase, and the view of marriage as a device for achieving immortality—ideas appearing in the Sophists and Scaliger—are expressed also in Erasmus's *De Conscribendis*, translated and made available to English readers in Wilson's *The Arte of Rhetorike*, which went through eight editions before 1585. Erasmus argues that marriage was instituted by God and renewed after the flood, and cites several Biblical passages expressing approval of marriage, along with arguments from Plutarch, Augustus Caesar, and Juvenal. Matrimony is natural, he contends; it would be a foul thing if beasts could observe the laws of nature and man could not. It is through carnal copulation that men make their kind immortal. Some of the examples from nature seen in the rhetoricians also appear in Erasmus's treatise. He quotes Pliny on the subject of marriage among trees:

> ... there is founde Mariage with some manifeste difference of bothe kyndes ... the housbande Tree do leane with his boughes even as thoughe he shoulde desire copulation upon the womenne Trees growynge rounde aboute hym ....[18]

He remarks that Pliny quotes other authors who think that male and female exist in all things that the earth yields, including precious stones. Even the sky or firmament, he writes, "Dothe it not playe the parte of a housbande, while it puffeth up the Earthe, the mother of all thinges, and maketh it fruictful with castinge seede ... upon it." Through marriage, all things exist and continue, but without marriage all decay and come to naught. Nations from ancient times have held marriage in esteem, he argues, and he mentions the ancient marriage-gods, Jupiter Gamelius, and Juno Lucina.

Erasmus refers to the tale of Orpheus "who did stirre and make softe ... the moste harde rockes and stones," and he interprets this to mean that a wise man called back the hardhearted, and brought them to live in accordance with the laws of matrimony. The man who has no mind for marriage, says Erasmus, is not a man but rather a stone, an enemy to nature, a rebel to God himself, seeking through his own folly, his "last ende and destruction." He argues that virginity is for angels, not men. "Virginity," he writes, "is a heavenly thyng ... wedlock is a manly thing." And he asks—rather wistfully, one might suspect—what can be more pleasant than to live with a wife "matched together both in harte and mynde, in body and soule, sealed together with the bond and league of an holy Sacrament, a swete mate in your youthe, a thankful comfort in your age."[19]

Erasmus's epistle is not labeled an epithalamium and it does not mention the word; it belongs, nevertheless, in the same tradition as certain of the prose works of the Sophists, which I have mentioned earlier. Even in form, it resembles, for example, the treatise of Dionysius on precepts for wedding orations. Addressed to a former student, the work of Dionysius is a combination of nuptial tribute arguing the advantage of marriage, and a demonstration of rhetorical techniques. Erasmus's epistle and Scaliger's treatise were the two most important documents available to guide the direction of the epithalamium as it developed in English. The other such discussion I have mentioned, Puttenham's chapter in *The Arte of English Poesie*, provides fewer aids for the poet. It praises the epithalamia of Catullus but says that the epithalamium of Secundus and his *De basis* "passeth any of the ancient or moderne Poetes in my judgment." Puttenham begins by praising married love in contrast with lust and says that marriage

> hath alwayes been accompted with every country and nation of never so barbarous people, the highest & holiest of any ceremonie apperteining to man; a match forsooth made for ever and not for a day, a solace provided for youth, a comfort for age, a knot of alliance and amitie indissoluble; great rejoysing was therefore due to such a matter and to so gladsome a time.[20]

It is therefore the duty of the civil poet to celebrate marriage, "as well Princely as others," just as much as it is to write ballads celebrating the births of children. Puttenham recalls that such ballads of rejoicing were in earlier times sung by musicians at the chamber door at specified times and were called "Epithalamies, or ballads at the bedding of the bride." Such songs were divided into three parts, the first to be sung outside the chamber door as the marriage was being consummated, the tunes of this part being loud and shrill to cover the "shreeking and outcry of the young damosell." Included in this part of the song were congratulations on the first acquaintance of the young couple, praise of the parents for making the match, and promises that the comfort of children and an increase of love will accompany the bride's submission. For the second part of the song the musicians returned to the door of the chamber about midnight or one o'clock, according to Puttenham. This part of the ballad was to "refresh the faint and wearied bodies and spirits and to animate new appetites with cheerful words . . . to advance the purposes of procreation." In the morning the same musicians returned for a third time "when it was faire broad day" to give the couple more advice on love-making, on living a frugal and thrifty life, and on bringing up the children in virtue and by good example. Finally, the singers encouraged the couple "to persever all the rest of their life in true and inviolable wedlocke."

Part Two
THE DEVELOPMENT
IN ENGLISH

VIII

Early English Epithalamia

The epithalamium had its greatest vogue in English after publication of Spenser's *Epithalamion* in 1595, but the genre was represented in English long before that time. In 1896 when Robert H. Case published his anthology, he remarked that the first epithalamium in English, original or translated, was Sir Philip Sidney's printed in the *Arcadia* of 1593 but believed to have been written in 1580–1581.[1] Writers after Case have repeated this assertion, but the fact is that a number of earlier epithalamia exist, representing several traditions. This chapter will consider a few of these, along with Sidney's and others written before 1595.

John Lydgate's "balade" of almost two hundred lines written in 1422 for the marriage of Humphrey, Duke of Gloucester, and Jacqueline, Countess of Holland, Zealand, and Hainault, bears little resemblance to the Sappho–Catullan lyric but stands rather in the tradition of the Statius–Claudian rhetorical epithalamium.[2] William Dunbar's *The Thrissil and the Rois*, written for the marriage in 1503 of James IV and the Princess Margaret Tudor, shows no influence of the early classical epithalamium; it is a nature allegory apparently related to the later Latin and medieval epithalamia.[3] The earliest classical lyric epithalamium I have seen in English is Henrie Wotton's translation of Jaques Yver's French adaptation of Catullus 62, which had appeared in Yver's collection of tales.[4] Wotton's translation of the tales was published in London in 1578 under the imposing title: *A Courtlie controversie of Cupids Cautels: Conteyning five Tragicall Histories, very pithie, pleasant, pitiful, and profitable: Discoursed uppon with Arguments of Love, by three Gentlemen and two Gentlewomen, entermedled with divers delicate Sonets and Rithmes, exceeding delightfull to refresh the yrkesomnesse of tedious tyme.* Within a few years Sidney's pastoral lyric epithalamium, and the similar poem by Bartholomew Yong, a translation of Gil Polo's Spanish pastoral epithalamium, were circulating in manuscript. In 1588 James I may have declaimed the epithalamium he wrote as part of a wedding masque.[5] And in the same year, an anonymous English translation of the epithalamium of Theocritus appeared in a little book of *Sixe Idillia* published in London.[6]

John Lydgate

John Lydgate's epithalamium for Gloucester is modeled on the rhetorical epithalamium, but he follows only in part the rhetoricians' guidelines. The main theme of the work is the hope that by means of marriage, harmony and peace may be attained between Holland and England. The wish that marriage may bring peace and concord to nations is, of course, a familiar motif in the epithalamium—we have seen it in the works of Aristophanes, Claudian, and some of the Italian and French poets. Lydgate's development of the idea is not very clear, but it appears to go something like this: The heavens predispose many things which the wit of man cannot comprehend. Wars, for example, and the fall of lords and kings are predetermined by the stars. Alliances, however, exclude strife, and although man may not go counter to things disposed by the stars, God is able to do so, and thus has instituted the order of marriage. But it is not only the Christian God who sanctions such union, for Cupid, Venus, and Nature have also regarded the present marriage favorably. Books and ancient chronicles give examples of the benefit of marriage for they tell

> Howe maryages / have grounde and cause be
> Betwene landes / of pees and unytee.

The poet expresses the hope that this marriage will bring:

> A nuwe sonne / to shynen of gladnesse
> In boothe londes / texcluden al derknesse
> Of oolde hatred and of al rancour
> Brought in by meen / of oon that is the floure
> Thoroughe oute the world / called of wommanheed
> Truwe ensaumple and welle of al goodenesse
> Benyngne of poorte / roote of goodelyheed
> Soothefast myrrour of beaute and fayrnesse . . . .

In keeping with the rhetoricians' advice, Lydgate compares the couple to mythological personages but adds Biblical and historical ones as well, the assembly including Esther, Judith, Polyxena, Dido, Hecuba, Lucrece, and Helen, along with Paris, Troilus, Hector, Solomon, Julius Caesar, and Cicero. The bride is described in terms which might fit a Christian saint—she is "aungellyk" and "celestyal"—and she is praised for her beauty and goodness, prudence, fortune, grace, reason, and compassion. The bridegroom is declared equal to the Nine Worthies and is complimented on his comeliness, mental attainments, bravery, and skill at poetry and rhetoric:

> Slouth eschuwing / he doothe his witt applye
> To reede in bookis / wheeche that beon moral
> In hooly writt with the Allegorye
> He him delytethe / to looke in specyal
> In understonding / is noone to him egal
> Of his estate expert in poetrye
> With parfounde feeling of Phylosofye
> With Salamoun hathe he sapyence
> ffaame of knighthoode / with Cesar Julius
> Of rethoryk and / eeke of eloquence
> Equypollent with Marcus Tulius . . . .[7]

His encomia concluded, the poet prays to the Christian God that there may be peace, and declares that people throughout the land are praying that the marriage may take place. The poet then appeals to Hymen and Juno to make "a knotte feythful and entiere" like that of Philology and Mercury. After an additional invocation to the gods and goddesses "above the firmament," Lydgate addresses an envoy to the bride, making the conventional apology for his inadequacy as a poet.[8]

The extravagant praise and devices characteristic of the rhetorical epithalamium are obviously intended by Lydgate to please his patron. The poet chooses to ignore the actual political situation and the fact that the marriage might increase the likelihood of war rather than bring peace. Characteristic of the age are the poet's unself-conscious blending of history, myth, and religion, and his reiteration of such commonplaces as the predetermination of man's destiny by the stars, the inevitability of the fall of princes, physical beauty as mirror of goodness, and delight in allegory. In one respect, the poem is almost unique among epithalamia: it has no nature imagery— no trees, birds, animals, breezes, streams or flowers. Except for the brief references to the stars and the "nuwe sonne" mentioned above, the only references to nature are lifeless metaphors—

the poet asks that the "dewe of grace distill shal and reyn Pees and accord," and he refers to the bride as "oon that is the floure . . . of wommanheed." Music, too, is missing from the poem except for mention of the wedding of Philology and Mercury

> Wher that Clyo / and eeke Calyope
> Sange with hir sustren / in noumbre thryes three.

William Dunbar

In striking contrast to Lydgate's marriage poems, Dunbar's *The Thrissil and the Rois* sparkles with the "May morning note" which C. S. Lewis remarked in some of the late Latin epithalamia.[9] Although the marriage of James IV and the Princess Margaret Tudor took place in August (1503), the poem was written earlier and has a spring setting:

> Quehn Merche was with variand windis past,
> And Appryll had, with hir silver schouris,
> Tane leif at nature with ane orient blast;
> And lusty May, that muddir is of flouris,
> Had maid the birdis to begyn thair houris
> Among the tendir odouris reid and quhyt,
> Quhois armony to heir it wes delyt;
>
> In bed at morrow, sleiping as I lay,
> Me thocht Aurora, with hir cristall ene,
> In at the window lukit by the day,
> And halsit me, with visage paill and grene;
> On quhois hand a lark sang fro the splene,
> Awalk, luvaris, out of your slomering,
> Se how the lusty morrow dois up spring.

The poet, after being awakened by Aurora, is ordered by the Month of May to write something in her honor and to describe

the "Ros of most plesance." In the beautiful garden of the
dream vision, Dame Nature summons the beasts, birds, and
flowers to receive her commands. The poet takes his allegorical devices from heraldry, the bridegroom being represented
by the Lion, whom Dame Nature crowns as king of beasts.
On the Royal Arms of Scotland he is portrayed

> Rycht strong of corpis, of fassoun fair but feir,
> Lusty of schaip, lycht of deliverance,
> Reid of his cullour, as is the ruby glance;
> On feild of gold he stude full mychtely,
> With flour delycis sirculit lustely.

The main symbol for the bridegroom, however, is the thistle
of Scotland, and for the bride the Tudor rose, which mingles
the red rose of Lancaster and the white rose of York. Dame
Nature gives the "awfull Thrissill" a crown of rubies because
he is an able warrior, and sends him forth as a champion,
with the instructions:

> And, sen thow art a king, thow be discreit;
> Herb without vertew thow hald nocht of sic pryce
> As herb of vertew and of odor sueit;
> And lat no nettill vyle, and full of vyce
> Hir fallow to the gudly flour delyce;
> Nor latt no wyld weid, full of churlichenes,
> Compare hir till the lilleis nobilnes.

> Nor hald non udir flour in sic denty
> As the fresche Ros of cullour reid and quhyt;
> For gife thow dois, hurt is thyne honesty,
> Conciddering that no flour is so perfyt,
> So full of vertew, plesans, and delyt,
> So full of blisfull angeilik bewty,
> Imperiall birth, honour and dignite.

The Rose is crowned as queen of flowers, and the flowers and songbirds join in exuberant rejoicing and welcome to the princess, concluding with a prayer that Christ may protect her from all adversity. Awakened by the singing, the poet composes his song:

> And thus I wret, as ye haif hard to forrow,
> Off lusty May upone the nynt morrow.

Dunbar's poem shows no specific debt to the classical epithalamium, although nature allegory existed as early as Claudian, and comparisons of the bridal couple to plants and flowers was so general in antiquity that the rhetoricians recommended it. Like Lydgate, Dunbar was a priest, and his description of the bride is reminiscent of the medieval Latin epithalamia to the Virgin. Such epithalamia also found their way into English in Dunbar's time, and one of his works, "Ane Ballat of our Lady," has among its epithets for the Virgin many floral terms—"rialest rosyne . . . fresche floure femynyne . . . rose of paradys . . . fair fresche flour delyce . . . green daseyne . . . flour delice of paradys . . . and ros virginall."[10] An anonymous poem of this genre, contemporary with Dunbar's, appears in two early manuscripts, and later in a book written in the hand of William Forrest, priest and poet who was a contemporary of Spenser.[11] Titled "Ros Mary: Ane Ballat of Our Lady," it begins "Ros Mary, most of vertewe virginale / Fresche floure on quhom the hevinlie dewe down fell . . ."; besides portraying Mary as a rose, it presents her as a star out-shining Phoebus (as hundreds of brides have done), and as the "cleir conclaif of clene virginite . . . tryumphand tempill of the Trinite." The epithets for the Virgin in the English ascetic epithalamia frequently cannot be distinguished from those for the bride in the nuptial poem. A seventeen-line wedding song, sometimes attributed to Dunbar,[12] describes the princess Margaret in the following terms, any of which would fit equally well in the poetry to the Virgin: "younge tender plant of pulcritud . . . fresche fragrant floure of fayrehede shene . . . Rose both rede and whyte . . . the floure of our delyte."[13]

Henrie Wotton

Henrie Wotton is unknown as a writer except for his collection of tales, *A Courtlie controversie of Cupids Cautels,* translated from *Le Printemps D'Yver* and published in London in 1578. The epithalamium in this work, unlike the poems of Lydgate and Dunbar which were written for actual marriages, is a song for a fictional wedding. It appears in the fifth tale of the series, and is a highly original adaptation of Catullus 62. The poem has received no attention, possibly because of the rarity of Wotton's book and because the poem is buried deep in the text.[14] It deserves to be brought to light, however, because of its historical interest as the earliest known epithalamium in English belonging to the Catullan lyric tradition, and because the poem itself has some freshness and vigor. Wotton's work is a fairly close translation of Yver's, but the English poet alters the tone considerably by his choice of vocabulary and meter (poulter's measure), and by changes in the refrain.

Jaques Yver's tales had been popular in French for some years before Wotton made his translation. First published in Paris in 1572, the year of Yver's death, the collection appeared in at least two and possibly three more editions in French before 1578. The tales are apparently original but influenced by Boccaccio in form, theme, and style,[15] the five "histories" being related on five successive days. The epithalamium appears in the final day's account, a tale of two Paduan students, reminiscent of *Decameron*, VIII, i, and *Bandello*, I, 17. Inasmuch as classical motifs and the amoebaean form had been popular in French epithalamia for many years, it is not surprising that Yver chose to adapt Catullus 62 for his inserted song, combining with it motifs seen in Catullus 5 and 61, Claudian, and the Italian epithalamia.[16] The variations which Yver works on conventional motifs may be illustrated by the first stanza, announcing the coming of night and the arrival of the evening star:

Ia du cristal voulé la lampe iournaliere
De ce grand univers emporte la lumiere
Ia mille, & mille, & mille, et mille feux et mille feux
Sallumans dans la ciel, assommeillent nos yeux
Et ia desia la nuict avec son aisle brune
Hatelle les chevaux de l'argentine Lune
Ie voy le beau Soleil dans la mer se plonger
Et de bien pres le suit l'estoille du berger
Sus doncques qu' entre nous soit ioye demenee
O Hymen, doux Hymen, Hymen, O Hymenee.[17]

The French poet retains the debate on marriage versus virginity, but for the final stanza substitutes a hymn in praise of Hymen the marriage-god, along with pleas that the couple may be free of jealousy, may be bound in love, and may serve as an example to the rest of the company whose turn will come:

Filles

O Hymen cree-tout, fils de nature heureux,
Hymen frere d'amour, soulas des amoreaux,
Qui crient apres toy, à fin que ta puissance
De leur bien desire leur donne ioussance:
Puis que de nostre rang ceste il t'apleu trasser
Pour au bras d'un mary doucement l'enlasser
De sa virginité luy rompant la ceinture
Recompence saperte en plus iuste mesure,
Rannis d'entour d'eux deux ialousie & mepris,
Et de sainte amitié enchaine leurs espris:
Fais qu'au lieu de pucelle, elle soit femme & mere,
Commençant à bastir sa famille prospere

Et que de nous chacune à son ordere, & son tour
Ayons ces gages seurs des soldats de l'amour
Qui la peine en fin rend de plaisir terminee
O Hymen, doux Hymen, Hymen, O Hymenee.

The "doux Hymen" of Yver's refrain does not occur in
Catullus, but may have been suggested by the "Blande Hymen,
iucunde Hymen" of Ariosto's version of Catullus 62. Wotton
ignores the "doux Hymen" of his French model, but he does
not go back to the Catullan refrain; instead, he introduces
another feature seen in Ariosto—the alternating refrain. It
seems likely, therefore, that both Yver and Wotton were familiar
with versions of Catullus 62 other than the original, and there
is at least the possibility that both knew Ariosto's poem.[18]

Wotton's work is less graceful than Yver's partly because
the poulter's measure seems jingly and verbose in comparison
to the French poet's more compressed line. But in Wotton's
hands the poem gains in energy. Below are the two versions of
the second stanza:

Les Garçons

Estoille que l'amour aprinse & reteneue
Pour messager certain de sa douce veneue.
Haste toy de verser cy hac le someil doux
Pour esteindre le feu de ce nouvel espoux,
Estoille que venus entre autre a choisie
Pour tesmoings de son ieu, plaisir & courtoisies,
Ie le prie haste toy d'une course empenee
O Hymen, doux Hymen, Hymen, O Hymenee.

The Young Men

O famous splendant starre by Cupid stayde above,
The pressed slave at all assayes, and messenger of
Love,

> Haste, haste thy wonted pace, and poure downe
>   pleasaunte sleepe,
> To quench the furious frying flames, that makes our
>   bridegrom wepe.
> Thou glorious starre, of whom dame Venus made hir
>   choice,
> For witnesse of hir pleasaunte sports wherein hir
>   thralles rejoyce:
> Make haste with penned course, I praye thee do not
>   staye
> But honoure Hymen at thys feaste, and blesse this
>   wedding daye.[19]

Wotton's generous use of alliteration, internal rhyme, and assonance may be seen in the lines above and also in additional phrases selected almost at random:

> daily lampe that leames . . . round about the rolling globe . . . glaring beames doth beare . . . scorching sun in seas to plunge . . . after him pursueth neare, the blasing sheppardes starre . . . Proceede then lustie youthes, let joy bear all the swaye . . . Vine that springeth up on hye . . . doth wither waste and dye . . . To daunce the preatie babes in satten mantels gaye . . . Proceede oh parch-ed spouse in flames of beauties beames . . . .

Wotton's poem brings into English the motif of love as a battle in the nuptial chamber, a motif not found in Catullus 62 but one which had been prominent in many Italian epithalamia, as I have indicated in Chapter VI. Here, however, the bold language of the Italian poems is absent. It is the thousand Cupids, familiar figures in the nuptial poems of the Pléiade, who signify that "the fielde is wonne."

Several motifs of the final stanza are to figure prominently in subsequent English epithalamia, among them the transformation of the bride from maiden to matron, the warning to contempt and jealousy to stay away, and the counsel to the bride on the importance of being a good housewife. Wotton writes, "Exile from them contempt, and jealousie of brayne," and not long thereafter Sidney instructs in his epithalamium, "But above all, away vile jealousy ... Go, snake, hide thee in dust."[20] In Wotton's poem the maidens arguing against marriage apparently view housekeeping chores with some displeasure, for they contend that the maiden who marries "Lives under yoke of toil and care, as keeping house doth prove." Later, however, after the maidens have conceded the argument, they take a different view, and ask Hymen to help the bride "To governe well hir familie in wifedomes holy trade." Sidney advises a little more bluntly: "Yet let not sluttery,/ The sink of filth, be counted housewifery." Wotton's poem concludes on a didactic note, the maidens expressing the wish that the bliss of the wedded couple may serve as an inspiration to others:

> And that eche one of us in order as they goe,
> By gauge thereof, the surest meane to love and
>   live may know,
> And knowing pleasure is the ende of payne alway,
> We honour Himen at this feaste, and blesse
>   this wedding day.

Sir Philip Sidney

Sir Philip Sidney's epithalamium is didactic, offering blunt marriage counsel, but the poet sets his advice against a cheerful pastoral background and decorates it with allegorical figures and nature comparisons, thus following his own precepts concerning the role of the poet:

> For he doth not only shew the way, but giveth so sweet a prospect into the way as will entice any man to enter into it. Nay, he doth, as if your journey should lie through a fair vineyard, at the very first give you a cluster of grapes, that, full of the taste, you may long to pass further .... And, pretending no more, doth intend the winning of the mind from wickedness to virtue ....[21]

Sidney's epithalamium honors a fictional wedding in the *Arcadia* and appears as the first of a group of five poems in the third eclogues of the work. It is a lyric of eleven stanzas of nine lines each, sung by the shepherd Dicus for the wedding of Lalus and Kala.[22] The metrical pattern and a few of the motifs indicate that Sidney's poem may have been inspired by the Spanish lyric of Gaspar Gil Polo in the continuation of Montemayor's pastoral romance, *Diana Enamorada*.[23] Sidney's poem, however, is not part of the general narrative of the *Arcadia* but of the eclogues inserted between books. This set of eclogues, as Ringler has observed, constitutes a marriage group and includes in addition to the epithalamium a humorous fabliau illustrating the effects of unfounded jealousy; a sonnet describing the ideal husband; a beast fable concerned with discovering the proper form of sovereignty for the state, as marriage is for the home; and a defense of marriage as a device in accord with Nature, designed that man may maintain his kind and preserve the commonwealth.[24] Thus the entire group of some six hundred lines seems to have as its purpose the "delightful teaching" which Sidney sees as the proper aim of a poet.

In the opening stanzas of the epithalamium, Sidney exploits Nature to entice the reader, knowing full well as he writes in the *Defense*, that

> Nature never set forth the earth in so rich tapestry as diverse poets have done—neither with so pleasant rivers, fruitful trees, sweet-smelling flowers, nor whatsoever else may make the too much loved earth more lovely.

The opening lines appeal to Mother Earth to "deck herself in flowers," and in each of the first six stanzas, we see one or two nature similes, all well-worn from centuries of use in epithalamia, but new in the English genre and skillfully used here. The "honest bridegroom and the bashful bride" are

> like the turtles fair . . . Like to the elm and the vine . . . like to lilies pure . . . like two rivers sweet . . . Like oak and mistletoe.

In a stanza addressed to Father Pan, the prospective offspring
of the couple are

> In number like the herd
> Of younglings, which thyself with love hast reared;
>
> Or like the drops of rain . . .

Sidney draws several morals. He contrasts "pure and plain"
married love with "lawless" lust. Urging the couple to be virtuous, he advises,

> That still he be her head, she be his heart,
> He lean to her, she unto him do bow,
>   Each other still allow;
>   Like oak and mistletoe,
> Her strength from him, his praise from her do grow.

He warns against quarrels and strife:

> All churlish words, shrewd answers, crabbed looks,
> All privateness, self-seeking, inward spite,
> All waywardness, which nothing kindly brooks,
> All strife for toys and claiming master's right,
>   Be hence, aye put to flight;
>   All stirring husband's hate
>   'Gainst neighbour's good for womanish debate,
>   Be fled, as things most vain:
>   O Hymen, long their coupled joys maintain!

After additional instructions against pride, sluttishness, and
jealousy, he promises the couple happiness.

Sidney's epithalamium has a meticulous structure which
reflects two aspects of the epithalamic tradition. In the classical epithalamium, as we have seen, a section is customarily
devoted to an appeal or prayer to the gods for blessings. In

Theocritus, for example, the closing lines appeal to Leto to bless the couple with children, Aphrodite to grant mutual and lasting love, and Zeus to bring prosperity. Such requests for blessings had already appeared in English, for in Lydgate's epithalamium there are appeals both to pagan deities and to the Christian God, and in Dunbar's a prayer to the Christian God to protect the bride from adversity. Sidney's epithalamium in its entirety is a series of appeals, their number being associated with the poem's structure: there are eleven appeals and eleven stanzas. The final stanza recapitulates the appeals and grants them.

Epithalamia had long been rhetorical playthings for poets. We have observed the amoebaean form with its symmetrical stanzas and parallel devices in Catullus 62 and its imitations, the repetitive techniques in the pastoral singing matches, the cento game played by Ausonius, the division into parts recommended by the rhetoricians, and the formula of describing the bride in four ways which medieval commentators superimposed upon the Canticle. Such devices are not peculiar, of course, to epithalamia. Sidney, in fact, chose for this epithalamium a rhetorical pattern which he had already used in other verse and which had been popular with neo-Latin and French vernacular poets for several decades—the *carmen correlativum* or *vers rapportes,* defined by Scaliger as a form in which "uerba ipsa modo regunt: ubi inter se respondent."[25] Typically, in this form, the poet discusses a series of items one by one and then summarizes or recapitulates. In the first six stanzas of Sidney's epithalamium, a series of blessings is requested from six sources, one in each stanza: the poet asks Mother Earth, Heaven, the Muses, the water-nymphs, Pan, and Virtue, each to grant a gift. In the next four stanzas, appeals are made to five aspects of evil to stay away from the couple: Lust, Strife, Pride and Sluttery (these two in the same stanza), and Jealousy. In the eleventh stanza, the poet summarizes the eleven requests and reports that they are being granted. Further, the refrain of the first ten stanzas has also been a request, "O Hymen, long their coupled joy maintain"; the refrain of the eleventh stanza reports the granting of this request, "For Hymen will their coupled joys maintain."

In Sidney's poem, the pagan deities are completely creatures of allegory. The Muses, the nymphs, and Father Pan are of the same order as Mother Earth, Heaven, and Virtue. In fact, the poet refers to Virtue as "if not a god, yet God's chief part." Cupid is "foul," and the symbol of Lust. Hymen appears only in the refrain, and Venus not at all.

The metrical pattern of Sidney's poem is closely related both to the Spanish epithalamium of Gil Polo and the translation into English by Bartholomew Yong, which was circulating in manuscript in the early 1580's.[26] The rhyme schemes of Yong and Sidney are identical, and they vary only slightly from that of the Spanish poem. The nine-line stanza with lines of varying lengths had appeared occasionally in Italian and French epithalamia. Some motifs of Gil Polo, especially those of the opening stanza, and the refrain of Gil Polo may have influenced Sidney,[27] but the strong didactic element, the appeals theme, and the rhetorical structure of Sidney's work did not come from the Spanish poem.

James I

The epithalamium written by James I about a decade later as part of a wedding masque is like Sidney's in that the entire poem is a series of appeals for blessings. The fact that appeals are made to seventeen gods and that the poem consists of seventeen couplets may be coincidence, inasmuch as the gods are not evenly apportioned. James's appeals are directed to an unusual assortment of Roman gods, the only conventional ones being Cupid, Talassio, and Venus. But the nature of his appeal to Venus is somewhat unconventional: James asks that Venus may amek the couple "brooddie"—inclined to breed—so that they may produce offspring quickly.[28] The other deities are more obscure, but except for two or three, all are to be found in St. Augustine's *De Civitate Dei*; King James might also have found them in some Latin grammar.[29] Included are Volumnia, the Well-Wisher, tutelary deity of newborn infants; Vitumnus, who gives vital breath to babes; Sentinus, who bestows the power of sensation; Prorsa, who presides over birth with the head foremost; Egeria, a Roman goddess of fountains worshipped as a goddess of childbirth who brings the child to light; Levana, who presides over the father's lifting up the child as a sign of acknowledgment; Vaticanus, who presides over the child's first cry; Cunina, guardian of the cradle; Rumina, protectress of infants at the breast; Educa, who presides over the child's eating; Potina, who supervises the child's drinking; Statilinus, who protects the baby on his first attempt at standing alone; and Fortune, the god who sways chance.

James's gentle concern for the prospective offspring of the couple, although slightly reminiscent of Catullus 62,[30] is unique in the tradition:

O thou Cunina cairefullie doe watche the cradle aye
Preserving it from sicknes or from harme in anie waye
Rumina with Edusa, and Potina joyn'd, doe see
That when it sucking is or wained, the foode may
　　　　　　　wholesome be . . . .

Although the greater part of the king's poem is devoted to the prospective offspring of the couple, the work is quite unlike the only other epithalamium we have seen which has the offspring as its principal theme, the Song of the Parcae in Catullus 64. The tender baby in James's epithalamium is in striking contrast with the bloody warrior Achilles, son of Peleus and Thetis.

Anonymous Translation of Theocritus 18

The same year as James's wedding masque, an anonymous translation of *Sixe Idillia* of Theocritus was published in Oxford, including Number 18, the epithalamium.[31] The anonymous poet handles the rhymed fourteener couplets with more finesse than did the youthful poet-king. Although A. H. Bullen pronounces the performance as worthy only of George Turberville or "that painful furtherer of learning" Barnaby Googe, the style has been defended by Douglas Bush as having "some charm and grace."[32] The light-heartedness contrasts with the didacticism and serious-ness of Sidney and James I, particularly in the playful remarks of the virgins addressed to the bridegroom:

> Fair Bridegroom do you sleep? Hath slumber all your
>   limbs possesst?
> What are you drowsy? or hath wine your body so
>   oppresst
> That you are gone to bed? For if you needs would take
>   your rest,
> You should have ta'en a season meet. Mean time, till
>   it be day
> Suffer the Bride with us, and with her mother dear,
>   to play!
> For, MENELAUS, She, at evening and at morning tide
> From day to day, and year to year, shall be thy loving
>   Bride.[33]

IX

Spenser

Of all English poets, Edmund Spenser was the most thoroughly versed in the epithalamic tradition. Although he did not write his *Epithalamion* until 1594, his first work in the genre was probably undertaken as early as that of Sidney and Yong, or possibly even earlier.[1] Spenser has long been praised for his *Epithalamion* and *Prothalamion,* but it has not been noted that before he wrote these two poems he had created two other works in the genre, and that each of the four represents a new strain in the tradition. In the classical era, Catullus is unique for having created the age's most brilliant nuptial lyric and two other great epithalamia as well, each very different from the others. In the Renaissance, it is Spenser who merits similar recognition for hav-

ing written the masterpiece in the genre and three other diverse
and novel works.

Spenser's *Epithalamion* is the first such poem for the poet's
own marriage.[2] His *Prothalamion* is a betrothal poem, and for
it he coined the title to indicate a song that preceded the nuptials.[3] A third work is his topographical epithalamium for the
union of the rivers Thames and Medway, which appears as Canto
xi, Book IV of *The Faerie Queene* and is probably a revision of
the lost *Epithalamion Thamesis* described in one of his 1580
letters as "a worke beleeve me, of much labour" that he intended "shortely at convenient leysure, to sette forth."[4] His
fourth contribution to the genre has not been discussed as an
epithalamium, so far as I know: it is the "Aprill" eclogue of *The
Shepheardes Calender,* published in 1579. An epithalamium to
the virgin queen, it utilizes conventions of the pagan nuptial
poem and the medieval tributes to the Virgin; the framework of
the French epithalamic eclogues, such as those of Ronsard and
Grévin; and metrical patterns and motifs reminiscent of Belleau and of the Gil Polo–Yong–Sidney group of pastoral lyric
epithalamia.

Spenser wrote another brief epithalamic passage, which
appears at the end of Book I of *The Faerie Queene,* celebrating
the betrothal of Una and the Redcrosse knight.[5] It is not an independent lyric, however, but is part of the fabric of the canto.
Spenser may have been author also of an additional work in
the epithalamic tradition, a translation of the Canticle, which
has been lost. William Ponsonbie wrote in "The Printer to the
Gentle Reader," which prefaced Spenser's *Complaints* volume
in 1591:

> To which effect I understand that he besides wrote sundrie others,
> namelie *Ecclesiastes,* and *Canticum canticorum* translated, *A se-
> nights slumber, The hell of lovers, his Purgatorie,* being all ded-
> icated to Ladies; so as it may seeme he ment them all to one
> volume. Besides some other Pamphlets looselie scattered abroad:
> as *The dying Pellican, The howers of the Lord, The sacrifice of a*

sinner, The seven Psalmes, & c. which when I can either by him-
selfe, or otherwise attaine too, I meane likewise for your favour
sake to set foorth.[6]

Spenser's familiarity with the Canticle and the Psalms as facets
of the epithalamic tradition is apparent in his other works.

Three of Spenser's epithalamia in some ways parallel the
three of Catullus. We have noted that Carmen 61 is a long lyric
with the poet as master of ceremonies directing the events of the
wedding day; Carmen 62 is dramatic in technique with the
amoebaean exchange between two choruses; Carmen 64 is a narrative and descriptive epyllion in which marital union has cosmic implications. Spenser's long lyric *Epithalamion* is mainly in
the general tradition of Catullus 61; his *Prothalamion* is a word-
painting of a dramatic performance—a description of a masque,
in effect—with inserted song and chorus; his Thames-Medway
canto is most nearly in the tradition of the narrative-descriptive
epic epithalamium, with the union of streams dramatizing the
age-old ideas of the cosmic generative force of water and (as
Thomas P. Roche, Jr., has so ably demonstrated) the fact that
"unity has momentarily emerged from the diversity of mutability."[7]

Spenser differs from Catullus, however, and is almost
unique in the epithalamic tradition in that his epithalamia are
more concerned with personal joy, love, admiration, and comment than with praise of marriage as an institution. Catullus's
epithalamia and most others, as we have seen, are mainly about
the subject of marriage. Spenser's are more clearly about human beings—himself, his bride, his friends, patrons, and queen
—and the land in which they live. The author is present as a
personality in the poem for his own marriage and in the others
as well.[8] All four epithalamia reflect Spenser's lifelong delight
in rivers and streams. The settings in *Epithalamion, Prothalamion,* and the Thames-Medway canto are real; instead of
mythological geography and palaces, one sees the Irish country-

side, the "scaly trouts and greedy pikes" of the Mulla,[9] the "bricky towres" of London, the castle of Leicester and Essex, Oxford and Cambridge universities, the softly-running Thames, and the multitude of other English and Irish rivers and details of landscape. All of his epithalamia are marked by his characteristic lavishness—great numbers of people, deities, rivers, flowers, birds, sounds, sights, and actions.

Paradoxically, although Spenser displays greater individuality than other English epithalamists and uses local, personal, and contemporary materials, he also makes the most extensive use of conventions. His epithalamia show influences of Hebrew, neo-Latin, Italian, French, Spanish, and English authors; pagan, Christian, and Neo-Platonic philosophies; and the literary traditions of lyric, pastoral, epic, hymn, topographical-antiquarian narrative, folk tale, dream-vision, emblem, *impresa,* and masque.[10]

Epithalamion

I shall not try to summarize the extensive criticism and scholarship on the *Epithalamion.*[11] My purpose here is to review briefly the main traditions which this poem represents, and the breadth of the influences which converge in it; I want to call attention also to a few of its distinctive elements which have not been the subject of previous comments, and to show some relationships between this poem and the "Aprill" eclogue.

The *Epithalamion* in its general structure and tone is in the style of Catullus 61 with the poet as master of ceremonies directing the rejoicing, and commenting upon the events of the wedding day in sequence. But Spenser's poem strongly represents two other major traditions also: (1) the narrative epic epithalamium with its nature allegory and mythological personages as in Claudian, and (2) the Christian epithalamium with its Biblical imagery, its devices of tribute to a saint, its cosmic implications, and its prayer for immortality. Critics have cited parallels in this poem with the epithalamia of Sappho, Aristophanes, and Theocritus; with all three of Catullus's marriage poems; and with those of Seneca, Statius, Claudian, Ausonius, Sidonius, Dracontius, Paulinus, Himerius, and Capella; and with the *Laurentian epithalamium.* Passages have been related to the epithalamia of neo-Latin poets in four or five countries, among them Micyllus, Cisnerus, Piccartus, Sabinus, Mellemannus, Bersmannus, Palearius, Pontanus, Altilius, Codicius, Lipsius, Beverinus, Gruterus, Baudius, Ogerius, Brissonius, Ennodius, Axonius, and Bonefonius. The French works of Belleau, Dorat, Marot, Du Bellay, Ronsard, and Buttet have been cited, along with the English poems of Sidney, Yong, and Dunbar. The Canticle, the Psalms, and the account in Revelations of the mystical marriage have been mentioned.[12] Additional works entirely outside the epithalamic tradition have also been suggested as possible sources. I have remarked earlier in this study that "sources" in the epithalamic tradition frequently break down, inasmuch as almost every epithalamic motif and image has appeared in more than one work. This list is of interest not so much because Spenser may have borrowed from a particular author, but because it demonstrates the range and diversity of motifs and techniques which critics have recognized in the *Epithalamion.*

To the list above I would add the names of Erasmus, James I, Tasso, and Pierre Poupo, not as "sources," but as epithalamists who preceded Spenser and expressed ideas parallel with some of those in the *Epithalamion.* In his "Epistle to perswade a yong Gentleman to marriage. . ." appearing in Thomas Wilson's *The Arte of Rhetorike,* Erasmus mentions Orpheus (see *Epithalamion,* 1. 16) and treats marriage as "a heavenly thing" and as a means of attaining immortality, a point of view in keeping with that of the *Epithalamion.* Further, the verse epithalamium by Erasmus has as its principal motif the role of the Muses, and Spenser begins his poem by summoning the Muses and asking them to help with the celebration, awaken his bride, and bring the nymphs.[13]

A passage in Spenser's Stanza 7, in which he appeals to Phoebus, is reminiscent of the opening lines of King James's epithalamium written six years earlier:

Spenser:

> If ever I did honour thee aright,
> Or sing the thing, that mote thy mind delight,
> Doe not they servants simple boone refuse,
> But let this day let one day be myne,
> Let all the rest be thine.
> Then I thy soverayne prayses loud will sing.
> That all the woods shal answer and theyr eccho ring.

James I:

> If ever I o mightie Gods have done you service true
> In setting furth by painefull pen your glorious
>   praises due
> If one the forked hill I tredd, if ever I did preasse
> To drinke of the Pegasian spring, that flowes
>   without releasse
> If ever I on Pindus dwell'd, and from that sacred hill
> The eares of everie living thing did with your fame
>   fulfill
> Which by the trumpett of my verse I made for to
>   resounde
> From pole to pole through everie where of this
>   immoble rounde
> Then graunte to me who patrone am of Hymens triumphe
>   here
> That all your graces may upon this Hymens band
>   appeare.[14]

It has been suggested that the stanza of Spenser's *Epithalamion* may have been modeled in part on that of the *canzone,* common in Italian poetry. I think it has not been pointed out in connection with Spenser, however, that Tasso is the author of several nuptial poems written in the *canzone* form, and that each concludes with a *tornata,* a stanza shorter than the preceding ones, addressed by the poet to his song and stating its purpose. Spenser's final stanza is of this nature. Also, in Tasso's epithalamia as in Spenser's, rivers and other aspects of topography are favorite themes. Tasso's repeated references to the swans on the river Po are of interest too in connection with Spenser's *Prothalamion*.[15]

Pierre Poupo, like Spenser in several ways, published his *Epithalames* for his own marriage four years before Spenser wrote his *Epithalamion*. The *Epithalames,* however, consist of nine nuptial sonnets linked by similarity in theme but not constituting a unified work. The sonnets are religious poems, several of them prayers, but in tone quite unlike the "festal sublimity"[16] of Spenser's prayers in the *Epithalamion*. In Poupo's sonnets the religious expression seems almost joyless, at times marked by the kind of tension which characterizes some of the devotional sonnets of the English metaphysical poets. The tremendous delight in experiences of the senses which permeates every stanza of Spenser's poem for his own marriage finds little place in Poupo's nuptial sonnets, but if we look back to Poupo's earliest epithalamium,[17] written before his conversion from Catholicism to Calvinism and first published in 1585, we find the same kind of vibrant joy in sensual experience which we see in the *Epithalamion,* particularly the poet's delight in music and other sounds of all kinds. Anticipating motifs to be seen in Spenser, Poupo's song rings with sounds from the shepherds' musical instruments and the songs of the larks in the happy woods. The streams and winds murmur, and the sun gives brighter light. At intervals, the rocks echo the joyful sounds. There is dancing to the sound of the tambourine, the lute, and the violin as a little spring chatters along its bank, and the woods are animated by the whistle of the wind and the humming of the bees. The nymphs of the rivers, plains, and forest gather flowers—roses, violets, lilies, buttercups, and other fragant blossoms—to decorate the bridal bed. The bride's virtues are praised, as well as her physical beauty, and she is described in Scriptural language as a pearl of unique value and as one who prefers to be estranged from her country rather than from her heart. The Muses arrive on the scene, and their song about the bridal couple is echoed by the rocks.

Spenser's refrain, although it varies as the poem pro-
gresses,[18] is concerned in each of the twenty-three stanzas with
the woods echoing the sounds of the wedding day. Poupo uses
the echo device three times. Brief quotations from the two
poems will illustrate some resemblances. In Spenser's Stanza 8,
boys run up and down the street shouting "Hymen, io Hymen,
Hymen," and the people standing about join in the song:

> And evermore they Hymen Hymen sing,
> That al the woods them answer and theyr eccho ring.

In Poupo's work the voice of an angel has announced that Hymen
is to be sung:

> A peine estoit en l'air ceste voix expandue
> Que desjà les rochers l-avoyent bien entendue,
> Et tous a l'environ d'un murmure soudain
> Se sont pris à jazer: "Hymen, hymen, hymen!"[19]

In Spenser the poet directs the Muses to summon the nymphs
to decorate the bridal bed:

> Bring with you all the Nymphes that you can heare
> Both of the rivers and the forrests greene:
> And of the sea that neighbours to her neare,
> Al with gay girlands goodly wel beseene.
> And let them also with them bring in hand
> Another gay girland
> For my fayre love of lillyes and of roses,
> Bound truelove wize with a blew silke riband.
> And let them eeke bring store of other flowers
> To deck the bridale bowers.

The nymphs have a similar task in Poupo's lines:

> Niphes, roines de Seine aux ondes argentines,
> Et des gayes forests qui rament ces colines,

Accourez pour ouyr le clairon de ma voix . . .
Allez vous pourmener en ces verdes prairies,
Couronnez-vous le chef de guirlandes fleuries,
Emplissez vos girons de roses et de lis . . . .[20]

Elsewhere in the poem the nymphs are pictured as gathering
an assortment of flowers "pour ceindre és environs / La couche
nuptiale . . . ."

The mood of rejoicing and the feeling of the participation
of all Nature are conveyed in somewhat the same manner by
the two poets, but in the French poem, although the poet functions as the conventional master of ceremonies, he is not person-
ally involved, as is Spenser. Poupo in this poem does not convey,
or even attempt to convey, the intense personal joy and spiritual elevation of the *Epithalamion.* Another of Poupo's epithalamia[21] concludes with a Christian motif similar to that of
Spenser's—the wish for children, and the prayer for blessing
and immortality—but its expression is prosaic compared to the
"haughty pallaces" and "heavenly tabernacles" of Spenser.

To summarize, both poets wrote several epithalamia, including poems for their own marriages; both translated the Canticle, presented Christian and Platonic motifs in their major
works, adopted the epithalamic poet's role from Catullus 61
and other motifs of pagan authors, used pastoral trappings and
the glories of nature as setting and symbol, and echoed Scriptural language and imagery, especially that of the medieval
epithalamia.

The "Aprill" Eclogue

Colin's song in the "Aprill" eclogue of *The Shepheardes
Calender* has long been praised as an original and graceful
pastoral tribute by the young Edmund Spenser to the Virgin
Queen Elizabeth.[22] Readers have noted that a few of its
lines anticipate some of those in the *Epithalamion* which Spenser
wrote some fifteen years later for another Elizabeth, his "beauti-
fullest bride," but no one has observed, so far as I know, that

the "Aprill" song is itself an epithalamium employing conventions which were common to nuptial epithalamia and to the medieval hymns called epithalamia which celebrated mystical marriage and usually paid tribute to the Virgin Mary. Recognition of the "Aprill" song as an epithalamium suggests an allegorical reading of the poem as a veiled commentary on Queen Elizabeth's proposed marriage to the Duke of Alençon, and provides a key to the baffling flower passage with its mysterious "Chevisaunce" which no one has been able to identify as a flower, even though E. K. declares pointedly in the Glosse, "all these be names of flowers."

Although modern critics have ignored the epithalamium as one of the forms of pastoral, it would not have seemed novel to Spenser to include in his collection of eclogues an epithalamium along with the more common kinds of pastoral such as complaint, elegy, and singing match. As we have seen, Theocritus's Idyll 18 is an epithalamium, and epithalamic eclogues were numerous in the work of sixteenth-century French poets. In fact, the framework of the "Aprill" might have been suggested by any of several French epithalamic eclogues, but particularly that of Jacques Grévin, written twenty years before *The Shepheardes Calender.*[23] Grévin's eclogue is a dialogue among three shepherds—Collin, Tenot, and Jaquet—and concludes with a nuptial epithalamium sung by Collin. We note the similar names in Spenser's "Aprill." Spenser's eclogue opens with Thenot and Hobbinoll discussing their friend Colin, who has ceased "his wonted songs" because of his dejection over his romance with Rosalind. To demonstrate Colin's skill as a poet, Hobbinoll says that he will sing a song written by Colin

> Of Fayre Eliza, Queene of shepheardes all;
> Which once he made, as by a spring he laye,
> And tuned it unto the waters fall.

Although it is not unusual for pastoral musicians like Spenser's Colin to "tune" their songs to the rhythm of the water, it is at least an interesting coincidence that in the epithalamium of

Grévin's Collin, the murmur of the moving waters of the Seine is also in accord with the rhythm of the song. Similarly, in the French poem the virgin bride, like the virgin queen in the "Aprill" eclogue, is the daughter of the shepherds' god, Pan.

It is not my purpose here, however, to enumerate resemblances of Spenser's "Aprill" to this particular epithalamium, although a few other likenesses could be cited. Rather, I shall point to some of the conventions of the epithalamic tradition in general which appear in the "Aprill" eclogue. One point I wish to concede initially is that some of these conventions are normal for other kinds of pastoral panegyrics, especially the elegy. My argument that these conventions help to make the "Aprill" poem an epithalamium rests on the particular assortment of conventions, the order in which they appear, and the similarity of the total pattern to that customary in epithalamia. I find it noteworthy that Spenser's "Aprill" employs stanzas of nine lines, a rather unusual length for English lyrics of the time. It seems more than coincidence that the pastoral lyric epithalamia of both Sidney and Yong, written at about the same time as Spenser's "Aprill," have nine-line stanzas, and that the rhyme patterns are similar in the three poems.[24]

In the "Aprill" song, as in the later *Epithalamion,* the poet assumes the role of master of ceremonies, summoning and directing nymphs, Muses, Graces, and shepherds' daughters, who join in praise and celebration of Elisa. Like the bride in Christian nuptial epithalamia and tributes to the Virgin, Elisa is praised in terms conventional for Venus and the Virgin Mary. In the opening stanza the poet summons water-nymphs and the Muses to help sing praises of Elisa, the passage resembling the opening lines of Belleau's epithalamium quoted on page 109 of the present study and the excerpt from Buttet quoted on page 112.[25] In the second stanza Elisa is described in language like that of the Canticle and medieval epithalamia as "the flowre of Virgins . . . without spotte." She is portrayed also as "of heavenly race," daughter of Syrinx and Pan. The bride in Grévin's epithalamium and in Ronsard's *Chant pastoral* is likewise the daughter of the god Pan.

> N'avez vous entendu comme Pan le grand Dieu,
> Le grand Dieu qui preside aux pasteurs de ce lieu,
> Par mariage assemble à sa fille Claudine
> Le beau pasteur Lorraine, de telle fille digne?[26]

Elisa's apparel includes a coronet of flowers and a "scarlot" gown, reminiscent of the flame-colored veil of Roman brides.[27] Her "angelick face . . . heavenly haveour," and "princely grace" are indeed fitting for a bride, and her eyes are "modest," as is traditional in bridal poems. The "redde rose medled with the White" in her cheeks is a traditional description of Tudor princesses but also of brides since the days of Catullus.[28] In three stanzas (4, 5, and 6) she is compared, as many a bride has been, to mythological figures representing the sun and moon, whom she outshines—Phoebe, Phoebus, and Cynthia. In the seventh stanza she is described as a "goddess" to whom the shepherd offers a milk-white lamb, conventional pastoral gift to the Virgin Mary.[29]

We see other familiar motifs and figures. Led by Calliope, the Muses play musical instruments and sing, the Graces dance, and the poet summons Elisa to become a fourth Grace. The passage reminds one of Du Bellay's epithalamium for the Princess Marguerite, in which the bride is not only the fourth of the Graces but the tenth of the Muses:

> Des Muses la dixieme,
> Des Graces la quatrieme,
> S'il en est plus de trois.[30]

Elisa then is crowned with olive branches because

> Olives bene for peace,
> When wars doe surcease.
> Such for a Princesse bene principall.

The war-and-peace motif had been common in epithalamia since Claudian, and had appeared in many Italian and French poems, as well as in Lydgate's epithalamium in English. Du Bellay's epithalamium, quoted above, devotes ten stanzas to the theme, including these lines:

> Des Dieux la prevoyance
> Gardoit ceste alliance,
> Instrument de la paix . . . .[31]

In the eleventh stanza the poet summons the shepherds' daughters to attend Elisa, warning them to bind up their locks and gird in their waists in order not to offend her. The further admonition is given that none may "adorne her grace" except virgins. It is traditional in epithalamia that the bride is attended by virgins, who help "adorn" her, although the women who serve as *pronubae* are sometimes, as in Catullus, matrons who have had but one husband. In this stanza, the line "And when you come whereas she is in place" seems to suggest the traditional "placing" of the bride on the nuptial couch.[32]

Following the "placing," appropriately enough, is the famous flower passage of Stanza 12. The flowers here are like those which adorn the nuptial chambers in many epithalamia and mark the consummation of the marriage. In Spenser's stanza the poet instructs the virgins to

> Bring hether the Pincke and purple Cullambine,
>> With Gelliflowres:
> Bring Coronations, and Sops in wine,
>> worne of Paramoures.
> Strowe me the ground with Daffadowndillies,
> And Cowslips, and Kingcups, and loved Lillies:
>> The pretie Pawnce,
>> And the Chevisaunce,
> Shall match with the fayre flowre Delice.

We recall that in the epithalamium of Statius the Loves and Graces strew roses, lilies, and violets on the couple as they embrace.[33] In Claudian the Loves scatter red spring flowers, roses, and violets in the nuptial chamber.[34] It was to "scatter flowers before the couches of the virgins of God" that the ninth-century monk, Radbert of Corbei, wrote his epithalamium to the nuns of Notre Dame de Soissons.[35] In one of Ronsard's epithalamia the dozen virgins who attend the bride are addressed as "Nymphes" and instructed to decorate the holy bridal bed with flowers:

> Nymphes, de vos couleurs
> Ornez leur couche sainte,
> Des plus vermeilles fleurs
> Dont la terre soit peinte . . . .[36]

After the flower passage, in the final stanza of the song, the poet addresses Elisa, "Now ryse up Elisa decked as thou art, in royall aray," a passage possibly reminiscent of the Virgin Mary's ascension in the mystical epithalamia. The poet then orders "And now ye daintie Damsells may depart, . . ." in keeping with the convention of sending the virgins away from the door of the nuptial chamber—a convention seen in epithalamia since the days of Sappho and Catullus.[37]

Perhaps the most convincing reason for regarding the "Aprill" as an epithalamium is to be found in Spenser's extensive borrowing from it in the epithalamium for his marriage. A few key words will indicate some of the parallel passages. The first quotation in each pair below is from "Aprill," the second from *Epithalamion*:

> Ye dainty nymphes . . .
> Ye learned sisters . . .
>
> Helpe me to blaze / Her worthy praise
> Helpe me mine owne loves prayses to resound
>
> Phoebus . . . how broade her beames did spredde
> His golden beame upon the hils doth spred

Bring hether the Pincke and purple Cullambine
Bring . . . lillyes . . . roses . . . bridale poses . . .

Strow me the ground with Daffadowndillies
And let the ground . . . Be strewed with fragrant flowers

Ye shepheards daughters . . . Binde your fillets faste
Ye Nymphes of Mulla . . . Bynd up the locks

No mortall blemishe may her blotte
No blemish she may spie

I saw Phoebus thrust out his golden hedde
And Phoebus gins to shew his glorious hed

Now rise up Elisa, decked as thou art
Now is my love all ready forth to come

Lo how finely the graces . . .
            dauncen deffly, and singen soote
Harke how the Minstrels . . . Damzels . . .
            doe daunce and carrol sweet

Like Phoebe fayre
Lyke Phoebe from her chamber of the East

Yclad in Scarlot like a mayden Queene
Golden mantle . . . like some mayden Queene

Upon her head a Cremosin coronet
And being crowned with a girland greene

Her modest eye
Her modest eyes

Tell me, have ye seene her angelick face,
            Like Phoebe fayre

Tell me . . . did ye see
    So fayre a creature

Ye shepheards daughters
Ye merchants daughters

Let none come there, but that Virgins bene
Of her ye virgins learne obedience

The Redde rose medled with the White yfere
    In either cheeke depeincten lively chere
How the red roses flush up in her cheekes
    And the pure snow with goodly vermill stayne

Of olive branches bears a coronall
Crowne ye god Bacchus with a coronall

And now ye daintie Damsells may depart
Now it is night ye damsels may be gon

Besides the similarity of the "Aprill" and the *Epithalamion* in motifs, diction, and tone, there is an additional resemblance in the rhyme pattern. Although the *Epithalamion* stanzas vary in length and pattern, twenty-two of the stanzas have the same rhyme scheme in the first nine lines.[38] This pattern is very close to that of the nine-line "Aprill" stanza:

           Epithalamion: ababccdcd
           "Aprill":   ababccddc

As we have seen, religious and moral allegory had for centuries been part of the epithalamic tradition, and elements of political allegory had crept into the Italian and French epithalamia. In addition, the epithalamium had long been a vehicle for poetic and rhetorical experimentation. It seems plausible that as a young poet interested in classical and medieval genres and in testing the English language as a poetic medium, Spenser might have been intrigued with the idea of using the epithalamium as a device for political allegory. *The Shepheardes Calender,* published anonymously, is prefaced by the letter in which E. K. asserts that the young poet had chosen to write in the eclogue form because he wished "to unfold great matter of argument covertly." Further, E. K. remarks that he had been "made privie" to the poet's "secret meaning" in the eclogues, but later in the argument of the book, E. K. adds "A few onely except, whose speciall purpose and meaning I am not privie to." Other eclogues of *The Shepheardes Calender* have been subjected to extensive interpretation as commentaries on contemporary events;[39] I suggest that the "Aprill" may have allegorical significance in connection with Elizabeth's proposed marriage. For several years Elizabeth had used the marriage negotiations as a device for political maneuvering, and had canceled and resumed them in keeping with political expedience. In the months just prior to publication of *The Shepheardes Calender,* late in 1579, it appeared that the marriage might take place. Spenser and his group opposed it, and it was during these months that Sidney wrote his letter to the queen arguing against the marriage.[40] *The Shepheardes Calender* was entered on the Stationers' Register December 5, 1579, by the printer, Hugh Singleton.[41] Four months earlier Singleton had printed the blistering attack opposing the marriage, written by John Stubbs, *The Discoverie of a Gaping Gulf whereinto England is Like to be Swallowed by another French Mariage, if the Lord forbid not the banes, by letting her Majestie see the sin and punishment thereof.*[42] Stubbs had attacked the French as untrustworthy and predicted Elizabeth would be "a doleful bryde in theyr bloody brydchambers." He prophesied that the marriage might mean the death of the queen in childbirth and the death of England as a nation. Angered by the attack, Elizabeth ordered that Singleton, Stubbs, and William Page should each be punished by the chopping off of his right hand. Singleton was pardoned, but on November 3—a month before the *Calender* was entered for publication—the grisly sentence of Stubbs and Page was carried out.

Paul McLane believes that Spenser revised portions of *The Shepheardes Calender* (although he does not mention the "Aprill" eclogue) just before publication, in order to express disapproval of the proposed alliance with Alençon. McLane sees the "November" elegy as a veiled criticism of Elizabeth, suggesting that such a marriage would be the death of England.[43] If the "Aprill" epithalamium was also intended to be read by the initiated as disapproval of the queen's proposed marriage, wherein is the disapproval expressed? I wonder if possibly the bride and bridegroom are hidden in the flower passage. The passage suggests royalty—*coronations* and *kingcups.* It suggests the French—*paramoures, pawnce, chevisaunce, flowre Delice.* It suggests a wedding and lovers—*paramoures,* and *sops in wine,* which besides being a flower is a wedding custom. And it mentions a "match":

> The pretie Pawnce,
> And the Chevisaunce,
> Shall match with the fayre flowre Delice.

Is Elizabeth the pretty pansy? And the Duke of Alençon the flowre Delice? The *fleur de lis* of the French Royal Arms has been a symbol for many French bridegrooms. And Baïf had written a poem in which the first line praised the Duke of Alençon as "François, fleuron François."[44] Why should Elizabeth be represented by a pansy instead of the more usual rose? Would the rose have been too obvious a symbol for her?

Agnes Arber has offered evidence that Spenser may have had access to a copy of Lyte's herbal published in 1578 and dedicated to Queen Elizabeth.[45] On a single illustrated page of this herbal are mentioned four flowers which appear in Spenser's flower passage: pinkes, gillofers, carnations, and soppes in wine. On another page of Lyte's herbal is this description of the *pance* or *Hartsease*:

> Faire and pleasant floures . . . like to a violet, each floure being of
> three divers colours, whereof the highest leaves for the most part

are of a violet and purple colour, the others are blewish or yellow, with black and yellow . . . .

. . . called in Latin viola flammea, Flamma, and at this time Viola tricolor, Herba trinitas, Iacea, and Herba Clauellata: in English, Pances, Love in Idlenes, and Hartsease: in French Pénsee, and Pensée menue . . . .

These floures boild and dronken, do cure and stay the beginnings of the falling evil . . . .[46]

The pawnce, then, is of royal colors, purple and gold. It is the. Herba trinitas—in flower lore often called the flower of the Trinity, and like the violet, the lily, and the rose, frequently associated with the Virgin Mary. Legend is that the pansy has special divine protection. It is the flower which signifies thought —"and there is pansies, that's for thoughts"—and thus appropriate to a learned princess. Louis XV of France is said to have selected this flower as an armorial bearing for his physician, Quesnay, whom he called his "thinker."[47] And, as Lyte points out, the pawnce is believed to have the power to cure the falling evil. Curing the falling evil, also called the "king's evil," is an attribute of kings and queens, who were believed able to do it by their touch. Is it not possible that "the pretie Pawnce" is Elizabeth?

But who or what is the third party of this "match"—the mysterious Chevisaunce? E. K.'s gloss, "All these be names of flowers," would seem odd and unnecessary if indeed all these are names of flowers.[48] Is he calling attention to the passage because Chevisaunce is not a flower? No one, to my knowledge, has been able to find it in the herbals of Spenser's time or any other. The Oxford English Dictionary offers only two examples of its use as a flower—Spenser's and a couplet by T. Robinson, which is imitating Spenser's. The OED says that "Dr. Prior has suggested the wallflower." Dr. R. C. Prior in *Popular Names for British Plants* made this suggestion because the Latin for wallflower is *Cheiranthus Cheiri*.[49] Agnes Arber proposes that Spenser may have meant *cherisaunce,* but *cherisaunce* is not a flower either—in Chaucer's time it meant "comfort" or "ease of heart"—and Miss Arber argues that this is more plausible than "chevisaunce" is. Renwick suggests the word may refer to the Chrysanthus of Virgil's *Culex*.[50] I think possibly Spenser himself, E. K., and the OED (in its first entry for the word *chevisaunce*) tell us what the word means. Spenser uses the word in the "May" eclogue: "They maken many a wrong chevisaunce."[51] E. K. glosses this: "sometime of Chaucer used for gaine; sometime of other for spoyle, or bootie, or enterprise, and sometime for chiefdome." The OED indicates that in Spenser's time the word was indeed used to mean gain, as well as shift, expedient, device, shiftiness, booty. It seems possible that in this passage Spenser's Chevisaunce simply had the word's customary meaning—expedience or shift. If so, the poet might have been using it to express his disapproval of the proposed match between the pretty pawnce and the *fleur de lis* because the match was indeed one of expedience and shiftiness, associated with political maneuvers.[52] It seems possible that Colin Clout, ostensibly strewing flowers before the couch of a virgin queen, may indeed have been attempting to convey "great matter of argument covertly."

Epithalamion Thamesis and the Thames-Medway Canto

A few months after *The Shepheardes Calender* was published, Spenser was apparently working on his *Epithalamion Thamesis*. In a letter to Harvey in 1580 he describes the work as "profitable for the knowledge, and rare for the Invention, and manner of handling."[53] He adds:

> For in setting forth the marriage of the Thames: I shewe his first beginning, and offspring, and all the countrey, that he passeth thorough, and also describe all the Rivers throughout Englande whyche came to this Wedding, and their righte names, and right

passage, & c. A worke beleeve me, of much labour, wherein not-withstanding Master Holinshed hath muche furthered and ad-vantaged me, who therein hath bestowed singular paines, in search-ing oute their firste heades, and sourses: and also in tracing, and dogging out all their Course, til they fall into the Sea.[54]

If Spenser completed the poem, it has been lost. It seems prob-able that the work described in the letter was revised to become the Thames-Medway epithalamium in *The Faerie Queene*. There is evidence that the canto borrows also from Camden's *Bri-tannia,* first published in 1586, and from the second edition of Holinshed, published in 1587.[55]

Rivers had long been prominent in nuptial epithalamia, the union of streams sometimes representing the union of two royal houses; and the rhetoricians had urged the wedding poets to com-pare marriage of human beings to unions of various elements of nature. In the Italian epithalamia, as we have seen, rivers and other aspects of topography, as well as voyages, were prev-alent. Creatures of the ocean and rivers—dolphins, whales, fish, the swans of Venus, and the swans on the river Po—had dec-orated hundreds of nuptial poems. The water-nymph Aganippe, deity of the Muses' sacred spring, had appeared in Catullus 61, and water-nymphs abounded in the works of the sixteenth-cen-tury French epithalamists. Other deities of ocean and rivers, especially those associated with Venus on her frequent ocean voyages, had long been common. In the epithalamium of Statius, Venus mentions her origin from the blue waters of the ocean.[56] And in medieval interpretations of the marriage of Peleus and Thetis, the bridegroom is portrayed as representing earth, and the bride as symbolizing water.[57] In the gloss to the "Aprill" eclogue of *The Shepheardes Calender,* E. K. explains the phrase "Ladyes of the lake" as follows:

Ladyes of the lake) be Nymphes. For it was an olde opinion amongste the Auncient Heathen, that of every spring and fountaine was a goddesse the Soveraigne . . . . For the word Nymphe in Greeke signifieth Well water, or otherwise a Spouse or Bryde.[58]

The association of rivers, streams, springs—and of water and its cosmic generative function—with the institution of human marriage thus had ample precedent in the epithalamic tradition.

In the nuptial epithalamium, the union of human beings is likened to the union of rivers, and the human beings take on the attributes of rivers. In Sidney's epithalamium, for example, after asking that the couple may live together, die together, and have one grave, the poet then makes the comparison:

> And like two rivers sweet
> When they, though divers, do together meet,
> One stream both streams contain:
> O Hymen, long their coupled joys maintain.

In the topographical epithalamium, the comparison is reversed: the union of two rivers is compared to the marriage of human beings, and the rivers assume the attributes of human beings, the bride, in particular, being described like a human bride. It seems possible that his reversal of the customary metaphor may have prompted Spenser to describe his *Epithalamion Thamesis* as "rare for the Invention."

The earliest poem of this kind by an English poet, so far as I know, is the Latin epithalamium *De Connubio Tamis et Isis,* in Camden's *Britannia.* Camden quotes the poem in several fragments, and from the manner in which he introduces each part, it seems probable that he wrote the epithalamium himself.[59] The longest quotation, appearing in the Oxfordshire section, is sixty-two lines, with the Isis as bridegroom and the Tame as bride. Introducing it, Camden remarks:

> Near this place Tame and Isis with mutual consent joyn as it were in wedlock and mix their names as well as their waters; being henceforth call'd *Tham-Isis* or the *Thames,* in like manner as the rivers *Jor* and *Dan* in the Holy Land, and *Dor* and *Dan* in France, from which composition are Jordan and Dordan . . . . Of the marriage of Tame and Isis I present you here with some verses from a Poem of that title, which you may read or pass over as you please.[60]

Isis, passing Radcot bridge, on his way to his wedding, is adorned for the occasion by Zephyr, Flora, and the Graces. Concord weaves chaplets of flowers for the pair. Hymen's torch lights the way, and the water-nymphs arrange the nuptial bed. The bed is decked—in a manner reminiscent of the bridal bed in Claudian—with all the spoils and trophies which Britons have won since Brute. The Tame, eager for marriage, speeds to join her lover, hurrying past Tame and Dorchester. She appears for her wedding with fresh blades of corn adorning her hair, lips like the rose, and hair which rivals the lilies:

> . . . nunc Tama resurgit
> Nexa comam spicis, trabea succincta virenti,
> Aurorae superans digitos, vultumque Diones:
> Pestanae non labra rosae, non lumina gemmae,
> Lilia non aequant crines, non colla pruinae:
> Utque fluit crines madidos in terga repellit,
> Reddit & undanti legen formamque capillo.[61]

Isis greets his bride and there is union of lips and souls:

> Oscula mille sonant, connexu brachia pallent,
> Labra ligant animos: tandem descenditur una
> In thalamum, quo juncta Fide Concordia sancta
> Splendida conceptis sancit connubia verbis.

Nymphs, satyrs, dryads, and the little Loves dance; the sound of musical instruments and the songs of birds fill the air; the woods echo the sounds; and all things rejoice. Britona, as *pronuba,* tells how she became an island, and mentions the visits of Hercules, Ulysses, Brutus, and Caesar. United now, the waters flow by Windsor, and the Thames speaks to the Castle, praising it and Elizabeth. Camden writes concerning this part of the poem, which appears in the section on Berkshire:

And now let it not be thought troublesom to run over these verses upon Windsor, taken out of *the marriage of Tame and Isis,* written some years since; in which Father Thames, endeavours to celebrate the dignity of the place, and the Majesty of Queen Elizabeth then keeping her Court there.[62]

The Thames salutes Windsor as the site of cradles, marriage-beds, and tombs of kings. The last twenty-nine lines are a pane-gyric of Elizabeth, praising her as a goddess and asking that she be blessed:

> Sit felix, valeat, vivat, laudetur, ametur;
> Dum mihi sunt fluctus, dum cursus, dum mihi ripae,
> Angligenum foelix Princeps moderetur habenas,
> Finiatuna dies mihi cursus, & sibi vitam.[63]

Camden's epithalamium thus is a masque-like panegyric of coun-try and queen. The personification of rivers dramatizes topo-graphical and historical details; and the implication that the off-spring of the union is Windsor, birthplace and home of kings, provides a context for the tribute to Elizabeth.

Although Camden's poem is an example of the same gen-eral type as Spenser's, the two differ substantially. In Camden's poem the Tame is the bride; in Spenser's the "Thamis" is the bridegroom, and he is the son of "th'auncient Thame" and his wife, the Isis. The bride in Spenser's canto, "the lovely Medua," is described in terms somewhat similar to those used of the bridal river in Camden:

> Then came the Bride, the lovely *Medua* came,
>   Clad in a vesture of unknowen geare,
>   And uncouth fashion, yet her well became;
>   That seem'd like silver, sprincled here and theare
>   With glittering spangs, that did like starres
>   appeare . . . .
>
> Her goodly lockes adowne her back did flow
>   Unto her waste, with flowres bescattered,
>   To which ambrosiall odours forth did throw

> To all about, and all her shoulders spred
> As a new spring; and likewise on her hed
> A Chaplet of sundry flowers she wore,
> From under which the deawy humour shed
> Did tricle down her haire . . . .[64]

The Medua, in observance of an ancient wedding custom,[65] had undergone a ceremonial foot-washing in preparation for the wedding:

> On her two pretty handmaides did attend,
>   One cald the *Theise,* the other cald the *Crane;*
> Which on her waited, things amisse to mend,
>   And both behind upheld her spredding traine;
>   Under the which, her feet appeared plaine,
> Her silver feet, faire washt against this day . . . .[66]

In keeping with the advice of Scaliger for epithalamists describing human brides, Spenser describes the Medway as a "proud Nymph . . . at last relenting" after long entreaty. In the manner of the epic epithalamium, he describes the "solemne feast . . . in honour of the spousals," attended by more than thirty "watry Gods," more than eighty English and Irish rivers, and fifty sea-nymphs, all identified by name, "And yet besides three thousand more."[67] A few of the names of sea-deities and nymphs are those of the entourage of Venus in Claudian's epithalamium for Honorius and Maria and other poems of this type. Spenser had other sources, however, for his comprehensive catalogue of deities, and he had personal knowledge of many of the rivers.[68] The identification by name of the guests at the wedding, the emphasis on the size of the crowd, and several additional aspects of this poem, suggest that Spenser may have recalled passages of Marc-Claude de Buttet's epic written for the marriage of the Princess Marguerite in 1559, a poem in which McPeek has noted several parallels with Spenser's *Epithalamion.*[69] Buttet's imaginative descriptions of the nymphs of the

Seine and the Marne presage something of the tone we find in
the Thames-Medway canto:

> Par un commun accord, tout l'univers s'égaie.
>   La belle nymphe Seine, issant du profond creux
>   De son vieillard palais, ses distillans cheveux
>   Et son beau front roial repousse hors des ondes,
>   Et, appelant à soi ses filles vagabondes,
>   A la grande cité va ses longs pas hâtant.
>   Marne, d'un cou panché, la suit, et va portant
>   Sur l'épaule sa cruche, en celeste azur peinte,
>   De trois grands arceaux verds bien proprement
>   enceinte.
>   Avec elle un troupeau de Naïades la suit;
>   Mais elle par sus tout divinement reluit.
>   A son grave marcher, et de beauté et grace,
>   Ainsi que de grandeur, toutes elle surpasse.
>   Elle choisit enfin un doux lit pour s'asseoir,
>   Dans une isle fleurie, et là la peult-on veoir
>   En ses grandes beautés, de son long étendue,
>   Couvrant de joncs sa hanche, au reste toute
>   nue . . . .
>   Les autres, qui aux fleurs ja intentives sont,
>   De beaux lis argentés lui couronnent le front.[70]

In the Thames-Medway canto the gods, rivers, and nymphs
assemble for the wedding feast in much the same manner as the
human guests in Buttet's poem:

> Des pais bien lointains elle a fait déloger
> Maint peuple paresseux et maint prince étranger,
> Accourans pour nous voir: L'Espagnol se déplace,
> Puis en nous saluant bienvegné nous embrasse;
> L'Alleman est ici, le Hongre et Thracien,
> L'Arabe parfumé, et la riche Indien,
> Et l'Anglois, maintenant non plus notre adversaire,
> Saute la mer, et vient pour à nous se retraire.

Tous peuples, tant soient-ils des Gaules écartés,
Debordans à grands flots, viennent de tous côtés,
Et se pressent ici en si grande abondance
Que je croi que l'Europe est maintenant en France.[71]

Buttet enumerates the wedding guests, "le roi dauphin . . . de l'Ecosse . . . le duc d'Orleans . . . et celui d'Angolesme . . . le grand roi navarrois . . . le prince de Condé . . . le duc de Montpensier," and others, and gives a brief description of each, much as Spenser does with the rivers. The crowd of wedding guests as they press toward the temple is compared to the overflowing Rhone river, increased by the water of rivers and lakes:

En longs hurts se poussant, le presse étrainte coule
D'un côté, puis de l'autre, emportée en la foule:
Non autrement qu'on voit aux neiges du printens
S'accroitre par les eaux des fleuves et étangs
Le Rosne debordé, qui assemble ses forces,
Puis en se dégorgeant en mille et mille entorces,
Accable tout à soi, et, rigoreaux flottant,
Ce qu'l treuve il élieve, et le va emportant
Rabatté par les eaux, d'une fuite lointaine
Entrainant les forests, et les champs, et la plaine.[72]

In the final stanzas of the Thames-Medway canto, Spenser identifies the great crowd of wedding guests—gods, nymphs, rivers— as the abundant progeny of the Sea. Buttet's crowd of wedding guests is characterized as a great sea of people:

Une grand' mer de gens, en ondoiante presse,
Par hurts se va portant aprés ceste princesse
Jusqu'à ce temple grand, qui, d'un front merveilleux,
De deux geantes tour semble toucher les cieux.[73]

Such profusion of people and descriptive details is characteristic of the epic epithalamium, and Spenser's Thames-Medway canto fits into this mode.

In its philosophical implication also, Spenser's canto is in the tradition of the rhetorical epithalamium. In the works of Statius, Claudian, and their followers, we have seen the goddess Venus emerge as the central figure, with the epithalamium becoming a panegyric of Venus and a declaration of the triumph of Love. Also in the epic, the marriage of Peleus and Thetis came to represent a union of elements, the rhetoricians recommending that one section of the epithalamium should celebrate the marriage of the elements which brought order out of chaos, and should glorify the love and concord which rule the world. Scaliger reiterated these precepts, urging the epithalamist to say that Love and Friendship were derived from the nuptials of Heaven and Earth, and that all things had their origin therefrom by generation. Spenser's canto is written as an illustration of Friendship, the main theme of Book IV of *The Faerie Queene*. He uses the union of rivers and the old idea of the cosmic generative force of water to symbolize the Love, Friendship, and Concord which hold the universe together—"And all mankinde do nourish with their waters clere."[74] In the preceding canto of Book IV, in his Hymn to Venus, Spenser had dramatized the role of Venus in the creation of the world:

> And when thou spredst thy mantle forth on hie,
> The waters play and pleasant lands appeare,
> And heavens laugh, and al the world shews joyous cheare.[75]

Venus is portrayed as responsible for union and generation of flowers, birds, beasts, "and all things else":

> Soone as with fury thou doest them inspire,
> In generation seeke to quench their inward fire . . .
>
> For all the world by thee at first was made . . . .[76]

This role of Venus is reiterated at the end of the Thames-Medway epithalamium.

I have been referring to the poem as Canto xi. It actually extends into the first stanzas of the following canto, where Spenser indulges in his frequent practice of summarizing the theme of the preceding canto. In the final stanzas of Canto xi and the first two stanzas of Canto xii, Spenser emphasizes the "abundant progeny" of the seas, and mentions Venus.[77] In Catullus 61 and other epithalamia, the joys of love are portrayed as more numerous than grains of sand or stars in the sky.[78] Spenser uses the metaphor twice in this passage to portray the vast number of "fruitfull seede" of the waters.

> For much more eath to tell the starres on hy,
> Albe they endlesse seeme in estimation,
> Then to recount the Seas posterity:
> So fertile be the flouds in generation,
> So huge their numbers, and so numberlesse their
> > nation.

> Therefore the antique wisards well invented,
> That *Venus* of the fomy sea was bred
> For that the seas by her are most augmented.[79]

Charles G. Smith has called attention to three especially significant lines in the Thames-Medway canto. Spenser is describing three rivers attending the marriage of the Thames and the Medway:

> All which long sundred, doe at last accord
> To joyne in one, ere to the sea they come,
> So flowing all from one, all one at last become.[80]

Smith sees these lines as illustrating Spenser's theory of Friendship in Book IV as "the operation in the world of man of a harmonizing and unifying principle of cosmic love." But the emergence of unity is in a sense only momentary, and it is this realization which accounts for the faintly melancholic tone at the conclusion of most epithalamia. It is a basic theme in all Spenser's works—the theme of mutability—and Thomas P. Roche, Jr., summarizes very well its expression in the Thames-Medway canto:

> Although it is not stated in the poem, the reader knows that this marriage must dissolve itself in the multiplicity of the sea and that this act of union will occur and dissolve again and again, and ultimately from his knowledge of the physical world that the act of union and dissolution are the same and inseparable.[81]

The Mulla-Bregog and Molanna-Fanchin Weddings

Spenser uses the union-of-rivers motif in two other passages —Colin's Mulla-Bregog lay in *Colin Clouts Come Home Againe,* and the account of the Molanna-Fanchin union in the "Mutabilitie cantos" of the fragmentary Book VII of *The Faerie Queene.*[82] Both are anti-epithalamic, the wedding imagery being used to dramatize improper unions which come to a bad end. The romance of the Mulla with the Bregog is improper because the Bregog is "her owne brother river," he is deceitful, and the Mulla's father, disapproving of the marriage, had arranged another alliance for his daughter. But the Mulla and Bregog are wed anyway, whereupon old Mole, the bride's father

> Did warily still watch which way she went,
> And eke from far observ'd with jealous eie,
> Which way his course the wanton Bregog bent,
> Him to deceive for all his watchfull ward,
> The wily lover did devise this slight:
> First into many parts his streame he shar'd,
> That whilest the one was watcht, the other might
> Passe unespide to meete her by the way;
> And then besides, those little streams so broken
> He under ground so closely did convay,

> That of their passage doth appeare no token,
> Till they into the Mullaes water slide
> So secretly did he his love enjoy . . . .[83]

But the secret is revealed by a shepherd's boy to the jealous
father, and he stones the Bregog to death:

> In great avenge did roll downe from his hill
> Huge mightie stones, the which encomber might
> His passage, and his water-courses spill.
> So of a River, which he was of old.
> He none was made, but scattred all to nought,
> And lost emong those rocks into him rold,
> Did lose his name: so deare his love he bought.

The romance of Molanna and Fanchin in Book VII also is
an improper one, having come about through the treachery of
Molanna. A sister of Mulla, "no less faire and beautifull then
shee," Molanna is described in bride-like terms. She is a favorite
of the goddess Diana:

> In her sweet streams, Diana used oft
>   (After her sweatie chace and toilesome play)
>   To bathe her selfe; and after, on the soft
>   And downy grasse, her dainty limbes to lay
>   In covert shade, where none behold her may:
>   For, much she hated sight of living eye.
>   Foolish God *Faunus,* though full many a day
>   Her saw her clad, yet longed foolishly
> To see her naked mongst her Nymphes in privity.[84]

Faunus corrupts Molanna with flattering words and gifts, and
promises that if she will arrange for him to see Diana bathing,
he will foster Molanna's romance with Fanchin, for whom she
has been pining. Molanna makes the arrangements, Diana dis-
covers the peeping Faunus, and she and her nymphs punish him,
drape him with a deerskin, and set the hounds upon him:

> They after follow'd all with shrill out-cry,
> Shouting as they the heavens would have brast:
> That all the woods and dales where he did flie,
> Did ring againe, and loud reeccho to the skie.[85]

Diana orders that the treacherous Molanna be "whelm'd with stones." Molanna weds Fanchin, and they combine "in one faire river spred," but Diana lays a curse upon the union, and henceforth the area harbors wolves and thieves.

Prothalamion

Spenser's interest in rivers and his association of them with the epithalamic tradition inspired one of the most memorable refrains in all of English literature, in his last published work, the *Prothalamion:* "Sweete Themmes runne softly, till I end my Song." The feature which most distinguishes the *Prothalamion* from all other nuptial hymns is related to the river, but it occurs in the poem because Spenser was celebrating two weddings instead of one. To represent the pair of brides, he chose the pair of swans who draw the car of Venus through the sky and on her journeys by river and sea. The two brides were sisters, the Lady Elizabeth and the Lady Katherine Somerset, and the poet puns on their father's name in the passage in which he identifies the swans with Venus and with the brides-to-be:

> Eftsoones the *Nymphes,* which now had flowers their fill,
> Ran all in haste, to see that silver brood,
> As they came floating on the Christal Flood.
> Whom when they sawe, they stood amazed still,
> Their wondring eyes to fill,
> Them seem'd they never saw a sight so fayre,
> Of Fowles so lovely, that they sure did deeme
> Them heavenly borne, or to be that same payre
> Which through the Skie draw *Venus* silver Teeme
> For sure they did not seeme

To be begot of any earthly Seede,
But rather Angels or of Angels breede:
Yet were they bred of *Somers-heat* they say,
In sweetest Season, when each Flower and weede
The earth did fresh aray . . . .[86]

This poem, like Spenser's other epithalamia, displays many motifs characteristic of the epic epithalamium, especially that of Statius. We can assume that Spenser even as a young man knew this work of Statius, because E. K. calls attention to it in the gloss to the "January" eclogue of *The Shepheardes Calender,* and we have heard its echoes in the "Aprill" and the *Epithalamion.*[87] It is in Statius that we have first seen the pair of white swans drawing the chariot of Venus, but other influences doubtless contributed to Spenser's choice of the motif. Real swans lived on the river Thames,[88] swans decorated the river Po in several of Tasso's nuptial poems, and there were at least two swan-journey poems on which Spenser might have drawn. The earliest is John Leland's *Cygnea Cantio,* a Latin work of 699 hendecasyllabic lines published in 1545, along with seventy-six pages of learned commentary.[89] A swan who lives at Oxford on an island in the Isis, wishing to see the wonders of the river, swims with twelve companions down the river, admiring the cities along the way. He is struck by the splendor of London. Deptford inspires him to review England's triumphs at sea. He concludes with a long encomium for Henry VIII and a farewell to the other swans in preparation for his journey to heaven. In his preface, Leland discusses the tradition of the swan song among Latin authors, and says that this poem is his own swan song before turning to more serious antiquarian studies.

The other swan poem generally cited as influencing the *Prothalamion* is W. Vallans' *A Tale of Two Swannes,* an English poem of 266 lines in blank verse, with a prose commentary, first published in 1590.[90] In a conventional spring setting, Venus orders Mercury to bring to her two beautiful swans, who are to draw her chariot and rule as king and queen of the Thames. In their old age the swan rulers go on progress through their kingdom. Attended by forty milk-white swans, they swim from the source of the Lea to its mouth, inspecting places of interest along the way. The poem ends with a swan of the *Thames* inviting the king and queen to see and celebrate "the marriage of two Rivers of great name."[91] Vallans, in his preface, associates his poem with the patriotic and topographical genre represented by *Epithalamion Thamesis.* He writes:

> I have seen it in Latine verse (in my judgment) wel done, but the Author, I know not for what reason, doth suppresse it. That which is written in *English,* though long since it was promised, yet is it not perfourmed . . . .[92]

We do not know if the Latin poem he had seen was Spenser's or some other, possibly Camden's. Vallans goes on to say that his own poem is meant as a swan song before he leaves the country, "not unlike the Swans, who before their death do sing, as Virgil, Ovid, Horace, Martial with all the Poets do constantly affyrme." Vallans' poem thus includes an assortment of motifs, some of which have been seen in various combinations in earlier epithalamia and in Leland, Camden, and Spenser's Thames-Medway canto. Among them are the swan song as a farewell, the swan journey, and the swans of Venus, in addition to panegyric of ruler, praise of country, topographical description, antiquarian reminiscence, and union of rivers.

Dan S. Norton believes that Spenser in his *Prothalamion* employs patterns not only from the epic epithalamium and topographical antiquarian poem such as those of Leland, Camden, and Vallans, but also from dream-vision, masque, *impresa,* and emblem.[93] He suggests too that although Spenser often explains the significance of his allegory, he does not do so here, and the reader is left to make his own interpretation of the symbols of the *Prothalamion.* Norton remarks that Spenser "opposes his middle-aged melancholy and the sad antiquity of the Temple to the enchanted youth of the swans," and concludes that with the *Prothalamion,* Spenser "made a swan-like end, but to unfading music."

The brief song which one of the nymphs sings midway in the *Prothalamion* typifies the music which Edmund Spenser contributed to the epithalamic tradition. It dramatizes the role of Love in conquering discord and attaining "endlesse Peace," "blessed Plentie," the pleasures of the marriage bed, and "fruitfull issue."

Ye gentle Birdes, the worlds faire ornament,
And heavens glorie, whom this happie hower
Doth leade unto your lovers blisfull bower,
Joy may you have and gentle hearts content
Of your loves couplement:
And let faire *Venus,* that is Queene of love,
With her heart-quelling Sonne upon you smile,
Whose smile they say, hath vertue to remove
All Loves dislike, and friendships faultie guile
For ever to assoile.
Let endlesse Peace your steadfast hearts accord,
And blessed Plentie wait upon your bord,
And let your bed with pleasures chast abound,
That fruitfull issue may to you afford,
Which may your foes confound,
And make your joyes redound,
Upon your Brydale day, which is not long:
Sweete *Themmes* run softly till I end my song.

X

Chapman

The extraordinary range of the nuptial poem in English can be seen by juxtaposing Spenser's lyric *Prothalamion* and another epithalamic allegory, Chapman's abstruse and rambling 643-line mythological narrative, the *Andromeda Liberata,* written in 1614 for the marriage of the Earl of Somerset and the Countess of Essex, the infamous couple later charged with the murder of Overbury.[1] Apparently modeled on Catullus 64, the *Andromeda Liberata* concludes with the "Parcarum Epithalamion," which in part imitates the song of the Parcae in the Catullan epyllion. This epic is the last of Chapman's three works in the genre, and in it he attempts one of the most elaborate metaphorical statements in the entire epithalamic tradition. His other works in the genre are the fifty-four-line "Epithalamion Teratos," a lyric which appears in his continuation of Marlowe's *Hero and Leander* (1598) and is significant to its theme, and an eighty-four-line lyric, *A Hymne to Hymen for the Most Time-Fitted Nuptialls,* written in 1613 for the Valentine's Day wedding of Elizabeth, daughter of James I, and Frederick, Count Palatine of the Rhine.[2]

All of Chapman's epithalamia are relatively original, although he borrows many passages and motifs from Catullus, Pontanus, Secundus, and their imitators. In addition, he goes to sources outside the genre for mythological plots and Platonic doctrine, the latter described by Douglas Bush as "both mystical and misty."[3] Dwelling on the Platonic "enterchange" between lovers, he creates entangled one-in-two and two-in-one paradoxes on the loss and redemption of self. Evident in the epithalamia also, as in his other poetry, are Chapman's doctrines of "night" and the virtue of obscurity if it "shroudeth it selfe in the hart of his subject . . . with fitnes of figure, and expressive Epethites . . . ."[4] For his elaborate development of the idea of marriage as microcosm, for the wit and beauty of many lines and passages, and for the sheer bulk of his work in the genre, Chapman ranks as a major English epithalamist, although none of his three poems is entirely successful.

"Epithalamion Teratos"

The first four stanzas of the "Epithalamion Teratos" from *Hero and Leander* are a hymn to Night and are reminiscent of Chapman's earlier "Hymnus in Noctem," published in 1595 as part of *The Shadow of Night,* which concludes with a brief epithalamic passage, with Night as the bride:

> See now ascends, the glorious Bride of Brides,
> Nuptials, and triumphs, glittring by her sides,
> Juno and Hymen do her traine adorne,
> Ten thousand torches round about them borne . . . .[5]

The "Epithalamion Teratos" opens with the poet calling Night as if it were a bride to come forth because "Loves glorie doth in darknes shine," and because Night is the attire of "naked vertue." After this summons, the conventional motif of love as a battle is introduced as the theme of a four-line refrain:

> Love cals to warre,
> Sighs his Alarmes,
> Lips his swords are,
> The field his Armes.[6]

Again the poet appeals to Night, in lines which are among Chapman's most memorable:

> Come Night and lay thy velvet hand
> On glorious Dayes outfacing face;
> And all thy crouned flames command,
> For Torches to our Nuptiall grace.

As in Catullus 62, the arrival of night is heralded by the evening star, which abruptly transports the reader to the nuptial feast where the youths and virgins are exchanging songs. The young people are urged to rise from the banquet tables and attend to the rites of love:

> Now love in night, and night in love exhorts,
> Courtship and Dances: All your parts employ,
> And suite nights rich expansure with your joy,
> Love paints his longings in sweet virgins eyes:
> Rise youths, loves right claims more than banquets, rise.
>
> Rise virgins, let fayre Nuptiall loves enfolde
> Your fruitles breasts . . . .

Unlike Henrie Wotton and Jaques Yver, who in their adaptations of Catullus 62 abandoned the Catullan tripartite division of virginity, Chapman insists upon using the figure, distorting it oddly

and marring a poem which is otherwise one of his happier achievements.[7]

The "Epithalamion Teratos" is of special significance because of its context in *Hero and Leander* as a song sung for the
wedding of Alcmane and Mya, a union attended by proper ceremony, unlike the unsanctioned union of Hero and Leander. Marlowe's and Chapman's *Hero and Leander* is a re-working and expansion of the brief tale by Musaeus, to which I have referred in
Chapter III, noting that Musaeus had marked the illicit union of
Hero and Leander by an anti-epithalamium. Some years after
publication of *Hero and Leander,* Chapman published a translation of Musaeus (1616) in which the anti-epithalamium reads
in part:

> Here weddings were, but not a musical sound;
> Here bed-rites offer'd, but no hymns of praise,
> Nor poet sacred wedlock's worth did raise.
> No torches gilt the honor'd nuptial bed,
> Nor any youths much-moving dances led.
> No father, nor no reverend mother, sung
> Hymen, O Hymen, blessing loves so young . . . .[8]

In the 1598 Hero and Leander, this brief passage has been
transformed by Chapman into a masque honoring the goddess
Ceremony. She enters, leading Religion and attended by Devotion, Order, State, Reverence, Society, Memory, Morality,
Comeliness, the Hours, and the Graces. Ceremony scolds Leander for his "plaine neglect of Nuptiall rites" and his ignoring
of "civill forms":

> Thus she appeard, and sharply did reprove
> *Leanders* bluntnes in his violent love;
> Tolde him how poore was substance without rites,
> Like bils unsignd, desires without delites;
> Like meates unseasoned; like ranke corne that growes
> On Cottages, that none or reapes or sowes:

Not being with civill forms confirm'd and bounded,
For humane dignities and comforts founded . . . .[9]

Her reproof moves Leander, and immediately he vows to celebrate "All rites pertaining to his married state." The poet turns
then to

> Sweet *Hero* left upon her bed alone,
> Her maidenhead, her vowes, *Leander* gone,
> And nothing with her but a violent crew
> Of new come thoughts that yet she never knew,
> Even to her selfe a stranger . . . .

Hero rationalizes the illicit union in a paradoxical argument of
"interchange" that echoes in later epithalamia of Chapman and
other poets as well:

> Had I not yeelded, slaine my selfe I had.
> *Hero Leander is, Leander Hero:*
> Such vertue love hath to make one of two . . . .
> Two constant lovers being joynd in one,
> Yeelding to one another, yeeld to none . . . .
> When life is gone death must implant his terror,
> As death is foe to life, so love to error . . . .

During the day which intervenes before Hero and Leander
may be married, Hero sends for the two lovers, Alcmane and Mya,
whom she had previously as a virgin priestess of Venus refused to
marry. Hero officiates at the wedding, and at the wedding feast
the nymph Tera recounts (in some three hundred lines) the tale of
the nuptial god Hymen and his romance and marriage.[10] She concludes by singing the "Epithalamion Teratos." Thus Chapman portrays in detail a marriage attended by proper ceremony in order
that it may serve as an object lesson for the erring lovers. Chapman's technique here may have been suggested by the contrast
of the two unlike unions in Catullus 64. In that work, however,

the improper union of Theseus and Ariadne, foreboding tragedy, is the inserted tale, and the legal union of Peleus and Thetis is the one with which the epyllion begins and ends.

A Hymne to Hymen

The influence of Catullus 64 is apparent also in the opening of Chapman's *A Hymne to Hymen,* printed at the end of a masque written for the wedding of Princess Elizabeth, although the greater part of the hymn is based on Catullus 62 as transmitted through Pontanus. The opening lines refer to Catullus's song of the Parcae, and to the recent death of Prince Henry. The poet salutes Hymen as an epic-like hero, and employing familiar conceits, praises him as the god able to contract two into one and one into two:

> Sing, Sing a Rapture to all Nuptiall eares,
> Bright Hymens torches, drunke up Parcaes teares:
> Sweet Hymen; Hymen, Mightiest of Gods,
> Attoning of all-taming blood the odds;
> Two into One, contracting; One to Two
> Dilating; which no other God can doe.
> Mak'st sure, with change, and lett'st the married try,
> Of Man and woman, the Variety.[11]

A favorite image of seventeenth-century poets, the circle, serves here to represent Hymen's arms: The "Circkle" of his arms charms away the anguish of "love-scorched" virgins, as well as that of fathers and mothers who are concerned about the future of their daughters. The enthusiasm of all nature for the ties of Hymen and the doctrine of increase are expressed in some of Chapman's most energetic lines:

> The whole court Io sings: Io the Ayre:
> Io, the flouds, and fields: Io, most faire,

Most sweet, most happy *Hymen*; Come: away;
With all thy Comforts come; old Matrons pray,
With young Maides Languours; Birds bill, build,
    and breed
To teach thee thy kinde, every flowre & weed
Looks up to gratulate thy long'd for fruites:
Thrice given, are free, and timely-granted suites:
There is a seed by thee now to be sowne,
In whose fruit Earth, shall see her glories show'n,
At all parts perfect; and must therefore loose
No minutes time; from times use all fruite flowes . . . .

Schoell has called attention to the fact that many lines of this poem, including those above, are a free translation of two of the Latin epithalamia written by Pontanus for his daughters, Aurelia and Eugenia.[12] The last fifty-three lines, including extensive development of the flower motif of Catullus 62, are chiefly from the epithalamium for Eugenia.

Andromeda Liberata

Again the influence of Catullus 64 is seen in one of the strangest and most interesting works in the epithalamic tradition, Chapman's *Andromeda Liberata*. The marriage of the Lady Frances Howard to the Earl of Essex had recently been annulled on grounds that he was impotent, and Chapman was one of the many poets to write epithalamia for her marriage to Robert Carr, a Scottish favorite of James I, soon to be made Earl of Somerset.[13] In the epyllion which was Chapman's model, Catullus had used the Peleus–Thetis and Theseus–Ariadne myths, but Chapman chose instead the Perseus–Andromeda tale. Perhaps this tale, often employed allegorically, occurred to Chapman because its hero, like Theseus in Catullus 64, slays a monster which had demanded innocent maidens as sacrifices. The myth describes the release by Perseus of the innocent Andromeda, who has been chained to a rock as a sacrifice to the monstrous beast. When the "whale" arrives, expecting to devour her, Perseus turns part of the monster into stone and with his sword slaughters the remainder, after which the hero marries Andromeda, the Parcae sing an epithalamium, and the poet adds an "Apodosis" in which the couple attain heaven and reign as constellations.

Like Catullus 64, Chapman's poem employs myth and an epithalamium as part of the intricate structure of a long work with cosmic implications. The main themes are familiar: Chaos and Death are conquered by orderly union, all things submit to Love, and it is through Love and generation that "heavens beauty" is attained.[14] In Chapman's allegory the gallant rescuer Perseus represents the bridegroom, the Earl of Somerset. "This match-lesse virgin" Andromeda is, of course, Frances Howard. The "monstrous beast" from whom the virgin is rescued is, in Chapman's words, "the ravenous multitude," the vulgar crowd whom he so much disliked. But Chapman's readers concluded that the "barraine Rocke" from which Andromeda was freed, or possibly even the "monstrous beast," was Frances Howard's ex-husband —the Earl of Essex. As a result, Chapman felt called upon to write his *A Free and Offenceles Justification of a lately publisht and most maliciously misinterpreted poeme entituled Andromeda liberata*. In it he attempted to explain the use of allegory in general and of his own in particular:

> . . . Poets in al ages . . . have ever beene allowed to fashion both, pro & contra, to their owne offencelesse, and judicious occasions. And borrowing so farre the privileg'd license of their professions; have enlarged, or altred the Allegory, with inventions and disposi-tions of their owne, to extend it to their present doctrinall and illustrous purposes. But which aucthority, my selfe (resolving amongst others, to offer up my poore mite, to the honor of the late Nuptials; betwixt the two most Noble personages, whose honored names renown the front of my Poeme) singled out (as in some parts harmelessly, and gracefully applicable to the occasion) The Nuptials of Perseus and Andromeda, an innocent and spotlesse virgine, rescu'd from the poulluted throate of a monster; which I in this

place applied to the savage multitude; perverting her most lawfully-
sought propagation, both of blood and blessing, to their owne most
lawlesse and lascivious intentions: from which in all right she was
legally and formally delivered. Nor did I ever imagine till now so
farre-fetcht a thought in malice (such was my simplicite) That the
fiction being as ancient as the first world, was originally intended
to the dishonor of any person now living: but presum'd, that the
application being free, I might *pro meo iure* dispose it (innocently)
to mine owne object . . . .[15]

Chapman's reasoning in defense of the annulment apparently follows Ficino's argument in his commentary on the *Symposium,* that if a marriage between great personages prove un-
fruitful, they should be allowed to dissolve that marriage easily
in the hope of producing children through a different union, for
"divine worth doth in generation shine." In this long dedicatory
epistle to the *Andromeda,* Chapman combines his doctrine of
poetry and the soul, reason, and sense with praise of the bride
and bridegroom as embodiments of virtue who have been attacked by slanderous tongues which "wold fain your honor sting."
The poem opens by attacking those who disapprove of the marriage, the "ungodly Vulgars . . . whispering their scandals,"
and then praises "all-creating, all-preserving Love." There follows a diatribe, partly adapted from Plutarch, against those whose
evil minds befoul the good: "No truth of excellence, was ever
seene, / But bore the venome of the Vulgares spleene." Then
comes a description of Perseus. In it Chapman states a tenet of
Renaissance Platonism and develops it at length:

> The minde a spirit is, and cal'd the glasse
> In which we see God; and corporeall grace
> The mirror is, in which we see the minde.
> Amongst the fairest women you could finde
> Then Perseus, none more faire; mongst worthiest men,
> No one more manly: This the glasse is then
> To shew where our complexion is combinde;
> A woman's beauty, and a manly minde . . . .

The "mind" of Perseus expatiates on the theme "Beauty breeds love, love consummates a man." After slaying the monster and rescuing Andromeda from her chains, Perseus speaks at length on the nature of love, and on the "enterchange" between two lovers, arguing that if the woman beloved does not return the passion and yield to the lover's embraces, she prevents the birth of children and thus is worse than a "homicide." All mortal good, according to Chapman, is defective and frail unless we "daily new beget."[16]

> In generation, re'creation is,
> And from the prosecution of this
> Man his instinct of generation takes.
> Since generation, in continuance, makes
> Mortals, similitudes, of powers divine,
> Divine worth doth in generation shine.

The Platonic interchange of lovers finds its longest and most tedious elaboration here. A few lines will illustrate:

> Love did both confer
> To one in both: himselfe in her he found,
> She with her selfe, in onely him was crownd:
> While thee I love (sayd he) you loving mee
> In you I finde my selfe: thought on by thee,
> And I (lost in my selfe by thee neglected)
> In thee recover'd am, by thee affected: ....[17]

As in Catullus 64, Jove and Juno and the subject deities attend the nuptial feast, and the song of the Parcae is sung there. Chapman's "Parcarum Epithalamion" of seven nine-line stanzas concludes with an onomatopoeic refrain based on Catullus's "currite ducentes subtegmina, currite, fusi." Like the original, Chapman's "Haste spindles haste" achieves something of the hissing sound of the wool on the spindles. He varies the refrain slightly, and at times there seems no reason for the variation ex-

cept that the practice is customary.[18] The poem is reminiscent of
the Catullan model chiefly in the refrain, the first stanza, and
the second line of the second stanza. It looks as if Chapman had
at first intended to translate the Catullan poem but changed his
mind. Compare the opening lines of the two poems:

Catullus's song of the Parcae:

> O decus eximium magnis uirtutibus augens,
> Emathiae tutamen, Opis carissime nato,
> accipe, quod laeta tibi pandunt luce sorores,
> ueridicum oraclum: sed uos, quae fata sequuntur,
>   currite ducentes subtegmina, currite, fusi.
> adueniet tibi iam portans optata maritis
> Hesperus, adueniet fausto cum sidere coniunx . . . .

Chapman's "Parcarum Epithalamion":

> O you this kingdomes glory that shall be
> Parents to so renownd a Progenie
> As earth shall envie, and heaven glory in,
> Accept of their lives threds, which Fates shal spin
> Their true spoke oracle, and live to see
> Your sonnes sonnes enter such a Progenie,
> As to the last times of the world shall last:
> Haste you that guide the web, haste spindles haste.
>
> See Hesperus, with nuptiall wishes crownd . . . .

At this point Chapman abandons Catullus 64, turns briefly to the
Perseus–Andromeda myth, and then reverts to the Neo-Platonic
arguments we have seen earlier in the long poem. There is, however, a good deal more warmth in the couple described in the "Parcarum" epithalamium than in the two puppet-like figures being
moved to and fro in the "two-made-one" and "one-made-two"
game earlier in the epic:

> She comes, o Bridegroom shew they selfe enflam'd
> And of what tender tinder Love is flam'd:
> Catch with ech sparke, her beauties hurle about:
> Nay with ech thoght of her be rapt throughout;
> Melt let thy liver, pant thy startled heart;
> Mount Love on earthquakes in thy every part:
> A thousand hewes on thine, let her lookes cast;
> Dissolve thy selfe to be by her embrac't,
> Haste ye that guide the web, haste spindles haste.[19]

Here also Chapman reiterates the Platonic motifs:

> Who bodie loves best, feedes on dantiest meats,
> Who fairest seed seekes, fairest women gets:
> Who loves the minde, with loveliest disciplines
> Loves to enforme her, in which verity shines.
> Her beauty yet, we see not, since not her:
> But bodies (being her formes) who faire formes beare
> We view, and chiefely seeke her beauties there.
> The fairest then, for faire birth, see embrac't,
> Haste ye that guide the web, haste spindles haste.

Chapman's "Apodosis," which follows the Parcarum song, ends on a note quite unlike that of Catullus.[20] In the Latin poem, because of the degeneration of mankind, gods no longer descend to earth. Here in Chapman's myth, human beings attain "Heavens beauty" by ascending to the sky and reigning as constellations. In the final lines of the "Apodosis," the bride and bridegroom are told:

> The Monster slaine then, with your cleere Seas, wash
> From spots of Earth, Heavens beauty in the minde
> In which, through death, hath all true Noblesse shinde.

XI

Jonson and Donne

Jonson and Donne each wrote three epithalamia, all relatively short, all marked by the verbal and structural ingenuity characteristic of the work of these two poets. Jonson's are deliberate exercises in craftsmanship, "made . . . both in form and matter to emulate that kind of poem which was called Epithalamium, and by the ancients used to be sung when the bride was led into her chamber."[1] Donne's are less conventional, but he too borrows motifs from classical as well as Christian and continental traditions. The goodly train of gods and goddesses is exiled, and the tales of the *Metamorphoses* are silenced in Donne's epithalamia, and, for the most part, in Jonson's. Catullan motifs and imagery appear in both, especially in Jonson's, along with Neo-Platonic and Christian doctrines and imagery, but none of the poems attempts an elaborate philosophical statement of the kind we have seen in Chapman. A central motif in the epithalamia of both poets is the idea that "perfection" may be attained through marital union, a theme especially prominent in the varied refrains which these two poets manage with exceptional skill. It appears in three of the four refrains exhibited below:

Jonson:

> So may they both ere day
> Rise perfect every way.[2]

> Make all that married be
>   Perfection see.
> Shine, Hesperus, shine forth, thou wished star![3]

Donne:

> Come glad from thence, go gladder than you came:
> Today put on perfection, and a woman's name.[4]

>   Should chance or envy's art
> Divide these two, whom Nature scarce did part,
> Since both have the inflaming eye, and both
>   the loving heart?[5]

Each of the refrains quoted is one of several variations. We have observed throughout the epithalamic tradition the use of varying refrains, a classical practice which Jonson remarks on in the notes appended to his first epithalamium:

> This poem had for the most part versum intercalarem or carmen amaebaeum: yet that not always one, but oftentimes varied, and sometimes neglected in the same song, as in ours you shall find observed.[6]

Ben Jonson

The first refrain quoted above is from the earliest of Jonson's epithalamia, the 120-line poem at the end of the *Masque of Hymen,* given in January, 1606, for the first marriage of the Lady Frances Howard, who was later to figure in the divorce and re-marriage noted in connection with Chapman's *Andromeda Liberata.*[7] Jonson wrote the masque late in 1605 for the celebration early in January, 1606, of her marriage to Robert Devereux, third Earl of Essex. It is at once apparent that what Jonson calls the "matter" of the poem is much like that of Carmen 61 of Catullus, although he borrows also from Catullus 62 and 64. In keeping with the formula of Catullus, the poem includes the invocation to Hymen; the summons to the youths and virgins to sing the hymeneal; description of the bride's conflicting emotions as she is urged to proceed to the bridegroom's house; the lifting of the bride over the threshold; the escorting of the bride to the marriage chamber; the assistance of the "good matrons" in placing the bride on the *lectus genialis;* the summons to the bridegroom to join the bride; the song before the couch urging the consummation of the marriage and the blessing by Venus of the marriage-bed so that there will be offspring; and the request to the youths and virgins to cease their song, to shut fast the door and leave the couple to themselves. These elements appear in Jonson's poem in the same order as in Catullus 61. Jonson, of course, borrows from others besides Catullus. In his notes to the poem he mentions, in order, Scaliger, Festus, Catullus, Cicero, Claudian, Servius, Plutarch, Alexander ab Alexandro, Constantius Landus, Theopholus, Phornutus, "the grammarians upon Homer," Homer, Lucretius, and Virgil. In his notes to the masque of which the poem is a part, among those he mentions in addition are Juvenal, Lucan, Ovid, Pliny, Varro, Terence, Macrobius, Brisson, Hotman, Martianus Capella, and Apuleius.[8]

As McPeek points out, eleven of the fifteen stanzas borrow their leading themes from Catullus.[9] Main themes of the remain-

ing four stanzas appear to come from Claudian, Johannus Secundus, Statius, the Emperor Gallienus, and Spenser. Although
Jonson uses many classical motifs, especially from Catullus
61 and 62, the poem is not a careless patchwork of translated
passages. His opening line uses a common theme—the passage
of time, a motif familiar from the opening lines of Catullus 62:

> Vesper adest, iuuenes, consurgite: Vesper Olympo
>   exspectata diu uix tandem lumina tollit.
>   surgere iam tempus, iam pinguis linquere mensas . . . .

But Jonson's use of "Glad time" is by no means a reproduc-
tion of Catullus:

> Glad *time* is at his point arriv'd,
> For which *loves* hopes were so long-liv'd.
>   Lead, HYMEN, lead away;
>   And let no object stay,
>   Nor banquets (but sweet kisses)
>   The *turtles* from their blisses.
>   'Tis *CUPID* calls to arme;
>   And this his last *alarme*.

The word "turtles" for the bridal couple had long symbolized
conjugal fidelity, and Sidney's first stanza had used it. The last
two lines of this stanza, introducing the theme of love as a battle,
also become the refrain of the second stanza; Chapman's 1598
epithalamium had used this motif as a refrain, and it appears
also in Claudian, Secundus, and some of the Italian vernacular
epithalamia.

The third stanza calls upon the youths and virgins to sing,
but the specific task Jonson assigns is that they "sing The
prize, which HYMEN here doth bring." The prize is the bride,
who is depicted as having been seized by force. Jonson's use of
the word "prize" is reminiscent of Tasso's description of the
bride as a trophy of battle.[10] Jonson comments on the convention:

The bride was always feigned to be ravished ex gremio matris: or (if she were wanting) ex proxima necessitudine, because that had succeeded well to Romulus, who, by force gat wives for him and his, from the Sabines. See Fast. and that of Catul. Que rapis teneram ad virum virginem.[11]

With the motif of Hesperus, the evening star, Jonson combines the perfection theme and the idea that the bride's name changes as does the name of the star:

> See, HESPERUS is yet in view!
> What *starre* can so deserve of you?
>   Whose light doth still adorne
>   Your *Bride,* that, ere the morne,
>   Shall farre more perfect be,
>   And rise as bright as he:
>   When (like to him) her *name*
>   Is chang'd, but not her flame.

The perfection motif is a favorite of Jonson. Earlier in the masque he uses the line, "Telia, for Hymen, perfects all, . . ." and in a note gives a long list of classical references to Telia, or Perfecta, as the symbol of the perfection of life and the maturity which there should be in matrimony.[12] The responsibility which the young bride is about to assume is dramatized by the poet as he urges her to enter the "covetous house" of which she is to be mistress. His addressing the bride as "tender lady" is especially suited to the bride being celebrated, for she was only thirteen years old. In a note, Jonson calls attention to the custom of giving the bride the keys to signify that "shee was absolute Mistris of the place, and the whole disposition of the family at her care." Jonson also explains his injunction to the bride to lift her "golden feet, Above the threshold, high" by describing another custom:

This was also another rite: that she might not touch the threshold as she entered, but was lifted over it. Servius saith, because it was sacred to Vesta. Plut. In Quaest. Rom. remembers divers causes. But that, which I take to come nearest the truth, was only the avoiding of sorcerous drugs, used by witches to be buried under that place, to the destroying of marriage, amity, or the power of generation. See Alexand. in Genialibus, and Christ. Land. upon Catul.[13]

Jonson's technique of combining motifs is illustrated in Stanza 6:

> Now, *youths,* let goe your pretty armes;
> The place within chant's other charmes.
>   Whole showers of *roses* flow;
>   And *violets* seeme to grow,
>   Strew'd in the chamber there,
>   As VENUS meade it were.
>   On HYMEN, HYMEN call,
>   This *night* is HYMEN'S all.

To the opening lines, compare Catullus 61:

> mitte brachiolum teres,
> praetextate, puellulae:
> iam cubile adeat uiri.[14]

With the motif from Catullus, Jonson combines the roses and violets gathered from Claudian's *Epithalamium of Palladius and Celerina:*

> Ut thalami tetigere fores, tum vere rubentes
> Desuper invertunt calathos largoesque rosarum
> Imbres et violas plenis sparsere pharetris
> Collectas Veneris prato.[15]

The good matrons who place the bride on the bridal couch in Jonson's poem are like those of Catullus 61:

> bonae senibus uiris
> cognitae bene feminae,
> collocate puellulam.[16]

Apparently referring to the fact that the fescinnine jests have ceased, Jonson says that the couple, "free from vulgar spite or noise" may now enjoy the pleasures of love. Neo-Platonic suggestions that "lips may mingle souls" and that embraces may "bind To each the others mind" seem far from Catullus, but they are reminiscent of lines in both the fescennine verses and the epithalamium of Claudian, especially the following:

> Vivite concordes et nostrum discite munus.
> Oscula mille sonent; livescant brachia nexu;
> Labra ligent animas.[17]

Jonson's technique of combining diverse motifs continues throughout the poem. A line or two of almost direct translation is frequently woven into a stanza which draws on motifs from other sources. Other poets imitated the technique, heeded his notes on the subject matter, and also imitated the assortment of conventions which Jonson included. Catullus 61 had provided a catalogue of conventions for generations of epithalamists, and Jonson's epithalamium provided a similar array for his successors. In its short lines and double-line refrain, Jonson's stanza suggests the glyconics of Catullus; thus his poem both in form and matter transmitted some of the flavor of Catullus 61.

Motifs of Catullus 61 dominate the entire wedding masque of which this epithalamium is a part. The theme of the Hymenaei masque is depicted in the opening scene, which exhibits an altar inscribed in gold with the word *Union*. In a note, Jonson explains the altar as "Mystically implying, that both it, the *place,* and all the succeeding *ceremonies* were sacred to marriage, or Union."[18] Five pages dressed in white and bearing five "tapers of virgin waxe" precede the bridegroom; Hymen appears as in Catullus 61, decked in saffron robe and yellow socks, crowned with roses and marjoram, and carrying a pine torch. Others follow in procession, including "a personated *Bride*" carefully delineated. *Reason* and *Order* participate in the rites, in a manner reminiscent of Chapman's epithalamic passage in *Hero and Leander*.[19]

As part of the festivities for the same wedding, the *Masque of the Barriers* was performed on the following night. Its theme is provided by the marriage-versus-virginity debate of Catullus 62; part of the argument by Opinion on behalf of virginity, and Truth on behalf of marriage, is an almost literal translation of the flower-maiden and vine-elm motifs of Catullus 62, bringing again to English readers the time-honored similes which had first appeared in English in Henrie Wotton's early epithalamium. Opinion speaks:

> Look, how a flower, that close in closes growes,
> Hid from rude cattell, bruised with no ploughes,
> Which th'*ayre* doth stroke, *sun* strengthen, *showres*
> shoot higher,
> It many *youths,* and many *maydes* desire;
> The same, when cropt by cruell hand, is wither'd,
> No *youths,* at all, no *maydens* have desir'd:
> So a *virgin,* while untouch'd she doth remaine,
> Is deare to hers; but when with bodies staine
> Her chaster flower is lost, she leaves to appeare
> Or sweet to *young men,* or to *maydens* deare.
> That conquest then may crowne me in this warre,
> *Virgins,* O *virgins,* flie from HYMEN farre.[20]

In answer to Opinion, Truth defends marriage:

> *Virgins, O virgins,* to sweet HYMEN yeeld,
> For as a lone vine, in a naked field,
> Never extolls her branches, never beares
> Ripe grapes, but with a headlong heavinesse weares

Her tender body, and her highest sproote
Is quickly levell'd with her fading roote;
By whom no *husbandmen,* no *youths* will dwell;
But if, by fortune, she be married well
To the 'elme her *husband,* many *husbandmen,*
And many *youths* inhabit by her, then:
So whilst a *virgin* doth, untouch't, abide
All unmanur'd, she growes old, with her pride;
But when to equall *wedlocke,* in fit time,
Her fortune, and endeavor lets her clime,
Deare to her love, and *parents* she is held.
Virgins O *virgins,* to sweet HYMEN yeeld.

In Catullus, the argument is won by the youths who are praising marriage. In medieval epithalamia, the argument is won by the champions of virginity. In Jonson's masque, the argument is a draw. The issue must be resolved in trial by combat, so champions of both sides address themselves to the struggle, performing—in Jonson's words—with "vigor" and "alacrity." Whereupon, Jonson writes, "on a suddaine . . . a striking light seem'd to fill all the hall, and out of it an angell or messenger of glory appearing"; Truth descends triumphant "in a second thunder" and announces that all yield to Hymen.[21]

Another masque, the *Hue and Cry after Cupid,* written in 1608 for the marriage of John Lord Ramsey, Viscount Haddington, and Lady Elizabeth Radcliffe, is the setting for Jonson's second epithalamium.[22] It is a shorter poem—seven stanzas of eleven lines each, four lines of which constitute a refrain. Lines are longer, and there is greater variation than in the previous epithalamium. The poem moves more freely, both because of the metrical variety and the fact that Jonson is less closely tied to his sources. Motifs resemble those of Catullus, Heinsius, Bonefonius, the Emperor Galienus, and Statius. The five-line refrain has three themes—love as a battle ("HYMENS warre"), attainment of perfection, and the wished-for arrival of the evening star. In the fifth stanza the maid-matron theme is the occasion of a pun and of an explanatory note by the poet:

> Why stayes the *Bride-grome* to invade
> Her, that would be a matron made?
>   Good-night, whilst yet we may
>   Good-night, to you a *virgin,* say:
>   To morrow, rise the same
> Your *mother* is, and use a nobler name.
>   Speed well in HYMEN'S warre,
>   That, what you are
>   By your perfection, wee
>   And all may see.
> Shine, HESPERUS, shine forth, thou wished *starre.*[23]

Jonson explains that when the maid rises "the same" as her mother, she has become "A wife, or matron: which is a name of more dignity, then *Virgin.*"

Jonson's third and last epithalamium, written about five years before his death, is his longest, a poem of twenty-four eight-line stanzas, *Epithalamion*; or "A Song: Celebrating the Nuptials of that Noble Gentleman, Mr. Hierome Weston, Son, and Heire, of the Lord Weston, Lord High Treasurer of England, with the Lady Frances Stuart, Daughter of Esme D. of Lenox Deceased, and Sister of the Surviving Duke of the Same Name."[24] The poem is addressed to the Sun, asking him to shine upon and observe the events of the wedding day. The poet asks the Sun to observe the wedding procession with its fine carriages all the way from Greenwich to Row-hampton chapel, to listen to the bells announcing the approach of the bride, and to marvel at her beauty as she "paceth forth in Virgin-white" lacking none of the attributes of "a Maiden Queene." The poet pays tribute to the bridegroom's father, the Lord High Treasurer, for his accurate and just performance of his official duties. Much of the epithalamium is matter-of-fact and undecorated, particularly the stanza describing the ceremony. The bride's father was not living, and she was given in marriage by the king:

See, now the Chappell opens; where the King
  And Bishop stay, to consummate the Rites:
The holy Prelate prayes, then takes the Ring,
  Askes first, Who gives her (I Charles) then he plights

    One in the other hand
      Whilst they both stand
    Hearing their charge, and then
The Solemne Quire cryes, Joy; and they returne, Amen.

The poem is dignified and restrained, the author commenting
at one point that he dare not speak in "Language *fescinnine.*"[25]
His use of a concluding alexandrine and lines of varying length
suggests Spenser's *Epithalamion,* but the form is more rigid and
the matter more prosaic. At some points, the tone suggests that
the poet is weary at the idea of saying again all the things that
are customarily said about weddings, but here and there Jonson
is at his best. Describing the roses and lilies which the virgins
strew in the path of the bride, Jonson calls them "The Emblemes
of their way," and continues:

    With what full hands, and in how plenteous showers
      Have they bedew'd the Earth, where she doth tread
    As if her ayrie steps did spring the flowers,
      And all the Ground, were Garden, where she led!

In this, his last wedding song, the aging poet envisions the distant future of the young bride and bridegroom, and wishes for
them

      That when you both are old
        You find no cold
      There; but, renewed, say
    (After the last child borne;) This is our wedding day.

John Donne

Donne's "Epithalamion made at Lincolnes Inn" has long been an enigma. No certain evidence exists as to when it was written, or for whom, or even whether it was written for a wedding. As a student, Donne was at Lincoln's Inn from 1592 to 1596; as a reader, he was there from 1616 to 1622.[26] In some of the manuscripts the poem is entitled simply "Epithalamion"; in others it is entitled "Epithalamion on a Citizen."[27] It has been suggested that the use by Donne's contemporaries of the latter title indicates their feeling that the poem was not entirely serious; David Novarr sees it as "a broadly satiric entertainment," written possibly for a performance at the Midsummer revels of Lincoln's Inn where Donne was a twenty-three-year-old student.[28] Most critics regard the poem as a serious epithalamium written early in Donne's career, although McPeek assigns it to the later period because of "the nature of the poem itself."[29] Parts of the work are indeed puzzling, particularly if the reader assumes that it is or ought to be in the style of Spenser's *Epithalamion* and ignores other elements of the tradition. It becomes a little less puzzling when one remembers the fescennine quality long present in epithalamia, the penchant of epithalamists for using the genre as a rhetorical plaything, the association of sacrificial rites with marriage and with the epithalamium (an aspect Scaliger had discussed),[30] and the literary devices characteristic of Donne and other poets of his time.

One must remember, I think, that in the later epithalamia generally the prettiness of some of the earlier poems has disappeared. Pierre Poupo in his mature work[31] casts off the adornments of his youthful poems and substitutes a stark Christianity. Jonson abandons most of the customary Renaissance decoration in favor of simplicity and controlled expression, retaining serious purpose but having none of Poupo's Calvinist intensity. Donne, too, prunes his diction, but in doing so achieves a paradox: for in the very process of removing elaborations of language, he loses some of the singleness of direction and earnestness of tone which had characterized earlier wedding hymns. In his hands the epithalamium becomes a mixed mode in which humor, satire, philosophical observations, and commentary on men and affairs accompany the more customary topics and devices. Like many of his other poems, Donne's epithalamia are marked by extended conceits, bold metaphors, exaggeration, ambiguity, epigrams, puns, colloquial language, a strong dramatic element, and argumentative structure. His familiarity with rhetorical techniques is exhibited in all three poems and especially in the *Ecclogue* with its division into sections to which he appends titles, as Ausonius had done.[32] His fourteen-line stanzas in the St. Valentine's Day song are in form reminiscent of the nuptial sonnets of Tasso, Marino, and Poupo.

It has been remarked that for mythology Donne substituted divinity,[33] but this is only partly true of the epithalamia. In the three nuptial poems Donne uses imagery from many areas, including religion, physiology, geography, music, commerce, government, and astronomy. The sun, moon, and stars had long figured prominently in epithalamia, and one of Donne's dominant motifs is the sun. He often mentions the seasons, especially winter, along with the globe, the round earth, the hemispheres, the West, the East, and the Northern pole. The "May morning note" is missing in Donne, although the birds in the St. Valentine's Day epithalamium seem to be somewhat in this tradition. Donne does not completely "ungod" the god of love, as he suggests in "Loves Deitie,"[34] but Cupid makes only a single brief appearance, and Venus is banned entirely. Bishop Valentine substitutes for Hymen.[35] The nuptial bed is an important motif in all of Donne's epithalamia. The poem which is probably his first work in the genre opens with a call to the bride to leave her "solitary bed" for the nuptial bed which is soon to be hers. Perhaps a playful echo of the traditional call to the bride to come forth may be heard in Donne's summons to her to "Put forth, put forth that warme balme-breathing thigh." The role of the bride is emphasized throughout the poem by the refrain "Today put on perfection and a woman's name," which with variations concludes the first four stanzas, and which changes to "Tonight put on perfection, and a woman's name" for the second half of the poem.[36]

The emphasis which this epithalamium places on the role of the bride has troubled some critics. It seems possible that it provides a key to the poem, especially if one accepts the suggestion of Grierson that the perfection theme is associated with the perfection attained by the Virgin in the mystical marriage with Christ. Grierson's comment is directed to only one passage of the poem:

> Till now thou wast but able
>   To be what now thou art; then that by thee
> No more be said, *I may bee,* but *I am,*
>   *To night put on perfection, and a woman's name.*[37]

Grierson explains the passage in the following manner: The bride has recognized her inner possibilities of development, namely to remain virgin, or to become a woman, has decided in favor of the latter, and has now really become that for which she had previously had the predisposition. Grierson cites passages from Thomas Aquinas and the *Metaphysics* of Aristotle, which place the action above the ability to act. He points out that the religious elevation of virginity does not contradict this metaphysical doctrine, because it is not virginity which is preferred to marriage, but the act of surrender of the virgin to God. Grierson summarizes, "Wedded to Christ, the virgin puts on a higher perfection." This association of the perfection theme with the Virgin places it in a Christian context instead of the pagan one of Jonson, who uses the term in reference to the Roman Juno Perfecta, contrasting the married Juno to the Juno Virgo.[38]

Grierson's interpretation of the quoted passage may be extended to become the major theme of the poem, for the perfection refrain appears in every stanza, and the emphasis throughout is on the bride. Thus, the poem becomes something of a tribute to human marriage, in that the human bride through earthly

marriage is portrayed as attaining a kind of perfection hith-
erto associated with the Virgin in mystical marriage. This view
of the poem is borne out by the fact that the attendants of
the bride are "Angels," the Temple is asked to unfold its gates
in order that the couple may be "mystically joyn'd," and devotional and sacrificial imagery marks the consummation of
the union. The nuptial bed becomes "loves altar," the bride is
compared to a faithful Christian who is content "that this life
for a better should be spent," and she is referred to as "a pleasing
sacrifice" and "an appointed lambe." The bridegroom receives
attention in Stanza 3, in which his attendants are directed
"This Bridegroom to the Temple bring," and in the final stanza
in which he is compared to a priest officiating at sacrificial rites.[39]

Donne's epithalamium thus applies to human marriage the
trappings of the medieval celebration of mystical marriage. But
he is not content to do only this. By the fescennine elements of
Stanzas 2 and 3 he emphasizes that the marriage is indeed an
earthly one. The "Daughters of London" who attend the bride
are not only labeled "Angels"—they bring with them "Thousands of Angels" (coins) on their marriage days; the bride is
one of them, fair and rich, and "As gay as Flora, and as rich
as Inde." The traditional fescennine teasing is aimed at both
bride and bridegroom; we recall that Scaliger suggested that the
jests involving the bride should be mild.[40] The taunts directed
at the groom and his associates are frequently pointed; here
the young men are described as:

> . . . frolique Patricians,
> Sonns of these Senators wealths deep oceans,
>   Ye painted courtiers, barrels of others wits,
> Yee country men, who but your beasts love none,
> Yee of those fellowships whereof hee's one,
>   Of study and play made strange Hermaphrodits . . .[41]

With its combination of sensual, fescennine, and ascetic
elements, this epithalamium thus becomes a paradoxical por-

trayal of earthly and heavenly aspects of marriage. There are elements in the poem, however, which make it seem only half-
serious—the familiarity with which the poet describes the bride's
bedchamber; the reference to her as "fit fewell" for love; and
the line which parodies the traditional bride whose beauty blinds
the onlookers, "except my sight faile, 'tis no other thing."[42] The
Sun, whose travels mark the events of the nuptial day, "stands
still" for the eager couple, but at noon he begins to "gallop lively
downe the Westerne hill" in anticipation of the nuptial night.
When the union has been consummated, the poet addresses the
couple and the Sun:

> Now sleep or watch with more joy; and O light
> Of heaven, to morrow rise thou hot, and early;
> This Sun will love so dearely
> Her rest, that long, long we shall want her sight;
> Wonders are wrought, for shee which had no maime,
> *To night puts on perfection, and a womans name.*[43]

A more successful wedding song is Donne's St. Valentine's
Day poem, one of the most ingenious epithalamia after Spenser
and the one which best demonstrates Donne's major contribution to the mode, the restoration of humor. We noted early in
the tradition that Sappho taunted the big-footed doorkeeper,
Theocritus teased the bridegroom who is in a hurry to go to bed,
and Claudian portrayed the playful Loves' circus-like antics as
well as Venus's artifice in carefully leaving part of her hair untended. English epithalamists, however, had tended to be a somewhat earnest and solemn breed. With Donne, the attitude changes.
He sets the new tone in the first stanza by brightly hailing not
Hymen but Bishop Valentine as the patron of lovers and marital
matchmaker in the bird kingdom. The entire sky is the bishop's
"Diocis"; the birds are his "chirping Choristers" and "Par-
ishioners." Every year the bishop performs marriage rites for

> The Lirique Larke, and the grave whispering Dove,
> The Sparrow that neglects his life for love,

The household Bird, with the red stomacher,
    Thou mak'st the black bird speed as soone,
As doth the Goldfinch, or the Halcyon;
The husband cocke lookes out, and straight is sped,
And meets his wife, which brings her feather-bed.
This day more cheerfully than ever shine,
This day, which might enflame thy self, Old Valentine.

As in the epithalamium discussed earlier, the marriage here
is a mystical one, but this time it is between

    Two Phoenixes, whose joyned breasts
Are unto one another mutuall nests,
Where motion kindles such fires, as shall give
Yong Phoenixes, and yet the old shall live.
Whose love and courage never shall decline,
But make the whole year through, thy day, O Valentine.

Assuming the traditional master-of-ceremonies role, the poet
awakens the bride:

Up then faire Phoenix Bride, Frustrate the Sunne,
    Thy selfe from thine affection
    Takest warmth enough, and from thine eye
All lesser birds wil take their Jollitie.
    Up, up faire Bride, and call,
Thy starres, from out their severall boxes, take
Thy Rubies, Pearles, and Diamonds forth, and make
Thy selfe a constellation, of them All,
    And by their blazing, signifie,
That a Great Princess falls, but doth not die;
Bee thou a new starre, that to us portends
Ends of much wonder; And be Thou those ends.
Since thou dost this day in new glory shine,
May all men date Records, from this thy Valentine.

Donne's reshaping of familiar conventions is seen in the stanza above and in the call to the bride to come forth:

> Come forth, come forth, and as one glorious flame
> Meeting Another, growes the same,
> So meet thy Fredericke, and so
> To an unseparable union growe.

The conventional complaint over the delay in the proceedings is voiced by the poet in a series of questions which include fescennine teasing of the bridal couple:

> But oh, what ailes the Sunne, that here he staies,
> Longer to day, then other daies?
> Staies he new light from these to get?
> And finding here such store, is loth to set?
> And why doe you two walke,
> So slowly pac'd in this procession?
> Is all your care but to be look'd upon,
> And be to others spectacle, and talke?

The wedding guests, the masquers, and the ladies who attend the bride are likewise playfully reproached:

> The feast, with gluttonous delaies,
> Is eaten, and too long their meat they praise,
> The masquers come too late, and, I thinke, will stay,
> Like Fairies, till the Cock crow them away.
> Alas, did not Antiquity assigne
> A night, as well as day, to thee, O Valentine?

> They did, and night is come; and yet wee see
> Formalities retarding thee.
> What meane these Ladies, which (as though
> They were to take a clock in peeces,) goe
> So nicely about the Bride;

A Bride, before a good night could be said,
Should vanish from her cloathes, into her bed,
As Soules from bodies steale, and are not spy'd.

The traditional reference to the ceremonial placing of the bride on the *lectus genialis* becomes in Donne the simple declaration, "But now she is laid." This accomplished, there is further delay: Where is the bridegroom? He comes and their union is reported. But the poet feels called upon to describe the event more elaborately and to make the conventional comparison of the couple to the sun and the moon. He exchanges the usual roles of bride and bridegroom, however, the bride becoming the sun, and the bridegroom the moon, in a Platonic interchange which Dr. Johnson was moved to describe as "Confusion worse confounded."[44] In the context of the epithalamic tradition and of the poem, the lines are somewhat less confusing than Dr. Johnson's comment leads us to believe:

Here lyes a shee Sunne, and a hee Moone here,
    She gives the best light to his Spheare,
    Or each is both, and all, and so
They unto one another nothing owe,
    And yet they doe, but are
So just and rich in that coyne which they pay,
That neither would, nor heeds forbeare, nor stay;
Neither desires to be spar'd, nor to spare,
    They quickly pay their debt, and then
Take no acquittances, but pay again;
They pay, they give, they lend, and so let fall
No such occasion to be liberall.
More truth, more courage in these two do shine,
Then all thy turtles have, and sparrows, Valentine.

The use here of commercial imagery in describing the consummation is perhaps "more remarkable for the invention" than any other such description in the English genre, but the reader may hear in it not only echoes of Chapman's earlier work but of some of the Italian epithalamia.

Donne's final stanza opens on a solemn note, with the union of lovers being related to the cosmos:

> And by this act of these two Phenixes
> Nature againe restored is . . . .[45]

Outside the nuptial chamber, the poet and other wedding guests wait for the sunrise and the emergence of the bridal couple. Some light is shed on Donne's remark, "Wee As Satyres . . . will stay Waiting," when one remembers the roles of the satyrs in early epic epithalamia: barred from the Paradise of Venus, they were frequently depicted as lurking in the vicinity waiting for a glimpse of the glory within.[46] The fescennine quality of Donne's humor is again apparent as the wedding guests place wagers as to

> whose hand it is
> That opens first a curtaine, hers or his;
> This will be tryed to morrow after nine,
> Till which houre, wee thy day enlarge, O Valentine.

Donne's third and longest epithalamium, the *Ecclogue* of 235 lines, is chiefly interesting for its form, a few brilliant passages, and its hint of the same melancholy we have seen in the final epithalamia of Spenser and Jonson. The format is that of the pastoral epithalamia of the French poets—Ronsard, Grévin, and Poupo, in particular—and of Spenser's "Aprill" eclogue. It opens with the conversation of two shepherds,[47] Allophanes and Idios, and after more than a hundred lines of conversation contrasting the Country and Court, Idios presents the song he has made, an epithalamium of eleven stanzas. Written for the notorious Somerset-Howard marriage, the *Ecclogue* opens with a statement of the argument:

Allophanes finding Idios in the country in Christmas time, repre-
hends his absence from court, at the marriage Of the Earle of
Sommerset, Idios gives an account of his purpose therein, and of
his absence thence.[48]

Grierson long ago suggested that Idios represents Donne, the
private man who has no place at court, and that Allophanes is
Sir Robert Ker. Grierson writes: "Allophanes is one who seems
like another, who bears the same name as another, i.e., the bridegroom. The name of both Sir Robert and the Earl of Somerset
was Robert Ker or Carr."[49] There seems to be the possibility
also that both speakers represent Donne in an argument with
himself, Idios expressing his actual viewpoint and Allophanes,
"appearing otherwise," arguing against it. The format of the
work is of interest, apart from its pastoral framework, in that
the eleven sections of the epithalamium are labeled: "The time
of the Mariage," "Equality of Persons," "Raysing of the Bride-
groome," etc.

In the opening dialogue, Allophanes' eloquent description
of the glory of the court, and his reproof of Idios for absenting
himself, cause Idios to defend the private life:

> So, reclus'd hermits often times do know
> More of heavens glory, then a worldling can.
>   As man is of the world, the heart of man,
> Is an epitome of Gods great booke
>   Of creatures, and man need no farther looke;
> So is the Country of Courts, where sweet peace doth,
>   As their one common soule, give life to both,
> I am not then from Court.

In response to Allophanes' renewed eloquence, Idios appears to
be convinced, but his speech reveals the disenchantment of a
man who is "a grave of his own thoughts." He dutifully, however, submits his nuptial song:

But since I'am dead, and buried, I could frame
    No Epitaph, which might advance my fame
So much as this poore song, which testifies
    I did unto that day some sacrifice.[50]

The eleven-stanza song lacks the buoyancy and rich imagery of the St. Valentine's Day poem, the conceits are generally more far-fetched, and the refrain is rather unhappily marinistic. The conceit which describes "The Bridegroomes comming" to join the bride is especially unfortunate:

As he that sees a starre fall, runs apace,
    And findes a gellie in the place,
    So doth the Bridegroome hast as much,
Being told this starre is falne, and findes her such.[51]

The varying refrain is at its worst in the final stanza, "The good-night":

This is joyes bonfire, then, where loves strong Arts
Make of so noble individuall parts
One fire of foure inflaming eyes, and of two loving hearts.

The gruesome image of the eyes and hearts in the flaming bonfire is intensified by the following remark of Idios:

As I have brought this song, that I may doe
    A perfect sacrifice, I'll burne it too.

Allophanes, however, says he will carry the song to Court and lay it upon "Such Altars, as prize your devotion."
    But the poet's expression of devotion seems somewhat dutiful and rhetorical. Sometimes emotion is lost in the intricacy of the conceits, as in the stanza on "Equality of Persons," which hints at both the ancient wedding rite of exchange of apparel by the wedding participants, as well as the Platonic interchange.[52]

Elsewhere the allusions and the choice of diction suggest dejection, as in "The Benediction" where Donne in addressing the couple as "Blest payre of Swans" calls to mind death, and wisdom grown "stale."

It seems ironic that the epithalamium, traditionally a song of rejoicing, should in the final poems of Spenser, Jonson, and Donne hint at melancholy and disenchantment.[53] Late in Donne's career, however, when in several of his sermons he mentions epithalamia, the genre has again come to signify for him a kind of rejoicing, but a rejoicing associated with death and mystical marriage. Donne expresses the paradox in a Whitsunday sermon at St. Paul's a few years before his death:

HEAVEN is Glory, and heaven is Joy; we cannot tell which most; we cannot separate them; and this comfort is joy in the Holy Ghost. This makes all Jobs states alike; as rich in the first Chapter of his Booke, where all is suddenly lost, as in the last, where all is abundantly restored. This consolation from the Holy Ghost makes my mid-night noone, mine Executioner a Physitian, a stake and pile of Fagots, a Bone-fire of triumph; this consolation makes a Satyr, and Slander, and Libell against me, a Panegyrique, and an Elogy in my praise; It makes a *Tolle* an *Ave,* a *Vae* an *Euge,* a *Crucifige* an *Hosanna;* It makes my death-bed, a mariage-bed, And my Passing-Bell, an Epithalamion.[54]

XII

Their Echoes Ring

Epithalamia became the fashion. The pervasiveness of the genre by 1601 is indicated by Thomas Dekker's mockery in *Satiromastix:* Ben Jonson, satirized as Horace, is depicted in the throes of composing an epithalamium. "Looke, sir," he tells Asinius Bubo, "tis an Epithalamium for Sir Walter Terrels wedding; my braines have given assault to it but this morning."[1] A number of poets did indeed give assault to the old motifs and devices, some of these efforts resulting in tortured conceits, fantastic comparisons, sensual extravagances, centos, emblems, shaped poems, acrostics, and huge epic-like conglomerations of mythological deities, Christian saints, personified virtues and vices, angels, cherubim, and human beings. Many fine poets, however, continued to draw effectively on the reservoir of traditional material, combining it with borrowings from their immediate predecessors and their contemporaries, as well as references to current history, manners, and customs. Herrick's five epithalamia are outstanding for both invention and technique, and there are graceful works in the genre by Thomas Campion, Michael Drayton, Henry Peacham, Thomas Carew, Thomas Vaughan, Francis Quarles, Andrew Marvell, and others.

Many of the most pleasant epithalamia are not separate entities but brief songs or soliloquies in drama and masque. With classical precedent, playwrights in England's great age of the drama used epithalamia symbolically in both tragedies and comedies. We see them in plays by Shakespeare, Beaumont and Fletcher, John Ford, Nathaniel Field, Richard Braithwaite, Samuel Daniel, Thomas Goff, and Philip Massinger, to name only a few. The growth of comedy, in particular, brought with it increasing numbers of epithalamia, for, as Robert Burton remarks in *The Anatomy of Melancholy,* it was customary to conclude a comedy with a wedding and shaking of hands—and frequently with an epithalamium as well.[2] Often the central motifs of the elaborate masques and pageants popular in the courts of James I and Charles I came from the epithalamic tradition.

The interest of James I in poetry generally, and in the epithalamium in particular (see Chapter VIII), may have added to the vogue for epithalamic panegyrics honoring royal weddings. Nearly five hundred epithalamia, most of them in Latin, appear in the collections published by the universities for the wedding of James's daughter Elizabeth to Frederick in 1613, and of his son Charles to Henrietta Maria just after Charles's accession to the throne in 1625.[3] James's interest in the Bible and in Scriptural treatises and sermons may have encouraged poets to resume the medieval practice of writing elaborate elucidations and translations of the Biblical epithalamia. Such works, frequently titled epithalamia, appear in both poetry and prose, sometimes on the occasion of a wedding but more often as sermons or religious treatises not marking a particular occasion.

It is not within the scope or purpose of the present study to treat in detail the multitude of epithalamia of these years. I wish, however, in the present chapter to give a sampling, to relate them to the traditional motifs already discussed, and to note some of the innovations and trends.

Robert Burton

One aspect of the epithalamic tradition is the tendency of poets to regard the epithalamium as a rhetorical plaything. No poem better illustrates this tendency than one by Robert Burton. After remarking on the frequency of weddings in comedy, Burton announces that he will conclude his discourse on love-melancholy with an epithalamium, and he does so, concocting a patchwork of excerpts from Catullus, Ausonius, Johannes Secundus, the Apocrypha, the Emperor Galienus, Theocritus, Erasmus, and others. His epithalamium is in effect a cento constructed by looser rules than those followed by Ausonius. Burton quotes a few lines of a Latin author, then translates into English, but his translation is far from literal, as may be seen in his handling of the following from Catullus 61:

> . . . ludite ut lubet, et brevi
> Liberos date . . .

> Then modestly go sport and toy,
> And let's have every year a boy.[4]

Burton's concluding passage is constructed largely of borrowings from Erasmus's *Epithalamium Peter Aegidii,* combined with lines from Ovid and Virgil. It echoes a motif of Sidney's epithalamium, that the couple may live and die together, and concludes with a favorite theme of Renaissance poets, especially popular with epithalamists, the idea that the poet's lines confer immortality upon the couple. This is the English translation Burton gives for the final lines of his epithalamium:

> Let the Muses sing, (as he said), the Graces dance,
> not at their weddings only, but all their days long;
> so couple their hearts, that no irksomeness or anger
> ever befall them. Let him never call her other
> names than my joy, my light, or she call him other-
> wise than sweetheart. To this happiness of theirs,
> let not old age any whit detract, but as their years,
> so let their mutual love and comfort increase.
> And when they depart this life,
> Because they have so sweetly liv'd together,
> Let not one die a day before the other,
> He bury her, she him, with even fate,
> One hour their souls let jointly separate.
> O happy both! if that my lines have power,
> No time shall ever make your memory fade.[5]

Burton's medley of some sixty lines, awkward as it is, is in a way representative, for it manages to echo classical, Biblical, and contemporary writers and to combine a fair number of the conventional epithalamic motifs.

Henry Peacham

Many seventeenth-century epithalamists were more skillful in their borrowings, especially those who chose to work primarily in the Catullan tradition, among them Peacham, Campion, and Herrick. One of Peacham's nuptial hymns in honor of the marriage of Princess Elizabeth and Count Frederick is the closest thing we have to a translation of Carmen 61.[6] Peacham's eighty-five-line poem translates and summarizes selected parts of Carmen 61, covering a little over one-third of it. His tetrameter lines do not duplicate the lightness and grace of Carmen 61, but he follows the chosen stanzas closely, and here and there conveys something of the tone of the original. An important motif of the original—praise of marriage as an institution for the perpetuation of family, state, and community—is preserved in the stanza:

> Wedlock, were it not for thee,
> We could not child nor parent see;
> Armies, countries to defend,
> Or shepherds, hilly herds to tend:
> Io, Hymen, Hymenaeus!

The chorus of virgins, the *deductio,* and the fescennine verses are omitted; other parts are abbreviated. Peacham substitutes Venus as *pronuba* for Catullus's good women who have had but one husband, and adds Vesper, Cynthia, and Lucina along with several references to seventeenth-century events. Rome's disappointment at a Protestant match is alluded to in the lines "She doth approach her bridal bed, / Of none save Tiber envyed." Tribute is paid to Frederick's royal line, and there is a wish for a young Frederick Henry[7] "Who mought to Europe give her law, / And keep encroaching Hell in awe."[8] A few contemporary allusions appear also in Peacham's fourth nuptial hymn for the same occasion, an undistinguished 212-line poem which is partly an imitation of Claudian. It concludes:

> Live, royal pair, in peace and sweetest love,
> With all abundance blest by Heaven above!
> A thousand kisses bind your hearts together;
> Your arms be weary with embracing either:
> And let me live to see between you twain,
> A Caesar born as great as Charlemain.[9]

Thomas Campion

The Catullan reminiscences are more graceful in Campion's and Herrick's epithalamia. Campion's "song in forme of a Dialogue," apparently suggested by the amoebaean form of Catullus 62, introduces elements of humor not found in the classical poem:

> Can.: Who is the happier of the two,
>   A maid or wife?
>
> Ten.: Which is more to be desired,
>   Peace or strife?
>
> Can.: What strife can be where two are one,
>   Or what delight to pine alone?
>
> Bas.: None such true friends, none so sweet life,
>   As that between the man and wife.
>
> Ten.: A maid is free, a wife is tied.
>
> Can.: No maid but fain would be a bride.
>
> Ten.: Why live so many single then:
>   'Tis not I hope for want of men.
>
> Can.: The bow and arrow both may fit,
>   And yet 'tis hard the mark to hit.
>
> Bas.: He levels fair that by his side
>   Lays at night his lovely bride.
>
> Cho.: Sing Io, Hymen! Io, Io, Hymen![10]

Robert Herrick

The light touch which we see in Campion is evident also in the five nuptial poems of Herrick. Herrick's poems, although in part "a twining of the Vine of Catullus around Jonson's Elm,"[11] refer to contemporary English marriage customs and are in other ways original. All are spirited and ingeniously constructed, especially the two major works, "An Epithalamie to Sir Thomas Southwell and His Lady," and "A Nuptial Song, or Epithalamie, on Sir Clipseby Crew and His Lady." The Southwell epithalamium is novel in having as its central theme the idea that time is passing and the couple must seize the day. The *carpe diem* motif, a favorite of Herrick, is here associated with the Catullan Fates spinning the thread of life, and is announced in the opening stanza:

> Now, now's the time; so oft by truth
> Promis'd sho'd come to crown your youth.
> > Then Faire ones, doe not wrong
> > Your joyes, by staying long:
> > Or let Love's fire goe out,
> > By lingring thus in doubt:
> > But learn, that Time once lost,
> > Is ne'r redeem'd by cost.
> Then away; come, *Hymen,* guide
> To the bed, the bashfull Bride.

Herrick uniquely combines Catullan motifs with sack-possets, the "codled" cook, girlish games, going-a-Maying, and barley-breaks.[12] As in Catullus 61, the virgins who attend the bride are told that their turn will come, and this motif is combined with the *carpe diem:*

> Virgins, weep not; 'twill come, when,
> As she, so you'l be ripe for men.
> > Then grieve her not, with saying
> > She must no more a Maying:
> > Or by Rose-buds devine,
> > Who'l be her Valentine.
> > Nor name those wanton reaks
> > Y'ave had at Barley-breaks.
> But now kisse her, and thus say,
> Take time Lady while ye may.[13]

Even Herrick's novel personification of the bridal bed is associated with the passage of time:

> And now, Behold! The Bed or Couch
> That ne'r knew Brides, or Bride-grooms touch,
>   Feels in it selfe a fire;
>   And tickled with Desire,
>   Pants with a Downie brest,
>   As with a heart possest:
>   Shrugging as it did move,
>   Ev'n with the soule of love.
>   And (oh!) had it but a tongue,
>   Doves, 'two'd say, yee bill too long.[14]

The penultimate stanza, leading up to the relentless spinning of the Fates, marks off one by one the divisions of time:

> On your minutes, hours, dayes, months, years,
> Drop the fat blessing of the sphears.
>   That good, which Heav'n can give
>   To make you bravely live;
>   Fall, like a spangling dew,
>   By day, and night on you . . . .

In the final stanza, we see one of Herrick's characteristic combinations of pagan and Christian elements as he moves from the opening lines on the Catullan Fates to the closing lines which echo the Book of Job's "Thou shalt come to thy grave in a full age, like as a shock of corn cometh in in his season."[15] Here the combination is likely to startle the unwary reader and may even disconcert him when he recognizes "Barn" as a metaphor for the grave or possibly the Christian Heaven:

> Let bounteous Fates your spindles full
> Fill, and winde up with whitest wooll.

Let them not cut the thred
Of life, untill ye bid.
May Death yet come at last;
And not with desp'rate hast:
But when ye both can say,
Come, Let us now away.
Be ye to the Barn then born,
Two, like two ripe shocks of corn.

Herrick's Southwell epithalamium, like Spenser's and others, offers marriage as a device to thwart time and mutability. It is probably no accident that in the 1648 edition of *Hesperides* the stanzas of this epithalamium are altar-shaped, for Herrick's arrangement of lines is often functional, even in poems which are not obviously shaped. Although the poem is in no sense devotional, the poet at one point does urge the participants "On, on devoutly." Through the marriage altar, the epithalamium suggests, man attains heavenly joys, "That good, which Heav'n can give."

The epithalamium for Sir Clipseby Crew is noteworthy for the hyperbole of the first three stanzas and for its expertly controlled metaphysical conceits, as in Stanza 13:

1. What's that we see from far? the spring of Day
Bloom'd from the East, or faire Injewel'd May
   Blowne out of April; or some New-
   Star fill'd with glory to our view,
      Reaching at heaven,
To add a nobler Planet to the seven?
   Say, or doe we not descrie
Some Goddesse, in a cloud of Tiffanie
         To move, or rather the
   Emergent Venus from the Sea?

2. 'Tis she! 'tis she! or else some more Divine
Enlightned substance; mark how from the Shrine

Of holy Saints she paces on,
Treading upon Vermilion
          And Amber; Spice-
ing the Chaste Aire with fumes of Paradise.
    Then come on, come on, and yeeld
A savour like unto a blessed field,
          When the bedabled Morne
Washes the golden eares of corne.

3. See where she comes; and smell how all the street
Breathes Vine-yards and Pomgranats: O how sweet!
    As a fir'd Altar, in each stone,
    Perspiring pounded Cynamon.
          The Phenix nest,
Built up of odours, burneth in her breast.
    Who therein wo'd not consume
His soule to Ash-heaps in that rich perfume?
          Bestroaking Fate the while
He burnes to Embers on the Pile . . . .

13. The bed is ready, and the maze of Love
Lookes for the treaders; every where is wove
    Wit and new misterie; read, and
    Put in practise, to understand
          And know each wile,
Each hieroglyphick of a kisse or smile;
    And do it to the full; reach
High in your own conceipt, and some way teach
          Nature and Art, one more
Play, then they ever knew before.[16]

The poem's most famous lines contain the fish motif, another
favorite of Herrick:

Blest is the Bride, on whom the Sun doth shine;
          And thousands gladly wish
You multiply, as doth a Fish.[17]

In one of his later nuptial poems, Herrick's wish for the couple is that they may

> Fish-like increase then to a million:
> And millions of spring-times may ye have . . . .

The figure is new in English nuptial poetry, although the fish had long been a symbol of fertility and as such had been associated with wedding rites.[18]

Herrick's *Connubii Flores, or the well-wishes at Weddings* is a novelty in the tradition in that it consists of alternate songs sung not by two choruses as in Carmen 62 but by a series of choruses, each of which has been given a Latin title—*Chorus Sacerdotum, Chorus Juvenum, Chorus Senum, Chorus Virginum, Chorus Pastorum, Chorus Matronarum,* and finally *Chorus Omnium.* The priests ask that blessings and joy may come to the couple as they go from the Temple to their home, the young men ask that night may come soon, and the old men advise moderation in love:

> Love is a thing most nice; and must be fed
> To such a height; but never surfeited.
> What is beyond the mean is ever ill:
> *'Tis best to feed Love; but not over-fill:*
> Go then discreetly to the Bed of pleasure;
> And this remember, *Vertue keepes the measure.*[19]

The virgins say that they have observed "luckie signes" to encourage the bride, and that the kissing Cupids they have seen flying about have their eyes open, an implication that Love is wise. Instead of the usual gift of a lamb, the shepherds bring a fleece to the bride, instructing her to make it into a piece of cloth and to be a good housewife:

> Nor Faire, must you be loth
> Your Finger to apply
> To huswiferie.

> Then, then begin
> To spin:
> And (Sweetling) marke you, what a Web will come
> Into your Chests, drawn by your painfull Thumb.

The chorus of matrons gives even more practical advice on the bride's responsibilities:

> Set you to your Wheele, and wax
> Rich, by the Ductile Wool and Flax.
> Yarne is an Income; and the Huswifes thread
> The Larder fils with meat; the Bin with bread.

The old men resume their advice, offering a series of well-worn proverbs:

> 'Tis haste
> Makes waste;
>
> Extreames have still their fault;
> The softest Fire makes the sweetest Mault.
> Who gripes too hard the dry and slip'rie sand,
> Holds none at all, or little in his hand.[20]

The virgins wish the couple the "blessing of encrease," and that Lucina, goddess of childbirth, may give tender attention to the bride "as her Aprill houre drawes neare." The final injunction of the young men—in fact, the didactic tone of the entire epithalamium—is reminiscent of Sidney's advice:

> Farre hence be all speech, that may anger move:
> Sweet words must nourish soft and gentle Love.

In Herrick's "The Entertainment: or, Porch-verse, at the Marriage of Mr. Hen. Northly, and the most witty Mrs. Lettice Yard," the speaker welcomes the couple at their own threshold, as might a priest, offering blessing to both and admonishing them to sacrifice to the god of the threshold as the marriage begins.[21] His other brief nuptial lyric, the sprightly "A Nuptiall Verse to Mistresse Elizabeth Lee, now Lady Tracie," urges the bride to hasten to her eager bridegroom and engage in love's "warre."[22] Herrick's poems, mainly in the Catullan stream, are indebted also to Jonson's nuptial masques, and Herrick's preoccupation with the bridal bed is akin to that which we have already noted in the epithalamia of Donne. All of his five poems demonstrate that an inventive poet may still give new life to old motifs.

Classical and Biblical Echoes

Some of the efforts of Herrick's contemporaries to inject new vigor into the classical epic epithalamium were less successful. One of these is Thomas Heywood's *Marriage Triumphe* of 756 lines, written in 1613 for the marriage of the Princess Elizabeth and Count Frederick, apparently in an attempt to demonstrate the poet's learning and to flatter the scholarly tastes of James I.[23] It is an unselective assortment drawn mainly from the neo-Latin epic epithalamia. Another long poem of this kind, written for the same marriage, is S. Hutton's translation of a Latin epithalamium of Joannes Maria de Franchis, which includes three books of 443 stanzas and an epilogue, a total of 2,674 lines.[24] The writer announces that he has translated it into English "to the end that the Ladies may be partakers." Such epithalamia were not limited to poetry, a fact amply evidenced by the 142-page prose "Epithalamium Gallo-Britannicum" of George Marceline, written in English for the marriage in 1625 of Charles I and Henrietta Maria.[25]

Long works are also to be found among the seventeenth-century epithalamia of the Christian tradition. Andrew Willet's volume celebrating the marriage of Elizabeth and Frederick is an example.[26] It opens with a verse translation of the 45th Psalm, followed by a verse "explication" of the Psalm, which the author refers to as the "marriage song" of Solomon. The book contains a fifty-six-page prose treatise in which the author "doth as it were descant upon" the Psalm, and makes "application of the text to the present marriage of these excellent Princes." Such commentaries as well as sermons giving allegorical interpretations of the Canticle were common. Less frequently, the Biblical epithalamia echo in drama. An early example is David's epithalamium in George Peele's play, *The Love of King David and Fair Bethsabe*.[27] The king, having observed Bathsheba bathing in a spring, has ordered that she be brought to him, and David's musings as he awaits her arrival echo the Canticle and other Biblical passages:

> Let all the grass that beautifies her bower
> Bear Manna every morn instead of dew . . . .
>
> See, Cusay, see the flower of Israel,
> The fairest daughter that obeys the king
> In all the land the Lord subdu'd to me;
> Fairer than Isaac's lover at the well,
> Brighter than inside-bark of new-hewn cedar,
> Sweeter than flames of fine perfumed myrrh,
> And comelier than the silver clouds that dance
> On Zephyr's wings before the King of Heaven.

And as Bathsheba approaches, David continues:

> Now comes my lover tripping like the roe,
> And brings my longings tangled in her hair . . . .
> Open the doors, and entertain my love;
> Open, I say, and, as you open, sing,
> Welcome fair Bethsabe, King David's darling.

Peele has introduced into his Biblical drama the Ovidian Salmacis motif used in one of the epithalamia of Poupo and in the marriage-of-rivers passage in Spenser's "Mutabilitie cantos."[28]

Topographical and Pastoral

Most of the motifs which we have seen in earlier centuries appear again in the seventeenth-century English genre. The marriage of rivers appears as a device in nuptial poems and masques—for example, in works of Wither and Beaumont—and as the central theme of a topographical epithalamium in Drayton's *Poly-Olbion.*[29] Pastoral motifs are less frequent than in the sixteenth century but have by no means disappeared; we have already observed them in Herrick. One of the most fanciful pastorals is the "Prothalamion" in the eighth Nimphall of Drayton's *The Muses Elizium,* which introduces English wedding customs into the plans for the wedding of Tita, smallest of the fairies, and her bridegroom who is "deft and wondrous Ayrye, / And of the noblest of the Fayry." Claia describes the wedding gown:

Of Pansie, Pincke, and Primrose Leaves;
Most curiously laid on in Threaves:
All all embroydery to supply,
Powthred with flowers of Rosemary:
A trayle about the skirt shall runne,
The Silke-wormes finest, newly spunne;
And every Seam the Nimphs shall sew
With th' smallest of the Spinners Clue:
And having done their work, againe
These to the Church shall bear her Traine:
Which for our *Tita* we shall make
Of the cast slough of a Snake,
Which quivering as the winde doth blow,
The Sunne shall it like Tinsell shew.[30]

The songs of the birds remind the reader of the music for Spenser's bride. The instrumental music is robust for so dainty a company:

> Violins, strike up aloud,
> Ply the Gitterne, scowre the Crowd,
> Let the nimble hand belabour
> The whisteling Pipe, and drumbling Taber:
> To the full the Bagpipe racke,
> Till the swelling leather cracke.

Drayton's "Prothalamion" is reminiscent of Shakespeare's brief epithalamic passage at the end of *A Midsummer-Night's Dream,* in which Oberon directs the fairies to consecrate with field dew the bridal beds in the palace, in order that the couples might be ever true in love and their offspring ever fortunate.[31]

The pastoral epithalamium of the seventeenth century was most often a part of drama or masque. Two such epithalamia appear in inserted masques in Shakespearean comedies. In *The Tempest* the brief song of Juno and Ceres emphasizes the fertility-and-increase theme seen many centuries earlier in the epithalamium in Aristophanes' *Peace.* Shakespeare's pun on "spring" and "offspring" is also somewhat reminiscent of the rustic humor of the hymn in the *Peace:*

> Juno: Honor, riches, marriage-blessing
>   Long continuance, and increasing,
>   Hourly joys be stille upon you!
>   Juno sings her blessings on you.
>
> Ceres: Earth's increase, foison plenty,
>   Barnes and garners never empty
>   Vines with clustering bunches growing,
>   Plants with goodly burthen bowing
>   Spring come to you at the farthest
>   In the very end of harvest!
>   Scarcity and want shall shun you;
>   Ceres' blessing so is on you.[32]

And the brief epithalamium at the end of *As You Like It,* as I have said earlier, signifies happiness at establishment of unity and peace out of confusion, and gives honor to marriage as a blessed mode of daily life, convenient and comfortable, and guaranteeing future citizens for the community.[33]

The Anti-Epithalamium

Like other aspects of the classical tradition, the phenomenon of the anti-epithalamium continues to appear from time to time in English, especially in drama. In *Romeo and Juliet,* the soliloquy of Juliet includes epithalamic devices presaging tragedy resulting from an improper union.[34] The invocation to Night and impatience for its arrival are common motifs in the epithalamium of the period, although it is not usual for these sentiments to be voiced by the bride. Her address of Night, "Thou sober-suited matron all in black," and her description of Romeo (lines 18–25) hint of the tragedy to come. In Webster's *The Tragedy of the Dutchesse of Malfy,* the marriage of the duchess also is unsanctioned, and one of the Madmen who participate in the masque just before the murder of the duchess sings this anti-epithalamic song:

> O let us howle, some heavy note,
> > some deadly-dogged howle,
> Sounding, as from the threatning throat,
> > of beastes, and fatall fowle.
> As Ravens, Schrich-owles, Bulls and Beares,
> > We'll bell, and bawle our parts,
> Till yerk-some noyce have cloy'd your eares,
> > and corasiv'd your hearts.
> As last when as our quire wants breath,
> > our bodies being blest,
> We'll sing like Swans, to welcome death,
> > and die in love and rest.[35]

Later Bosola rings a bell and intones the following lines, ordering the duchess to make herself ready for death by preparing as does a bride for her wedding:

> Hearke, now every thing is still—
> The Schritch-Owle, and the whistler shrill,
> Call upon our Dame, aloud,
> And bid her quickly don her shrowd:
>
> . . . .
>
> Strew your haire, with powders sweet:
> Don cleane linnen, bath your feete,
> And (the foule feend more to checke)
> A crucifixe let blesse your necke,
> 'Tis now full tide, 'tweene night, and day,
> End your groans, and come away.[36]

The presence of the birds and other elements of evil omen, the swan-song motif, the adorning of the bride, and the arrival of the "full tide 'tween night and day" are all elements from the epithalamic tradition, used to anticipate the tragedy resulting from an unsanctioned union not attended by proper ceremony.

We have noted the anti-epithalamic motifs in the classical drama, especially in Seneca's *Medea*. The interest of Renaissance dramatists in Senecan tragedy may have encouraged the use of these motifs during the period.[37] John Studley, in his sixteenth-century translation of *Medea,* had omitted the epithalamium, substituting a chorus of his own, because in the original he saw "nothing but an heape of prophane idoles."[38] He had included, however, the anti-epithalamic passage which follows the epithalamium. Sir Edward Sherburne's seventeenth-century translation of *Medea,* including not only the epithalamium but extensive notes concerning it may have contributed toward the continuing popularity of the genre at mid-century.[39]

Satires, Imitations, Novelties

In England's great age of the drama, the epithalamium was most at home in romantic and pastoral comedy and masque. With the changing character of comedy after the Restoration and the altered attitudes toward love and marriage depicted in much of the drama, came an increase in satiric and broadly witty epithalamia, exemplified by Richard Brome's poems in the *City Wit* and *The Merry Beggers;* the anonymous "On Dr. Corbet's Marriage" in *Wit Restored;* Richard Duke's "Epithalamium upon the Marriage of Captain William Bedlowe"; and William Wycherley's "An Epithalamium on the Marriage of Two Very Ill-Natured Blacks."[40] The satiric epithalamia, although they accompanied the decline of the tradition, were probably a symptom rather than a cause. Epithalamia had become so numerous, and the same themes, metaphors, and rhythms had been repeated so many times that people simply became weary of them. Spenser, Chapman, Jonson, Donne, and Herrick, although selectively imitating models from the classical and Christian traditions, were able to create new and original works. Few of their imitators, however, were blessed with the skill of the masters, and many of the works were little more than trite panegyrics, echoing long-familiar phrases. Among the lesser poets who chose Spenser as their principal model were Michael Drayton, George Wither, Phineas Fletcher, and Christopher Brooke.[41] Relatively few poets chose to imitate Chapman and Donne, and those who did were not very successful. Sir Henry Goodere's poem illustrates the difficulty encountered by a minor writer attempting a metaphysical epithalamium in the manner of Donne. The poet, having referred to the bridegroom as "destiny's great instrument," the bride as a mine, the bridal bed as a sea, the bridegroom as an argosy, the bride as an island, and the romance as a voyage, goes on to describe the couple:

> Now like two half-spheres set
> On a flat table, on these sheets they lie;
> But grow a body perfectly,
> As half-spheres make a globe by being met.
> Still may you happy be,
> So as you need not spend
> So much as one wish to your end!

> We'll wish and pray whilst you enjoy, and we
> What length of life you wish shall plainly see
> By your now length'ning out by sweet delays
> This night, for which this year may spare a
>   month of days.[42]

Robert Herrick was the most successful of Ben Jonson's followers. Others included Thomas Randolph and James Shirley. The renewed interest in form and structure, with less concern for the matter of the poem, may in part be due to Jonson, but he can hardly be blamed for the anagrams and acrostics of Thomas Heywood, Joshua Sylvester, and Thomas Jordan.[43] Jonson's influence may have led to the preference for shorter epithalamia among Cavalier writers. Some of their brief lyrics are bright and ingenious, taking their main motifs from circumstances pertaining to the couple or wedding being celebrated. An example is Thomas Carew's "On the Marriage of Thomas Killigrew and Cecilia Crofts, the Morning Stormy," which uses the storm as its central motif:

> Let tempests struggle in the air, but rest
> Eternal calms within thy peaceful breast.[44]

Carew's poem is novel also in that its content is pagan, but its technique is in part derived from the sacred meditation.[45]

The mixture of sacred and secular should be mentioned in connection with epithalamia of Frances Quarles, Richard Crashaw, and Henry Vaughan. Like Sidney in the *Arcadia,* Quarles inserted nuptial poems in his *Argalus and Parthenia.* Each of his five brief songs refers to an individual rite of the pagan marriage ceremony. Part of his prayer to Juno echoes Sidney:

> From satiety, from strife,
>   From jealousy, domestic jars,
>   From those blows that leave no scars,

Juno protect your marriage life.
Let Juno's hourly blessing send ye
As much joy as can attend ye.[46]

Quarles's prayer here is addressed to one deity rather than to the several usually mentioned in the pagan poems.[47] Quarles is author also of a Christian epithalamium, "An Epithalamium to the Bridegroom" (in the *Sions Sonnets*), which paraphrases the Canticle, and of a poetic translation of the 44th Psalm in his book of emblems.[48]

Henry Vaughan's brief Christian lyric is one of the finest in the waning epithalamic tradition.[49] Richard Crashaw makes extensive use of epithalamic motifs in his Christian hymns, and contributes a bizarre nuptial epithalamium mainly in the Catullan tradition.[50] One of Andrew Marvell's songs for the marriage in 1657 of Lord Fauconberg and Lady Mary Cromwell, third daughter of the Protector, praises the bridegroom as the only "demigod" able to meet with the approval of "Jove" as a son-in-law.[51]

Epic and Allegory

The declining years of the tradition are marked not only by the hundreds of short lyrics but by many poems in the heroic mode, some of them depicting Venus in a manner reminiscent of Statius, Claudian, and their neo-Latin followers. Although the poems do not rely as extensively on mythology as their classical forerunners, there are dutiful references to Jove, Apollo, Neptune, sea-nymphs, and dolphins. A few remind the reader of Lydgate's epithalamium for Gloucester: the epithalamium in English seems almost to have come full circle. In epic fashion the bridal couple are compared to Adam and Eve, or Penelope and Ulysses. The bridegroom is praised as a Noah, a Joshua, or an Alexander, and the bride as another Helen of Troy. The epithalamia for the wedding of Charles II in 1662 are concerned more with politics than with love, describing Charles's restoration to the throne; his qualities as a leader in peace and war;

England's internal struggles and her relations with Spain, Portugal, and France; and the fact that the marriage brought Bombay and Tangier to England as part of Catherine's dowry. The dominant motif of these poems is the same as that of Lydgate, the hope for future unity and peace among nations.[52] Love conquers War.

The general tenor of the poems for royal marriages during the second half of the century may be illustrated by lines from John Oldham's epithalamium for the wedding in 1677 of the Prince of Orange and the Lady Mary, who in 1688 took the throne as William III and Mary II:

> Hail happy Pair! kind Heav'ns great Hostages!
> Sure Pledges of a firm and lasting Peace!
> Call't not a Match, we that low Stile disdain,
> Nor will degrade it with a Term so mean;
> A League it must be said,
> Where Countries thus Espouse, and Nations Wed:
> Our Thanks, propitious Destiny!
> Never did yet thy Pow'r dispence,
> A more Plenipotentiary Influence . . . .[53]

With a few exceptions, notably the epithalamia of Matthew Prior and the translation of Theocritus 18 by John Dryden,[54] the epithalamia of the closing years of the century were patriotic and general rather than personal. The death-blows to the genre were perhaps dealt late in the seventeenth century and early in the eighteenth by Elkanah Settle, who maintained a standing epithalamium which he provided in elaborate bindings to a series of customers, altering a page or two on each occasion to give recognition to the ancestry of the couple.[55] The opening lines demonstrate the cosmic aspects which the epithalamium had come to assume again and again in both pagan and Christian traditions:

> When the Great FOUNDER this vast Pile began,
> And ended with his Sixth Day's Labour, MAN,

His greatest Work the Last; stampt in his Own
Bright IMAGE, call'd to th' Universal Throne:
Yes Earth, Heav'n, Stars, and Sun, the whole wide
                                        Round
All built for Him, all to his Service bound,
These humbler Glories in the Front appear,
Whilst MAN, true SOVERAIGN-like, brought up the Reer. . .[56]

In the hundreds of English epithalamia that were written in
the century between Sir Philip Sidney and Elkanah Settle, we see
represented nearly all the motifs and conventions of the Hebrew,
Greek, Roman, neo-Latin, and continental vernacular epithalamia which preceded the English genre. The epithalamium in
English had its greatest success as a nuptial lyric; it was less
successful when poets attempted epic-like works with general or
allegorical application.

The decline in numbers was gradual. It remained the custom throughout the eighteenth century to write epithalamia for
royal weddings and for a few less exalted rites; in lyrics by Christopher Smart in the eighteenth century, and by Shelley and
Tennyson in the nineteenth, the genre glows briefly. Even in
the twentieth century the old conventions and motifs have been
fanned into life by A. E. Housman, John Masefield, James
Joyce, W. H. Auden, Robert Graves, Edith Sitwell, Gertrude
Stein, e. e. cummings, Yvor Winters, Dylan Thomas, Ann Stanford, James Merrill, and others.[57]

Conclusion

Reviewing the assortment of literary works which poets have called epithalamia, I have concluded that there are two concepts which underlie all of them: *union* and *order*. It may be union of man and woman, of the Virgin and Christ, of the human soul and Christ, of two rivers, or trees. Through union, there is generation, rebirth, immortality, perfection, salvation, peace. Rivers unite, and the area of their confluence becomes the birthplace of kings; or their coming together symbolizes the fertility and fair prospects of the realm, its ruler, and its people. However it is accomplished, the union must be a proper and orderly one, sanctioned by deity or society, in accord with nature, attended by suitable ceremony. The epithalamium is part of the ritual. In the classical era the genre dealt with human wedlock; in the Middle Ages it was more often concerned with mystical union and virginity. The humanism of the Renaissance, fostering the conviction that virginity is a heavenly state but marriage a human one, provided a favorable climate for the re-development of the classical epithalamium and the blending of pagan and Christian conventions. When the typical Renaissance practice of relating human marriage to the cosmos—the microcosm to the macrocosm—appears in the genre, it is often accompanied by the ancient theme of the unions of rivers and other forces of nature. The epithalamium thus becomes mirror and model of favorite Renaissance concepts—the doctrine of increase, the notion that marriage and generation are in accord with nature, the belief that wedlock and poetry are means of attaining immortality. The genre was supported by, and helped to perpetuate, the doctrines of order and degree and the divine right of kings.

Although in the late seventeenth century the genre began to decline into dutiful and repetitious panegyric of influential patrons, it carried with it, even if in degraded form, the signs of its mythic origins. These origins of the epithalamium account in part for its being a more various literary type than criticism has generally taken it to be. Beginning as a folk song in the pre-history of literature, the epithalamium is rooted in fertility rites and dramas of generation and death, out of which the great modes of comedy and tragedy probably developed. From being a folk song, a more or less spontaneous expression of love and rejoicing, it grew into a literary form, attracting the talents of fine poets in every stage of its history. Through the centuries, its associations with comedy have been far more numerous and extensive than those with tragedy: this book records some examples of the handshakings, kisses, pledges, treaties, banquets, fêtes, happy beddings, and hopes for amity and offspring which unite nuptial hymns and the last acts of dramatic comedies.

The connections of the epithalamium with tragedy are fewer; and even those, as I have said earlier, seem to have gone unnoticed. But surely the origins of the "anti-epithalamium" are to be found in tragedy, and perhaps as well in the types of satire which lean toward the tragic. When procreation, order, and increase are the leading themes, love transcends death and confers immortality on married couples and their poets. When the counter-statement invades the mode, then some of the conditions of tragedy prevail. Propitious signs and emblems are reversed to presage disunion; if the ritual of order exists at all in a poem, it will be an improper one; evil spirits are summoned up; and darkness dispels light.

As we have seen, the English epithalamium draws upon all the resources of this diverse tradition, and every English wedding hymn reveals some indebtedness to it. But as we might expect, English poets pick and choose to suit themselves, establishing their own attitudes toward the received materials. Edmund Spenser is in some ways the most conventional and in others the most original of English epithalamists: the greatest wedding hymn in English is a personal love poem as well as a public encomium of marriage. Such particularity is rare, and so is any tendency toward romance. The English epithalamium is in general more realistic than romantic, seldom raising marriage to divine estate or making goddesses and gods of English brides and grooms. It embodies the assumption that marriage is a practical condition of adult life.

Therefore, on the whole the English epithalamists are pleasant, moral, and didactic, even though they play with the inevitable *double-entendre* of the fertility theme. Less sensuous than the Italian, less frivolous than many of the French poets, they look upon marriage as an orderly procedure for the realization of maturity and fulfillment for the individual—the Juno Perfecta of Ben Jonson. From this point of view, marriage is a union sanctioned by God and man for easing the burden of daily life, providing the comforts of the nuptial bed, and perpetuating the community, an attitude epitomized in Shakespeare's wedding song in *As You Like It.*

The English epithalamium throughout its history has been didactic, and during the days of its flowering—in the hands of Sidney, Spenser, Jonson, and Donne—it taught delightfully the blessing of orderly union. Its functions—nuptial, devotional, topographical, and patriotic—are expressed in Ben Jonson's description of the role of Poesy: "It ... offers to mankinde a certaine rule and Patterne of living well and happily, disposing us to all Civill offices of Society." The "rule and Patterne" offered by the epithalamium extend beyond the individual to the entire human race. Grounded in the act of love, which consummates the union of every man and woman, and made moral and instructive by ages of reflection upon marriage as a holy state and a conservative social institution, the epithalamium through its own rituals enacts the patterns of order. By means of the poetry of marriage, disruptive elements—often personified by Mars and Venus—have been subdued in men and resolved by art into an exhibition of harmony, peace, and hope.

From the earliest known bridal songs, cited in the first chapter of this book, to the passage from Edith Sitwell's *Prothalamium* for the marriage of the Duke and Duchess of Kent, June 8, 1961, with which this last chapter closes—a recorded history of 3,000 years maintained through the best and worst of times—the epithalamium reiterates its promises of procreation, joy, and union for mankind and all nations:

> Love is all life, the primal law,
> The sun and planets to the husbandman,
> The kernel and sap; it is the power
> That holds the Golden Rainers in the heavens, bringing us
> The calyx of the flower of the world, the spirit
> Moving upon the waters, the defeat
> Of all time's ravages . . . .
>
> Who was it cried, "This is no time for sowing or begetting.
> The East is yellow with fear, and the West is red with its
>   setting?"
>
> Although a gray bough drips
> With dews of death, still the lost floras of the world
>   Lie on young cheeks, young lips.

Notes

Introduction

1. Sidney's epithalamium may have been composed between 1577 and 1580, although it was not published until the *Arcadia* of 1593. See comments of W. A. Ringler in the introduction to *The Poems of Sir Philip Sidney* (Oxford, 1962), p. xxxvi.

2. James's fragmentary wedding masque appears in MS. Bodley 165 and MS. Add. 24195 in the British Museum. James Craigie, editor of the Scottish Text Society's edition of the king's poems (Edinburgh and London, 1958), includes the texts from both manuscripts.

3. The song, "Roses, their sharp spines being gone," which opens *The Two Noble Kinsmen,* has also been called an epi-

thalamium and has been attributed to Shakespeare or John Fletcher. E. K. Chambers in *William Shakespeare, A Study of Facts and Problems* (Oxford, 1930), I, 532, writes, "Either might have written the song in i.I." See Chapter IX of the present study for discussion of epithalamia in *The Faerie Queene*. The epithalamic passages in *Paradise Lost* include the "Hail wedded Love" hymn, Book IV, lines 750–775, and some preceding lines in the same book, 689–719, describing the nuptial bower.

4. The principal collections are *Epithalamia Sive Lusus Palatini in Nuptias Celsissi* . . . (Oxford, 1613); *Epithalamia Oxoniensia, Potentissimi* . . . (Oxford, 1625); *Epithalamia Illustriss. & Felicis* . . . (Cambridge, 1625); *Epithalamia Cantabrigiensia* . . . (Cambridge, 1662); and *Domiduca Oxoniensis* (Oxford, 1662).

5. A discussion of classical lyric epithalamia, particularly those of Sappho, Theocritus, and Catullus, is found in E. A. Mangelsdorff's dissertation, *Das lyrische hochzeitgedicht bei den Griechen und Romern* (Hamburg, 1913). English epithalamia are related to a variety of classical models in the dissertation of Kurt Wöhrmann, *Die englische Epithalamiendichtung der Renaissance und ihre Vorbilder* (Leipzig, 1928) and that of Adelheid Gaertner, *Die englische Epithalamienliteratur im siebzehnten Jahrhundert und ihre Vorbilder* (Coburg, 1936). Wöhrmann considers some of the epithalamia of Sidney, Spenser, Chapman, Peacham, and Jonson. Miss Gaertner with considerable discernment examines the works of seventeenth-century English epithalamists, giving particular attention to Donne, Jonson, Heywood, Herrick, and Randolph and touching more briefly on a great number of others. Another classical approach is the unpublished paper of Hilda Schön, "Catulls Epithalamion und seine englischen Nachahmer bis 1660" (Vienna, 1940), which relies heavily on Wöhrmann and Gaertner and paraphrases at length the epithalamia of Spenser, Chapman, Peacham, Fletcher, Donne, Herrick, and Jonson, and compares selected passages with lines from Catullus.

Robert H. Case in the introduction to his anthology, *English Epithalamies* (London, 1896), gives a general view of the English epithalamium in relation to its classical predecessors. The best study of English in relation to Catullus is found in James A. S. McPeek's *Catullus in Strange and Distant Britain* (Cambridge, 1939). His chapter on the Catullan marriage songs relates them to the works of Sidney, Spenser, Jonson, Donne, Campion, Peacham, Herrick, and Crashaw, and describes the role of the Pléiade in transmitting Catullan influence. Other classical scholars whose work is helpful as background for the English genre are Camillo Morelli and Arthur Leslie Wheeler. Morelli's "L'epitalamio nella tarda poesia latina," *Studi italiani di filologia classica,* XVIII (1910), 319–432, deals in particular with the rhetorical Latin epithalamium, with emphasis on the works of Statius and Claudian, but includes also such poets as Apollonius, Sidonius, Ennodius, Fortunatus, Martianus Capella, and Dracontius. Wheeler's book, *Catullus and the Traditions of Ancient Poetry* (Berkeley, 1934), has a good chapter on the wedding poems, pp. 183–217. An older treatise by M. l'Abbé Souchay, "Discours sur l'origine et le caractére de l'épithalame," *Historie de l'académie royale des inscriptions et belles-lettres,* IX (Paris, 1736), 305–319, is of value for its varied approach and for the author's recognition of Christian as well as classical representatives of the genre.

The most useful single guide to specific items among the multitude of classical, medieval, and later continental predecessors of the English genre is found in Cortlandt Van Winkle's introduction, detailed notes, and extensive bibliography in his edition of Spenser's *Epithalamion* (New York, 1926). Additional light is shed on Spenser's work in the genre by the dissertation (Princeton, 1940), of Dan S. Norton, "The Background of Spenser's *Prothalamion*," which offers evidence that prothalamia, or spousal songs, never became an independent literary type but depended primarily on established forms, particularly the epithalamium. Norton makes especially valuable contributions by his survey of English betrothal and marriage customs, by the analysis of the bridal poems of Lydgate and Dunbar, and by relating such poems

generally to the traditions of dream-vision, epic-epithala-
mium, topographical-antiquarian poems, pastoral songs,
heraldry, *impresa,* emblem, and masque. Thomas M.
Greene's paper, "Spenser and the Epithalamic Convention,"
Comparative Literature, IX (Summer 1957), 215–228,
points out a few of the most important epithalamia among
the classical, neo-Latin, Italian, and French predecessors of
Spenser, and from them and the critical discussions defines
the major conventions of the traditional nuptial poems.

6. As translated from *De Elocutione* of Demetrius Phalereus
by J. M. Edmonds in *Lyra Graeca* (London, first printed
1922), pp. 173–174.

CHAPTER I

The Greeks: Sappho, Aristophanes, Theocritus, and The Beginnings of Pastoral

1. George Chapman, *The Whole Works of Homer, Prince of
Poetts, In his Iliads, and Odysses* (London, 1616), p. 263.
For description of Achilles' shield, see Book XVIII, lines
491–496. For wedding of Peleus and Thetis, see Book
XXIV, lines 57–63.

2. See Arthur Leslie Wheeler, *Catullus and the Traditions of
Ancient Poetry* (Berkeley, 1934), p. 185, and Christian
James Fordyce, *Catullus* (Oxford, 1961), p. 235.

3. See H. G. Evelyn-White's translation, *Hesiod, The Homeric
Hymns and Homerica* (Cambridge, rev. 1936), pp. 239–
240.

4. The poem on Alcman is translated by Edwyn Robert Be-
van in *Leonidas of Tarentum* (Oxford, 1931), p. 92.

5. C. M. Bowra, *Greek Lyric Poetry* (Oxford, 1961), pp. 108–109.

6. See J. M. Edmonds, *Lyra Graeca* (Cambridge, 1927), I, 231.

7. Henry Thornton Wharton, *Sappho* (London, 1895), pp. 140–141.

8. Demetrius says that when Sappho celebrates the charms of beauty she does so in lines that are themselves beautiful and sweet. So too when she sings of love and springtime. It is in a different key that she mocks the clumsy bridegroom and the porter at the wedding. See the translation of Demetrius by W. Rhys Roberts, *Demetrius on Style* (Cambridge, 1902), p. 149. Demetrius also praises Sappho's lines on the evening star. See Roberts, p. 139.

9. Edmonds, pp. 289, 219.

10. See Bowra, pp. 214 ff.

11. Kurt Wöhrmann, *Die englische Epithalamiendeichtung der Renaissance und ihre Vorbilder* (diss. Leipzig, 1929), p. 2.

12. John Addington Symonds, *Studies of the Greek Poets,* I, 122.

13. See Fordyce, p. 235, and Bowra, p. 215. J. Hookham Frere's comments appear in *Aristophanes, Four Plays in English Verse* (Oxford, 1912), p. 264.

14. Gilbert Norwood, *Greek Comedy* (Boston, 1932).

15. Bowra, pp. 107 ff.

16. The *Sixe Idillia* were reprinted by A. H. Bullen in *Some Longer Elizabethan Poems* (Westminster, 1903). See p. 140.

17.   Idyll 18 of Theocritus has been a favorite among English
       translators. Of most interest are the translations of the
       anonymous poet in *Six Idillia* (Oxford, 1588), and John
       Dryden in *Sylvae: or the Second Part of Poetical Miscel-
       lanies* (London, 1685), pp. 100–106. Others are by Thomas
       Creech, in *The Idylliums of Theocritus with Rapin's Dis-
       course of Pastorals Done into English* (Oxford, 1684),
       pp. 100–103; Charles Stuart Calverly in *Theocritus* (Lon-
       don, 1896), pp. 104–109; Andrew Lang in *Theocritus,
       Bion and Moschus* (London, 1889), pp. 97–100 and Rich-
       ard Polwhele in *The British Poets* (Chiswick, 1822), XCII,
       77–79. The tone of the lines in which the chorus of virgins
       teases the bridegroom may be illustrated by a few lines
       from Dryden's translation:

> This was their song: Why happy Bridegroom, why
> E're yet the Stars are kindl'd in the Skie,
> E're twilight shades, or Evening dews are shed,
> Why dost thou steal so soon away to Bed?
> Has *Somnus* brush'd thy Eye-lids with his Rod,
> Or do thy Legs refuse to bear their Load,
> With flowing bowles of a more generous God?
> If gentle slumber on thy Temples creep,
> (But naughty Man thou dost not mean to sleep)
> Betake thee to thy Bed thou drowzy Drone,
> Sleep by thy self and leave thy Bride alone:
> Go leave her with her Maiden Mates to play
> At sports more harmless, till the break of day:
> Give us this Evening; thou hast Morn and Night,
> And all the year before thee, for delight.

18.   Creech, pp. 26–27.

19.   See comment of J. M. Edmonds, *The Greek Bucolic Poets*
       (London, 1950), p. 397. For the Greek text and English
       translation, see Edmonds, pp. 398–401. For the translation
       by Francis Fawkes, see *The Works of the British Poets,*
       ed. Robert Anderson (London, 1795), XIII, 214.

CHAPTER II

Catullus

1. See Elmer Truesdell Merrill, *Catullus* (Cambridge, 1893), p. 96.

2. For discussions of the role of the epithalamic poet as master of ceremonies, see Arthur Leslie Wheeler, *Catullus and the Traditions of Ancient Poetry* (Berkeley, 1934), p. 200, and Thomas M. Greene, "Spenser and the Epithalamic Convention," *Comparative Literature,* IX (Summer 1957), 215–228.

3. The term *amoebaean,* also spelled *amebean,* is applied to songs which are alternately or reciprocally responsive.

4. See Merrill, p. 130.

5. Quoted by James A. S. McPeek, *Catullus in Strange and Distant Britain* (Cambridge, 1939), p. 332.

6. The term is believed to relate to the ancient festivals of Fescennium, a town in Etruria, and to the rude jests and licentious verses that characterize the festivals. Christian James Fordyce describes the custom as representing "a familiar form of primitive superstition, the attempt, at moments of human happiness, to cheat the power of the evil eye, or *inuidia* . . . by 'taking down' the fortunate person." Fordyce provides helpful commentary and notes on all three marriage poems in his edition of the poems of Catullus (Oxford, 1961). See especially pp. 235–261 and 315–325.

7. Merrill, p. 105.

8. *Ibid.,* p. 109.

9.   Fordyce, p. 236.

10.   This outline has been influenced by Merrill and by Robinson Ellis, *A Commentary on Catullus* (Oxford, 1889), pp. 208–251.

11.   As Fordyce and others have pointed out, Hymen is dressed like the bride herself, with the *flammeum,* yellow shoes, and chaplet of flowers. *Luteum,* which is regularly used of the bridal color, is a reddish-yellow or yellowish-red, according to Fordyce, p. 240.

12.   E. A. Mangelsdorff, *Das lyrische hochzeitgedicht bei den Griechen und Romern* (diss. Hamburg, 1913), p. 36: "Das Gedicht führt uns also durch die verschiedenen Stadien einer Hochzeit, von dem kletischen Hymnos (an der Hochzeitstafel?) bis zu dem Augenblick, wo sich die Türen des thalamos schließen. Jeder Vers richtet sich an eine der Personen, die bei der Hochzeit agieren oder doch als agierend gedacht sind."

13.   Ben Jonson and Henry Peacham, in particular.

14.   The role of water-nymphs is discussed further in connection with the French epithalamia and those of Spenser, Chapters VI and IX.

15.   For these references, see Merrill, pp. 96, 98, 99, 101, 105, 110, 111.

16.   Fordyce, p. 254. See also Edward Fraenkel, "Vesper Adest," *Journal of Roman Studies,* XLV (1955), 1–8.

17.   Fordyce, p. 254.

18.   *Ibid.*

19.   Fraenkel, p. 8.

20.   Fordyce, p. 255.

21.   See Ellis, p. 280, and Wheeler, pp. 131–132. I am indebted to Patricia Wickham for permitting me to read her unpublished paper, "Unity in Catullus 64."

22.   McPeek, p. 147.

23.   Clyde Murley, "The Structure and Proportions of Catullus 64," *Transactions and Proceedings of the American Philological Association,* LXVIII (1937), 305–317.

24.   George Chapman translated brief passages into English.

25.   This outline is based in part on Merrill.

26.   See R. A. Mynors, *Catullus* (Oxford, 1960), lines 24, 34, 45, 46.

27.   *Ibid.,* lines 278 ff.

28.   *Ibid.,* lines 331–332, 334–336.

29.   *Ibid.,* lines 132 ff.

30.   See Fordyce, p. 317.

31.   Mynors, line 316.

32.   McPeek, p. 148.

33.   Mynors, lines 405–408.

34.   *Ibid.,* lines 50 ff.

35.   See Wheeler, p. 133.

36.   Greene, p. 221.

CHAPTER III

The Anti-Epithalamium

1. Inga-Stina Ekeblad in "The 'Impure Art' of John Webster," *RES*, N. S. IX (1958), 253–257, calls attention to several anti-epithalamic passages in English literature but does not give the phenomenon a label or indicate its relevance to the classical epithalamic tradition.

2. H. J. Rose, *A Handbook of Greek Literature* (New York, 1960), p. 187.

3. See Catullus 64:

   alta Polyxenia madefient caede sepulcra,
   quae, uelut ancipiti succumbens uictima ferro,
   proiciet truncum submisso poplite corpus.
   currite ducentes subtegmina, currite, fusi.

4. Translated by Ann Stanford.

5. Rose, pp. 234–235.

6. Several interpretations have been made of the fragments. See Rose, p. 201.

7. Tr. Thomas Love Peacock, *Works* (London, 1926), X, 53.

8. Tr. Ella Isabel Harris in *An Anthology of Roman Drama,* ed. Philip Whaley Harsh (New York, 1960), p. 209.

9. See *Troas,* tr. James Talbot (London, 1686), p. 33.

10. In *Titus Andronicus,* Lavinia is portrayed as turning the pages of Ovid's *Metamorphoses* to the tale of Philomela to give word of her plight.

11. *The Fifteene Bookes of P. Ovidius Naso Entituled Meta-morphosis,* tr. Arthur Golding (London, 1612). Compare Golding's translation of this passage with that of George Sandys, *Ovid's Metamorphosis Englished, Mythologiz'd and Represented in Figures* (Oxford, 1632), Book VI, p. 210:

> Pandion, Progne joynes
> To him in marriage. This, nor Juno blest,
> Nor Hymen, nor the Graces grac't that feast.
> The snake-haird furies held the sputtering light
> From funeralls snatcht, and made the bed that Night.
> Th'ill boading Owle upon the roofe was set.
> Progne and Tereus with these omens met:
> Thus parents grew. . . .

12. See *Lucans Pharsalia: Containing the Civil Warres be-tweene Caesar and Pompey,* translated by Spenser's friend, Sir Arthur Gorges (London, 1614). See also the translation of Thomas May (London, 1635).

13. May, sig. B8.

14. *Ibid.,* sig. C3v.

15. Douglas Bush points out that Marlowe's 818 lines carry the story as far as the first 281 lines of Musaeus; Chap-man's portion, of nearly sixteen hundred lines, corresponds to the remaining sixty-two lines of Greek. See Bush's com-ment on the alien material, p. 217, *Mythology and the Renaissance Tradition in English Poetry* (London, 1932).

16. In 1592 Abraham Fraunce remarked that "Leander and Heroes love is in every mans mouth." The tale was known in the Renaissance both from the *Heroides* and the many versions of Musaeus, including those of Bernardo Tasso, Baldi, Marot, and Boscan, according to Bush. Chapman's continuation places special emphasis on the anti-epitha-lamic motif. His translation of Musaeus was published eight years later in 1616.

17.   *Hero and Leander,* tr. Sir Robert Stapylton (London, 1647), sig. B5 and B5*v*.

18.   *Ibid.,* sig. B11.

19.   The epithalamic celebration of death is related to both classical and Christian epithalamic traditions. (See Chapter V.) Milton's "Epithaphium Damonis," for example, concludes with an epithalamic tribute to virginity primarily in the Christian tradition, but uses pagan imagery also.

    Similarity of elegy to epithalamium may be seen also in Spenser's "November":

> The water Nymphs, that wont with her to sing
>   and daunce,
> And for her girlond Olive braunches beare,
> Now balefull boughes of Cypres doen advaunce:
> The Muses, that were wont greene bayes to weare,
> Now bringen bitter Eldre braunches seare,
>   The Fatall sisters eke repent,
>   Her vitall threde so soone was spent
>   O heavie herse.

    Marvell's elegy for Lord Hastings, who died on the eve of his wedding, refers to "drooping Hymeneus ... Who for sad Purple, tears his Saffron coat, / And trails his Torches through the Starry Hall / Reversed ...."

20.   See *Poems,* Thomas Stanley (London, 1651), sig. C2 and C2*v*.

CHAPTER IV

The Rhetorical Epithalamium: Statius, Claudian, and Their Followers

1.   See D. A. Slater's introduction, pp. 26–27, to *The Silvae of Statius* (Oxford, 1908). For the epithalamium, see pp. 46–57.

2.   See *Claudian,* tr. Maurice Platnauer (London, 1922), pp. 205–215, and 231–267.

3.   See Chapter VII of this study.

4.   Cortlandt Van Winkle's introduction to his edition of Spenser's *Epithalamion* gives a brief review of the history of the epic epithalamium.

5.   Camillo Morelli, "L'epitalamio nella tarda poesia latina," *Studi italiani di filologia classica,* XVIII (1910), 347.

6.   Slater, p. 46.

7.   Cf. Catullus 61.

8.   Slater, p. 57.

9.   *Ibid.,* p. 51.

10.   E. Faye Wilson, "Pastoral and Epithalamium in Latin Literature," *Speculum,* XXIII (1948), 35–57.

11.   *Ibid.,* p. 38.

12.   Slater, p. 57.

13.   *Ibid.*

14.   Platnauer, p. 204.

15.   *Ibid.,* p. 247.

16.   *Ibid.,* p. 249.

17.   *Ibid.,* p. 251.

18.   *Ibid.,* p. 255.

19.   Platnauer, p. 263. The parting of the hair with the spear was a relic of marriage by capture.

20.   *Ibid.*, p. 263.

21.   *Ibid.*, p. 267.

22.   The *Fescennina* are pp. 231–239, Platnauer.

23.   This fescennine verse has something of the "May morning note" which C. S. Lewis describes in the later Latin epithalamia. See *The Allegory of Love* (Oxford, 1936), pp. 76–111.

24.   The union of streams, here representing two royal houses, becomes significant in the later tradition.

25.   See Gaspar Gil Polo's *Diana Enamorada*, tr. Bartholomew Yong and ed. Raymond L. Grismer and Mildred B. Grismer (Minneapolis, 1959). The poem opens:

De flores matizadas se vista'l verde prado,
    retumbe el hueco bosque de bozes deleytosas
    olor tengan mas fino las coloradas rosas,
    floridos ramos mueua el viento sossegado:
El rio apressurado
    sus aguas acresciente.
    y pues tan libre queda la fatigada gente
    del congoxoso llanto,
    moued hermosas Nymphas regozijado canto.

26.   Platnauer, p. 237.

27.   This had become a customary section of the epithalamium.

28.   In keeping with a wedding custom common in many cultures.

29.   Platnauer, p. 239.

30. *Ibid.,* p. 207.

31. See Chapter IX, the discussion of the "Aprill" eclogue of Spenser as an epithalamium. Hymen, as a shepherd in this epithalamium, seems to anticipate the role of Colin.

32. Platnauer, p. 215. The union of souls through kisses becomes a commonplace of Renaissance epithalamia, perhaps influenced by *The Courtier* as well as the epithalamic tradition.

33. Platnauer, p. 215.

34. Thomas M. Greene, "Spenser and the Epithalamic Convention," *Comparative Literature,* IX (Summer 1957), 216.

35. See *Ausonius,* tr. Hugh G. Evelyn-White (London, 1919), pp. 370–393, and intro., xvi–xvii.

36. *Ibid.,* p. 387.

37. *Ibid.,* p. 391.

38. *Sidonius, Poems and Letters,* tr. W. B. Anderson (Cambridge, Mass., 1936), pp. 200–211.

39. For Donne's use of the Phoenix, see Chapter XI.

40. Sidonius, pp. 220–241.

41. C. S. Lewis, p. 76, *Allegory,* remarks that in many ways Sidonius is more medieval than Claudian, and calls attention to the allegorical "houses" of Pallas Athena. The house of philosophy, Lewis says, is described in terms "that might have been used by Lydgate." Lewis translates:

Here sit the Seven Wise Men, the source and fount
Of more philosophies than I can count; . . .
Shut out, but near the door, the Cynics are,
But Epicurus Virtue keeps afar.

Sidonius's interest, Lewis comments, is not so much in the allegory as in the trappings—the effect of light and water, etc. "It is strange and bright places that he wishes to describe, not moral realities."

42.   Fifth century, before 439.

43.   See Wilson, pp. 43–46.

44.   In the view of William Matthews, unpublished lecture, October, 1961.

45.   Wilson, p. 45.

CHAPTER V

The Medieval Epithalamium and the Christian Tradition

1.   A detailed treatment of the history of the epithalamium in the Middle Ages is found in E. Faye Wilson's unpublished dissertation (University of California, Berkeley, 1930), "A Study of the Epithalamium in the Middle Ages: an Introduction to the *Epithalamium beate Marie virginis* of John of Garland." Miss Wilson's examination of the role of hundreds of neo-Latin epithalamia is invaluable to any student of the genre. This chapter is based in part on her work.

2.   See E. Faye Wilson, "Pastoral and Epithalamium in Latin Literature," *Speculum,* XXIII (1948), 45–46.

3.   The influence of the Psalms is especially evident.

4.   See *Claudian,* tr. Maurice Platnauer (London, 1922), p. 207.

5. Wilson, diss., p. 39. References in the notes which follow are to Miss Wilson's dissertation unless the *Speculum* article is specified.

6. *Ibid.*

7. *Ibid.,* pp. 8–16.

8. Wilson, *Speculum,* pp. 40–41.

9. This is the forty-fifth Psalm in the Authorized Version. The first three lines as quoted here are from the Book of Common Prayer.

10. The role of the poet as one who by his epithalamium can make his subject immortal also appears early in the pagan epithalamium. It recurs throughout the tradition; we recall the concluding line in Spenser's *Epithalamion,* the wish that his poem may be "for short time an endlesse moniment."

11. See St. Augustine, *City of God,* tr. John Healy (London, 1610), p. 648.

12. *Ibid.*

13. *Ibid.*

14. *Ibid.*

15. Hugh J. Schonfield, *The Song of Songs* (New York, 1959), p. 67.

16. *Ibid.,* p. 54.

17. Wilson, pp. 3–4. For an interesting interpretation of the "Song of Songs" in some detail, see the excellent book by Stanley Stewart, *The Enclosed Garden* (Madison, 1966), pp. 3–30 in particular.

18.   Morris Jastrow, Jr., *The Song of Songs* (Philadelphia, 1921), p. 81.

19.   *Ibid.*, p. 82.

20.   Wilson, pp. 18–21.

21.   *Ibid.*, p. 23.

22.   *Ibid.*, pp. 24–25.

23.   Christus ubique pii voce sonet populi
       Nulla per ornatas insultet turba plateas
       Nemo solum foliis, lumina fronde tegat.
       Net sit Christicolam fanatica turba per urbem
       Nolo profana pios polluat ambitio.

       Quoted by Wilson, p. 25.

24.   Wilson, pp. 28–29.

25.   Wilson, *Speculum,* p. 42.

26.   Wilson, p. 55.

27.   The Mozarabic liturgy is that of the Spanish Christians who kept their religion in a modified form during the domination of the Moors. See Wilson, p. 47 and footnote.

28.   *Ibid.*, pp. 49–52.

29.   *Ibid.*, p. 53. Richard Crashaw, *Carmen Deo Nostro* (Paris, 1652), "Prayer, an Ode, which was Prefixed to a Little Prayer-book Given to a Young Gentlewoman."

30.   Wilson, p. 55.

31.   *Ibid.*, pp. 177 ff.

32.   *Ibid.*, p. 182.

33.   Quoted from Matthew of Vendôme. See Wilson, p. 185.

34.   The 516-line epithalamium of Conrad of Hirschau is sum-
        marized and quoted at length by Miss Wilson, pp. 113–
        118.

35.   See Miss Wilson's discussion of the *Epithalamium* of John
        of Garland, pp. 214–330.

36.   *Ibid.,* p. 212. "Phyllis and Flora is the goliardic version of
        the classical epithalamium, and it may very well be a con-
        scious glance at the sacred epithalamium . . . . Instead
        of a hymn to the Christian God, it is a panegyric to the
        Love god."

37.   See Robert H. Case, *English Epithalamies* (Chicago,
        1896), pp. xiv–xvi, for a discussion of some of these
        works.

38.   Wilson, *Speculum*, p. 41.

39.   *Ibid.,* p. 42.

40.   *Ibid.,* p. 44.

41.   *Ibid.,* p. 46.

42.   Thomas M. Greene, "Spenser and the Epithalamic Con-
        vention," *Comparative Literature,* IX (Summer 1957),
        216.

CHAPTER VI

Neo-Latin and Continental Vernacular
Epithalamia of the Renaissance

1.   Many epithalamia mingle rhetorical and lyrical con-
        ventions.

2.   See Cortlandt Van Winkle's introduction to his edition of Spenser's *Epithalamion* (New York, 1926), p. 18.

3.   Some of these tendencies have been observed earlier in the classical poems.

4.   For a bibliography of these collections, see Van Winkle, p. 69.

5.   *Ibid.,* p. 18.

6.   See Robert H. Case's introduction to his anthology, *English Epithalamies* (London and Chicago, 1896), pp. xxiv–xxv, for discussion of these works.

7.   *Ibid.,* p. xvii.

8.   *Ibid.*

9.   *Ibid.,* p. xix.

10.   Quoted by Case, p. xviii.

11.   *Pontani Opera* (Venice, 1513), p. 195.

12.   See Ariosto's *Opere Minori* (Firenze, 1857).

13.   *The Familiar Colloquies,* tr. Nathaniel Bailey (London, 1733).

14.   Case, pp. xxiii–xxiv.

15.   Case, p. xxvi.

16.   George Puttenham, *The Arte of English Poesie,* ed. G. D. Willcock and A. Walker (Cambridge, 1936), p. 53.

17.   See *The Love Poems of Joannes Secundus,* ed. F. A. Wright (New York, 1930), pp. 216–237.

18. *The Love Poems of Joannes Secundus*, p. 236.

19. Both Carmen 5 and Carmen 7 of Catullus, the famous "kissing" poems, provide motifs for many epithalamia.

20. James A. S. McPeek, *Catullus in Strange and Distant Britain* (Cambridge, 1939), p. 152.

21. Case, p. xxi.

22. *Ibid.,* p. xxiii.

23. *Ibid.,* p. xxiv.

24. McPeek, p. 334.

25. Van Winkle, p. 19.

26. George Buchanan, *Scoti Poemata* (London, 1686).

27. C. Hagberg Wright, "Italian Epithalamia," *Edinburgh Review,* CCI (1914), 105–121.

28. See Thomas M. Greene, "Spenser and the Epithalamic Convention," *Comparative Literature,* IX (Summer 1957), 216.

29. Wright, p. 107.

30. *Ibid.*

31. *Ibid.,* p. 112.

32. *Ibid.,* p. 109.

33. Maud F. Jerrold, *Italy in the Renaissance* (London, 1927), p. 243, remarks that the feeling for antiquity is a notable feature of poetry generally at this time.

34.   Greene, p. 216, says, "Tasso wrote no formal 'epi-
        talamio,' but he did write thirteen nuptial poems . . . .
        These poems did not adhere strictly to the Catullan
        pattern but borrowed elements freely from that pat-
        tern."

35.   *Epitalami del Cavalier Marino* (Venice, 1628). The col-
        lection was first published in 1616.

36.   Gaspar Gil Polo, Bartholomew Yong, and Sir Philip
        Sidney are among those to use the nine-line stanza.

37.   *Le Rime di Torquato Tasso* (Bologna, 1900), III, 50.

38.   *Ibid.,* p. 90.

39.   See lines 20–23 and 83–85.

40.   *Ibid.,* p. 321.

41.   The effect of verbal legerdemain of this kind is discussed
        by Jefferson Butler Fletcher, *Literature of the Italian
        Renaissance* (New York, 1934), p. 319. "In Tasso's
        Gerusalemme Liberata," Fletcher remarks, "the over-
        abundance of conceits trivializes what was meant to be
        heroic."

42.   Tasso, p. 91.

43.   *Ibid.,* pp. 90–94.

44.   *Ibid.,* pp. 92–93.

45.   *Ibid.,* pp. 93–94.

46.   *Ibid.,* p. 353.

47.   *Ibid.,* pp. 50, 53.

48.   *Ibid.,* p. 497.

49.   The more conventional comparison is to the sun and the moon.

50.   Tasso, p. 498.

51.   *Ibid.,* p. 499.

52.   Marino, *Epitalami.*

53.   L'Abbé Souchay, "Discours sur l'origine et le caractére de l' épithalame," *Historie de L'académie royale des inscriptions et belles-lettres,* IX (Paris, 1736), 316.

54.   *Ibid.,* pp. 315–316.

55.   See Fletcher, p. 323.

56.   Giambattista Marino, *Poesie Varie* (Bari, 1913), p. 327.

57.   *Ibid.,* pp. 332–335.

58.   Marino, pp. 336–341.

59.   Marino, p. 340.

60.   Walter Starkie describes ancient marriage rites as practiced by Spanish gypsies, descendants of the band from Greece which in 1417 spread through western Europe. In "Raggle-Taggle in South Spain," *Uclan Review,* IX (Spring 1963), 12, he mentions their observing the ritual of the groom's mock capture of the bride. He describes also how the old woman, who in the ceremony is called the *picaora,* entered the bridal apartment on the morning after the consummation of the marriage and displayed to the guests evidence that the bride had been a virgin, whereupon the celebrated gypsy poem of virginity was sung.

61.   Marino, p. 341.

62.   Most of them wrote more than one.

63.   C. S. Lewis, *The Allegory of Love* (Oxford, 1936), pp. 77 ff.

64.   *Ibid.,* p. 75.

65.   *Ibid.,* p. 77.

66.   *Ibid.,* p. 82.

67.   *Ibid.,* p. 78.

68.   McPeek, p. 163.

69.   See discussion of the blazon in Hallett Smith's *Elizabethan Poetry* (Cambridge, 1952), pp. 26–27.

70.   See *Oeuvres complètes de Clément Marot,* ed. M. Pierre Jannet (Paris, 1868), II, 97.

71.   The frequent presence of the gamesome Cupids contributes to this effect.

72.   See *Oeuvres complètes de Remy Belleau,* ed. A. Gouverneur (Paris, 1867), II, 88.

73.   *Ibid.,* pp. 91–98.

74.   *Ibid.,* pp. 327–335. There is also a Latin version.

75.   See pp. 88, 98–100 as examples.

76.   Marguerite, sister of the king, was much praised for her learning and for her patronage of literature.

77.   McPeek, p. 155, comments on this.

78.   *Poésies Françaises et Latines de Joachim Du Bellay,* ed. E. Courbet (Paris, 1931), II, 429.

79.   *Ibid.,* p. 436.

80.   *Ibid.,* p. 441:

    Comme d'un vase ayant estroicte bouche,
      Lequel est d'eau remply jusques au bord,
      L'eau goutte à goutte, et à grand' peine sort,
      Et son passage elle mesme se bouche:
    Ainsi chantant este Royale couche,
      L'ayse qui faict de sortir son effort,
      Pour en sortir ne se trouve assez fort,
    Et d'un seul verse ma Muse a peine accouche.

81.   *Oeuvres poétiques de M.-C. de Buttet,* ed. P. L. Jacob (Paris, 1880), I.

82.   McPeek, pp. 159–184.

83.   Buttet, p. 138.

84.   McPeek, pp. 162–163.

85.   Buttet, pp. 60, 63, 64.

86.   *Euvres in Rime de Ian Antoine de Baïf,* ed. Ch. Marty-Laveaux (Paris, 1883), II.

87.   *Ibid.,* p. 352.

88.   *Ibid.,* p. 398.

89.   *Ibid.,* p. 316.

90.   Pierre de Ronsard, *Oeuvres Complètes,* ed. Paul Laumonier (Paris, 1931), IX. See pp. 75 and 84 for identification of the shepherds.

91.   *Ibid.,* pp. 91, 92.

92.   *Ibid.,* p. 95.

93.   *Ibid.,* pp. 85, 86.

94.   *Théâtre complet et poésies choisies de Jacques Grévin,* ed. Lucien Pinvert (Paris, 1922), pp. 219–237.

95.   Dan S. Norton in his unpublished dissertation, "Background of Spenser's *Prothalamion"* (Princeton, 1940), discusses the role of the dream-vision in the tradition generally.

96.   Ronsard, IV, 4.

97.   According to Ralph Marion Hester, Jr., unpublished dissertation (University of California at Los Angeles, 1963), pp. 1–4.

98.   For Poupo, see Hester, p. 1. For Spenser, see Alexander C. Judson, *The Life of Edmund Spenser* (Baltimore, 1945), p. 1.

99.   Hester, p. 1.

100.   *Ibid.,* p. 79.

101.   *Ibid.,* p. 105.

102.   *Poésies Diverses Tirées de La Muse Chrestienne de Pierre Poupo,* ed. Ernest Roy (Paris, 1886), pp. 85–101.

103.   Lewis, p. 77.

104.   Hester, p. 198.

105.   Hester remarks that the *Epithalame pastoral* is one of the few poems whose composition definitely antedates Poupo's conversion to Calvinism.

106.   Poupo, p. 92.

107.   *Ibid.,* p. 96.

108.   *Ibid.,* pp. 96–97.

109.   See Ernest Roy's introduction, pp. vii–viii.

110.   Poupo, pp. 103–111.

111.   *Ibid.,* p. 105.

112.   Similar references to the Salmacis bathing scene are discussed in connection with Spenser, p. 189, and Peele, p. 244.

113.   Poupo, pp. 107, 108.

114.   *Ibid.,* p. 108.

115.   *Ibid.,* pp. 109, 110.

116.   *Ibid.,* p. 121.

117.   *Ibid.,* p. 120.

118.   "A. E. B. Son Frere." This is the introductory sonnet as printed by Roy.

119.   *Ibid.,* p. 114.

120.   *Ibid.,* p. 115.

121.   Yver's work was published in eleven editions before the end of the century.

122.   All were court poets. Renée, daughter of Louis XII, was accompanied to Italy by a considerable French suite including the poet Marot.

123.   See *Gaspar Gil Polo, Diana Enamorada,* tr. Bartholomew Yong, and ed. Raymond L. Grismer and Mildred B. Grismer (Minneapolis, 1959).

CHAPTER VII

Critical Theory

1. The influence of the Greek and Roman teachers of rhetoric is summarized by E. Faye Wilson in Chapter I of her unpublished dissertation (University of California, Berkeley, 1930), "A Study of the Epithalamium in the Middle Ages . . . ," and by A. L. Wheeler in "Tradition in the Epithalamium," *American Journal of Philology,* LI, 3 (July 1930), 205–223. Part of Chapter VII appeared in my article, " 'High Wedlock Then Be Honored'—Rhetoric and the Epithalamium," *Pacific Coast Philology,* I (April 1966), 32–41.

2. Wilson, pp. 18–22, and 148.

3. *Liber* III, *Caput ci,* 150–155.

4. Thomas Wilson, *The Arte of Rhetorike* (London, 1553). Robert Hood Bowers in his introduction to a facsimile of the 1533 edition remarks that Erasmus's treatise was a popular text, available in English as early as 1530, translated from the Latin by R. Tavenour and entitled "A ryght frutefull epystle in laude and prayse of matrymony."

5. J. W. Lever in *The Elizabethan Love Sonnet* (London, 1956) argues convincingly that Erasmus's epistle, *De Conscribendis,* translated and accessible to the Elizabethan common reader in Wilson's book, had a profound influence on Elizabethan poetry. With its profusion of rhetorical analogies, the epistle furnished Wilson a model for his textbook and later writers with a pattern. Sidney drew on it twice in *Arcadia,* Lever points out, summing up the theme in the verse dialogue of Geron and Histor in the third eclogues, and in the prose discourse of Cecropia urging Pam-

ela to break her vows of chastity. Marlowe extended the doctrine in *Hero and Leander* to include not only human procreation and natural fertility but commercial expansion: "Treasure is abused when misers keep it ... Lone women, like to empty houses, perish." Marlowe portrays beauty as a capital asset, analogous to bullion and real estate: a miser's hoard and celibate's body are sterile; investors' capital and wedlock are fruitful, and required by the law of nature. Lever argues that the doctrine of increase, as presented by Erasmus, is a major concept of Shakespearean drama, *Venus and Adonis,* and the sonnets. Lever points especially to the use of the doctrine in the sonnets urging a young male friend to marriage. Such had been the original occasion of the *De Conscribendis.*

6.   George Puttenham, *The Arte of English Poesie,* ed. G. D. Willcock and A. Walker (Cambridge, 1936).

7.   See Chapter XI of the present study for discussion of Jonson's notes.

8.   *Medea,* tr. Sir Edward Sherburne (London, 1648). Sherburne includes twelve pages of notes describing ancient marriage customs and explaining the poem's references to Jupiter, Pluto, Lucina, Juno, Mars, Amalthea, Hymen, Venus, Lucifer, Jason, Bacchus, Apollo, Diana, Castor and Pollux, etc. He also explains geographical and astronomical references, cites Scaliger's comments on various matters, and quotes Hesiod, Catullus, and Martianus Capella, translating fourteen lines of Capella into English.

9.   Thomas M. Greene, "Spenser and the Epithalamic Convention," *Comparative Literature,* IX (Summer 1957), 218–219.

10.   Wheeler, pp. 211–212.

11.   *Dionysii Halycarnasei praecepta de oratione nuptiali,* sig.
N8. *(Per Theodorum garzen é graeco in latinū traducta.)*

12.   Wheeler, p. 211.

13.   Dionysii, *Praecepta,* sig. N8v and sig. 01, and Wheeler,
p. 211.

14.   E. Faye Wilson, p. 4.

15.   Scaliger on Catullus:

> Manes maximi & optimi poetae,
> Et quantum pote plurimum diserti
> Seu vos Elysiis Thalia campis
> Lentos dulcibus entheat susurris.

16.   Henry Peacham, *The Compleat Gentleman* (London,
1622), Chapter X.

17.   Scaliger, *Poetices, Liber* III, 154 ff.

18.   Thomas Wilson, p. 47.

19.   *Ibid.,* pp. 52, 55.

20.   Puttenham, pp. 50–53.

CHAPTER VIII

Early English Epithalamia

1.   Robert H. Case, *English Epithalamies* (London and Chicago, 1896), p. xxvii. Nearly every writer who mentions the
genre assumes that Sidney's is the earliest in English.

Some have excluded the works of Lydgate and Dunbar on the assumption that they are not "really" epithalamia because they are not Catullan lyrics.

2.   See *The Minor Poems of John Lydgate,* ed. Henry Noble MacCracken (London and New York, 1911). The editor titles the poem "Epithalamium for Gloucester" and gives a good account of the historical background, pp. 142–145. See also the notes, pp. 435–436.

3.   *The Poems of William Dunbar,* ed. W. Mackay Mackenzie (London, 1960), pp. 106–112.

4.   *Le Printemps D'Yver* (Paris, 1588). The collection was first published in 1572.

5.   See *The Poems of James VI of Scotland,* ed. James Craigie (Edinburgh and London, 1958).

6.   Theocritus, *Sixe Idillia* (Oxford, 1588), rep. A. H. Bullen, *Some Longer Elizabethan Poems* (Westminster, 1903), p. 125.

7.   Lydgate, p. 148.

8.   Lowly I prey / un to youre hyeghe noblesse
          Of my Rudenesse/not to taken heed
          And where so it be/this bille that yee reed
          Hathe mercy ay/on myn Ignoraunce
          Sith I it made/bitwix hope and dreed
          Of hoole entent/yowe for tyl do plesaunce.

9.   C. S. Lewis, *Allegory of Love* (Oxford, 1936), pp. 76–111.

10.   Dunbar, pp. 160–162 and 226–227.

11.   *Ibid.,* pp. 175–177, 230.

12.   Mackenzie includes this poem, pp. 178–179.

13.   These epithets were frequently used in later poetry of tribute to Queen Elizabeth.

14.   The translator is not to be confused with Sir Henry Wotton. Arthur Tilley in *The Literature of the French Renaissance* (New York, 1959), II, 182, says that only two copies of Wotton's translation are known, one in the British Museum and the other in the Bodleian. I am indebted to Marian Kaplan for calling the poem to my attention.

15.   See Mary Augusta Scott, *Elizabethan Translations from the Italian* (New York, 1916).

16.   Especially the motif of love as a battle.

17.   Yver, p. 320.

18.   Wotton, p. 307. For poem of Ariosto, see *Opere Minore* (Firenze, 1857).

19.   Wotton, p. 306.

20.   See *The Poems of Sir Philip Sidney,* ed. W. A. Ringler (Oxford, 1962), p. 93.

21.   Sir Philip Sidney, *The Defense of Poesy* (London, 1595).

22.   Thyrsis and Kala in other editions.

23.   See *Gaspar Gil Polo, Diana Enamorada,* tr. Bartholomew Yong, and ed. Raymond L. Grismer and Mildred B. Grismer (Minneapolis, 1959).

24.   See discussion of Erasmus's *De Conscribendis,* Chapter VII of the present study.

25.   Quoted by Ringler, p. 406.

26.   See Case, p. xxvii.

27. For detailed discussion of the possible relationships of these poems, see Kurt Wöhrmann, *Die englische Epithalamiendichtung der Renaissance und ihre Vorbilder* (diss. Coburg, 1936).

28. See Craigie's edition of the king's poems, pp. 134–136 and notes.

29. This suggestion is made by Allan F. Westcott, ed., *New Poems by James I of England* (New York, 1911), in his notes to the poem. Identification of the gods here is based on Westcott's notes.

30.   Torquatus uolo paruulus
                    matris e gremio suae
                    porrigens teneras manus
                    dulce rideat ad patrem
                    semihiante labello.

31. The six pieces are reprinted by Bullen; see note 6 above.

32. Douglas Bush, *Mythology and the Renaissance Tradition in English Poetry* (first pub. 1932, rev. New York, 1963), p. 54.

33. Bullen, p. 142.

CHAPTER IX

Spenser

1. In a letter to Harvey in 1580 Spenser mentions his work on *Epithalamion Thamesis*. He had completed the "Aprill" eclogue before that date and possibly had worked on his translation of the Canticle.

2. Pierre Poupo had written sonnets for his own marriage but no long epithalamium.

3. See the unpublished dissertation (Princeton, 1940) by Dan S. Norton, "The Background of Spenser's *Prothalamion,*" p. 8. Apparently Spenser invented the title, changing the prefix of *epithalamion* to *pro,* meaning "before in time or place."

4. For discussion of the possible extent to which Canto xi utilizes material from the lost *Epithalamion Thamesis,* see the *Variorum* Spenser, IV, 239–242.

5. The epithalamic passage begins with the fifth stanza from the end of the canto:

    > Than gan they sprinckle all the posts with wine,
    > And made great feast to solemnize that day . . . .

    The passage is reminiscent of both the classical and Christian epithalamic traditions. Kitchin suggests Claudian's *Epithalamium de Nuptiis Augusti* as a source (see *Variorum* I, 310), and Upton notes the allusions to the song sung at the marriage of the Lamb, Revelations 19: 6–7. Sidney's epithalamium may have suggested the lines in Canto xi:

    > Ne wicked envie, ne vile gealosy
    > His deare delights were able to annoy . . . .

6. *Three Proper, and Wittie, Familiar Letters* (1580).

7. See comment of Lotspeich, *Variorum,* IV, 276, and Thomas P. Roche, Jr.'s fine study of the third and fourth books of *The Faerie Queene, The Kindly Flame,* pp. 167–184 (Princeton, 1964).

8. In the *Prothalamion* the poet speaks in the first person throughout, and the refrain, "Sweet Themmes runne softly, till I end my Song," reminds the reader at the end of each

stanza that the poet is the speaker. More personal information is given here than in any of his other works. In Stanza 1 he expresses his own melancholy:

> When I whom sullein care,
> Through discontent of my long fruitlesse stay
> In Princes Court, and expectation vayne
> Of idle hopes, which still doe fly away,
> Like empty shaddowes, did aflict my brayne,
> Walked forth to ease my payne
> Along the silver streaming Themmes . . . .

In Stanza 8 he describes the journey of the swans:

> At length they all to mery London came,
> To mery London, my most kyndly Nurse,
> That to me gave this Lifes first native sourse;
> Though from another place I take my name,
> An house of auncient fame . . . .

In Stanzas 8 and 9, he describes Essex House as once the abode of Leicester:

> Next whereunto there standes a stately place,
> Where oft I gayned giftes and goodly grace
> Of that great Lord, which therein wont to dwell
> Whose want too well now feeles my freendles case
> But Ah here fits not well
> Old woes but joyes to tell . . . .

In the Thames-Medway canto the author speaks in the first person early in the epithalamium, expressing the wish that he may be able to tell the names of all the rivers who came to the wedding:

> All which not if an hundred tongues to tell,
> And hundred mouthes, and voice of brasse I had,
> And endlesse memorie, that mote excell,
> In order as they came, could I recount them well.

At intervals throughout the canto, the poet continues to remind us that he is speaking.

9.   *Epithalamion,* line 56. The Mulla is Spenser's name for the Awbeg river. The realism of the setting is evidenced by Renwick's comment, "There are good trout in Awbeg still." See *Variorum,* VII, ii, 464.

10.   See Norton for discussion of the literary traditions of topographical-antiquarian narrative, dream-vision, emblem, *impresa,* and masque as background for the *Prothalamion.*

11.   Generations of literary critics have extolled the *Epithalamion,* and many have suggested that its "triumphant fusion of many elements," to use the words of C. S. Lewis, is significant to its success. Cortlandt Van Winkle in the introduction to his edition (New York, 1926), p. 5, writes of its richness "in musical cadence, in joyousness of spirit, in vitality of language and thought, and in the exuberance and intensity of personal feeling." H. S. V. Jones in *A Spenser Handbook* (New York, 1930), p. 353, remarks on its "dignity of movement" and "formal pageantry." James Russell Lowell praises its "organ-like roll and majesty of numbers," and R. W. Church its "strong and harmonious government over thought and image, over language and measure and rhythm" (both quoted, *Variorum,* VII, ii, 645).
　　C. S. Lewis, p. 372, writes that with the perfection of the *Epithalamion* the "Drab" in English literature is completely purged away. He calls attention to the fescennine jollity of Stanza 14, the hushed sensuousness of Stanza 17, the grotesque night fears of Stanza 19, the realism of "those trouts and pikes" in Stanza 4. He notes the transformation whereby a small Protestant church becomes a Salomonic or even a pagan temple and at the same time a great cathedral of the old religion, with high altar, roaring organs, and crowds of hovering angels. The device which harmonizes all the different traditions, in Lewis's view,

is "the steady procession of the bridal day," the technique of Catullus 61. He concludes: "The intense desire for posterity (who will people not only earth but heaven) and the astrological connexion of this with the 'thousand torches flaming bright' above the housetops add not only a public but almost a cosmic solemnity to the poem; which remains, none the less, a thoroughly personal love poem."

W. L. Renwick in *Edmund Spenser* (London, 1925), pp. 204–205, characterizes the poem as a "perfect reconciliation of Italian form, Roman matter, Irish landscape, literary tradition, and personal emotion."

Thomas M. Greene in "Spenser and the Epithalamic Convention," *Comparative Literature,* IX (Summer 1957), 228, sees the *Epithalamion* as distinguished ultimately by its "amplitude," complemented with an elegant symmetry and an intricate harmony. Because the role of the bridegroom and the poet are fused, the wedding is seen from within, not without, and it is "above all a private emotional event." This kind of unconventionality is, in Greene's view, the most basic.

12. Most of these possible sources are cited by Van Winkle, pp. 89, 100, 107, *et al.* See also James A. S. McPeek, *Catullus in Strange and Distant Britain* (Cambridge, 1939), pp. 159–184, and 341–352.

13. See Wilson, pp. 40–64, for this work. It is true that the Muses are summoned in many epithalamia, however.

14. *The Poems of James VI of Scotland,* ed. James Craigie (Edinburgh and London, 1958), p. 134.

15. See discussion of Tasso, Chapter VI.

16. C. S. Lewis uses this expression.

17. *Poésies Diverses Tirées de La Muse Chrestienne de Pierre Poupo,* ed. Ernest Roy (Paris, 1886), pp. 85–101. The *Epithalame pastoral* antedates his conversion.

18. The most significant variation in Spenser's refrain has been much discussed by earlier writers. It is, of course, the change when night falls. Up to Stanza 17 the refrains are positive, on the general pattern of "The woods shall to me answer and my Eccho ring." In the remaining stanzas, except for the envoy, the refrains are negative, on the general pattern of "The woods no more shal answere, nor your echo ring." Spenser has thus taken the motif of the echoing woods—used by Claudian, Poupo, and other predecessors in the tradition—and worked it into a refrain with intricate variations. A. Kent Hieatt in his book *Short Time's Endless Monument* (New York, 1960) has presented a convincing argument on the time symbolism of the numbers in Spenser's poem. He sees the twenty-four stanzas of the poem as an allusion to the hours of the marriage day, and attaches special significance to the fact that the change in the refrain from day to night occurs in Stanza 17. On the day of the wedding (the longest in the year) and in the latitudes in southern Ireland where the marriage took place, the number of hours of daylight is sixteen and a fraction. Thus the seventeen stanzas with the positive refrain of the echoing woods indicate the seventeen hours of daylight, and the seven stanzas with the negative refrain—the woods no longer echoing—indicate the seven hours of darkness, in Hieatt's view.

  Poupo's use of the motif of the echoing woods bears a possible relationship to Spenser only because Poupo repeated the motif three times in the same poem. It seems possible that the *repetition* of the motif may have suggested its use as a refrain.

19. Roy, p. 87.

20. Roy, p. 95.

21. Roy, p. 112, "Epithalame de S. Bruneau et Nic. Le Bey."

22. Herford (quoted in *Variorum,* VII, ii, 275) labels the "Aprill" eclogue "a romantic rapture of eulogy to a virgin queen." Herford, Renwick, and others place this eclogue

in the tradition of the panegyric upon a monarch, citing Theocritus's Idyll 16 and Virgil's "Pollio" as ancestors. E. C. Wilson in *England's Eliza* (Cambridge, 1939), besides naming these forerunners, argues also that the poem combines courtly and learned conventions with the popular and native tradition of ballad and broadside, recalling too that the conventional encomium had been revived by continental poets to compliment princes of the Italian and French Renaissance. Wilson's discussion of Elizabeth as a bride and as Elizabeth Virgo, and the poems he quotes in relation to these subjects, are significant to the present study; Wilson does not, however, associate these tributes with the epithalamic tradition. See Wilson, pp. 5, 6, 26–28, 59, 76, 129–136, 163, 195–208, 213–215, and 218.

Josephine Waters Bennett in *The Evolution of "The Faerie Queene"* (Chicago, 1942), pp. 7 and 47, expresses the opinion that the poem employs the subject matter and tone of courtly entertainments and masques to provide a graceful compliment to the queen, who is "simply an English Diana, or Venus." Walter F. Staton, Jr., in "Spenser's 'Aprill' Lay as a Dramatic Chorus," *Studies in Philology* LIX, (April 1962), 111–118, sees similarities between the poem and the choruses in Ronsard's *Bergerie* in that both are inserted lyrics with varying line lengths, both imitate courtly entertainments addressed to a queen, and both reflect, though in different ways, the technique of the classical dramatic chorus. Staton points specifically to the "Avril" stanza of the French poets, and its variants, the stanza which took its name from a lyric in the 1572 edition of Belleau's *Bergerie*. Both of Belleau's epithalamia appeared in the *Bergerie*.

I think the "Aprill" eclogue may indeed be indebted to all these predecessors, but I am suggesting that it is more specifically indebted both in content and form to the long tradition of the epithalamium—classical, medieval, and Renaissance—and particularly to the epithalamia of the Pléiade.

23.   *Théâtre complet et poésies choisies de Jacques Grévin,* ed. Lucien Pinvert (Paris, 1922), pp. 220–237.

24.   See Chapter VIII.

25.   *Oeuvres complètes de Remy Belleau,* ed. A. Gouverneur (Paris, 1867), II, 88–98, and 327–332. *Oeuvres poétiques de M.-C. de Buttet,* ed. P. L. Jacob (Paris, 1880), I, 60.

26.   Pierre de Ronsard, *Oeuvres Complètes,* ed. Paul Laumonier (Paris, 1931), IX, 88.

27.   The *flammeum* of the bride in Catullus 61 and other Latin epithalamia is described as of a reddish-yellow color like flame. According to Robinson Ellis in his *Commentary on Catullus* (Oxford, 1889), p. 212, the *flammeum* was of large dimensions, sufficient to cover the whole person from head to foot.

28.   The complexion of the bride in Catullus 61 is described as follows:

> uxor in thalamo tibi est
> ore floridulo nitens
> alba parthenice uelut
> luteumue papauer.

Christian James Fordyce in his commentary on Catullus (Oxford, 1961), p. 252, remarks that the *parthenice* is presumably the white camomile which Pliny calls *parthenium,* and that the poppy is *luteum,* i.e., red.

29.   Among the pre-Spenser paintings which portray the shepherd's gift of a white lamb to the Virgin are those of Domenico Ghirlandajo (1449–1494) and Lorenzo Lotto (1480–1556), but there are many in this tradition. As I have pointed out in Chapter V, medieval epithalamia frequently describe the bride as a combination of Venus and the Virgin Mary. We recall that in Stanza 2 Spenser described Elisa as "without spotte." Here he refers to her as a "goddesse" but suggests her likeness to the Virgin Mary by the gift of the white lamb. Spenser's reference to the "younglings

cryen for the dam" is reminiscent of lines in Theocritus's epithalamium for Helen, "the suckling lambs/Desire the strouting bags and presence of their tender dams" (1588 anon. tr.). It is also reminiscent of Sidney's pastoral epithalamium, in which the poet wishes that "Father Pan" may make the offspring of the couple "in number like the herd/Of younglings."

30. *Poésies Françaises et Latines de Joachim Du Bellay,* ed. E. Courbet (Paris, 1931), II, 429.

31. Du Bellay, p. 438. See also the succeeding stanzas.

32. In Latin epithalamia the term for the ceremonial placing of the bride is *collocate.* In Catullus 61 the attendants are instructed by the poet to set the damsel in her place:

> [uos] bonae senibus uirus
> cognitae bene feminae,
> collocate puellulam.

Fordyce, p. 252, calls attention to the use of *collocate* as a technical term for such an occasion, as Donatus notes on Ter. *Eun.* 593 "deinde eam in lecto conlocarunt."

33. *The Silvae of Statius,* tr. D. A. Slater (Oxford, 1908), p. 47.

34. *Claudian,* tr. Maurice Platnauer (London, 1922), p. 213.

35. See the unpublished dissertation (University of California, Berkeley, 1930), by E. Faye Wilson, "A Study of the Epithalamium in the Middle Ages . . . ," pp. 113–118. See also Chapter V of the present study.

36. Pierre de Ronsard, *Les Odes* (Paris, 1952), IV, 216–217.

37. In Sappho the maidens are told to leave the door when the dawn shall come. See Chapter I. In Catullus 61, the virgins are told to close the door, that they have sung enough.

38.   Van Winkle calls attention to this, p. 38.

39.   See in particular Paul E. McLane's *Spenser's Shepheardes Calender: A Study in Elizabethan Allegory* (Notre Dame, 1961). See also the older study of J. J. Higginson, *Spenser's Shepheardes Calender in Relation to Contemporary Affairs* (New York, 1912).

40.   For background of these events, see McLane, Chapter II, "Alençon Courtship," 13–26; Chapter IV, "Elizabeth as Dido," 47–60; also "Chloris of 'Aprill,' " 346–348. See also Conyers Read, *Mr. Secretary Walsingham and the Policy of Queen Elizabeth* (Cambridge, 1925), pp. 1–117, and the same author, *Lord Burghley and Queen Elizabeth* (London, 1960), pp. 51–66, and 203–234.

41.   On December 5, *The Shepheardes Calender* was entered on the Stationers' Register by Singleton, and must have been published between December 5 and March 24, since the title page is dated 1579. See Alexander C. Judson's *The Life of Edmund Spenser* (Baltimore, 1945), p. 63.

42.   See John Stubbs, *The Discoverie of a Gaping Gulf . . .* (London, 1579).

43.   See McLane, pp. 13–26 and 47–60.

44.   In *Euvres in rime de Ian Antoine de Baïf,* ed. Ch. Marty-Laveaux (Paris, 1883), IV, titled "A Monsieur le duc d'Alençon" and opening with the words: "François fleuron François . . . ." The poem requests Alençon to patronize the arts as had his noble grandfather (François I).

45.   Agnes Arber, *Herbals, Their Origin & Evolution* (Cambridge, 1953), p. 127. Miss Arber points out that seven of the flowers Spenser uses, including pawnces, appear within sixteen pages in Lyte's 779-page book. Also see Miss Arber's article, "Edmund Spenser and Lyte's 'Niewe Herball,' " *Notes and Queries,* CLX, xiii, (May 16, 1931), 345–347.

46.   Lyte, p. 149.

47.   Hilderic Friend, *Flowers and Flower Lore* (New York, 1891), p. 396. The idea that flowers may convey a message, long popular, is expressed in John Donne's lines in Elegie VII:

> I had not taught thee then, the Alphabet
> Of flowers, how they devisefully being set
> And bound up, might with speechlesse secrecie
> Deliver errands mutely . . . .

Among the books which treat of the folklore and symbolism of flowers are J. Foord, *Flowers* (London, n.d.); Ernst and Johanna Lehner, *Folklore and Symbolism of Flowers, Plants and Trees* (New York, 1960); Henry Phillips, *Floral Emblems* (London, 1825); and Robert Tyas, *The Language of Flowers; or Floral Emblems of Thought, Feelings and Sentiments* (London, n.d.), which bears on the title page this message:

> How oft doth an emblem bud silently tell
> What language could never speak half so well!

48.   E. K.'s gloss to the flower passage seems redundant unless it is intended to convey some hidden meaning to the initiated. After remarking that "all these be names of flowers," he goes on, "Sops in wine a flowre in colour much like to a Coronation, but differing in smel and quantitye. Flowre delice, that which they use to misterme, Flowre de luce, being in Latine called Flos delitiarum."

49.   Arber, *NQ,* p. 345.

50.   Renwick edition of *SC,* p. 192.

51.   Line 92.

52.   There is the possibility also that the word *Chevisaunce*

may refer to Lord Burghley, who favored the marriage and was active in promoting it. See Read, *Lord Burghley and Queen Elizabeth,* for Burghley's role in the matter.

53. *Three Proper, and Wittie, Familiar Letters* (London, 1580).

54. Paragraph 3 of the first letter.

55. C. G. Osgood, *Spenser's English Rivers* (New Haven, 1920), pp. 70, 107.

56. Describing the bride, Venus says she is "worthy to have been born like me from the blue waters, and to sit in my car of pearl." See Slater's translation, *The Silvae,* I, 51.

57. E. Faye Wilson, "Pastoral and Epithalamium in Latin Literature," *Speculum,* XXIII (January 1948), 44.

58. E. K.'s gloss provides an additional clue that the "Aprill" is related to the epithalamic tradition.

59. See William Camden, *Britannia,* pub. Edmund Gibson (London, 1695). The preface states: "The verses which occur in Mr. Camden's text were all translated by Mr. Kennet of Corpus Christi College in Oxford. . . . Of all in the Book, the *Wedding of Tame and Isis* seems to run in the best vein; whether we look upon the Smoothness, the Thought, or the Composition. Who the Author of it was, is not certainly known; but if we should fix upon Mr. Camden himself, perhaps there would be no occasion for a second conjecture."

60. *Ibid.,* p. 264.

61. *Ibid.*

62. *Ibid.,* pp. 147–150. See also edition of William Camden's *Britannia* (London, 1789), enlarged by Richard Gough from the edition of 1607, in three volumes. The poem on Eliz-

abeth in both Latin and English is found in I, 152–153. The preface details the history of the several editions of the work from the time of its first publication in 1586.

63.   In 1595 edition see p. 147; in 1789 edition, p. 153.

64.   Stanza 45.

65.   Edward Westermarck, *A Short History of Marriage* (New York, 1926), p. 203, describes the ceremonial "feet-washing" and mentions that it prevailed in Northumberland. It is one of the many rites intended to avert ill fortune and dispel evil influences which Westermarck refers to as "prophylactic or cathartic rites." The idea long prevailed that the bride and bridegroom are in a state of danger, exposed to magical tricks or evil looks, or the attacks of evil spirits, and therefore stand in particular need of protection or purification. Among such rites are the bathing or washing of bride and bridegroom or sprinkling them with water, the lighting of fires and waving of torches, the disguising of the bride and bridegroom in clothing of the opposite sex, and the contracting of mock marriages with trees or animals or inanimate objects. For another reference to the ceremonial "feet-washing" of the bride, see the anti-epithalamic passage in Webster's *The Tragedy of the Dutchesse of Malfy,* discussed in Chapter XII of this study. The duchess is ordered to make herself ready for death, and the preparations are those a bride might make for her wedding:

> Strew your haire, with powders sweete:
> Don cleane linnen, bath your feete . . . .

66.   Stanza 47.

67.   Stanza 52.

68.   Osgood, pp. 68–69. Spenser apparently had personal knowledge of the Irish rivers, but the passage about the English rivers, in Osgood's view, "breathes in comparison a faint

odor of lucubration and bookishness," although Spenser knew some of the English rivers at firsthand. His catalogue of deities is probably based on Natalis Comes. See *Variorum*, IV, 242–247.

69.   James A. S. McPeek, *Catullus in Strange and Distant Britain* (Cambridge, 1939), pp. 160–184.

70.   *Oeuvres poétiques de M.-C. de Buttet,* ed. P. L. Jacob (Paris, 1880), I, 142.

71.   *Ibid.,* pp. 143–144.

72.   *Ibid.,* p. 148.

73.   *Ibid.,* p. 150.

74.   Stanza 52.

75.   Stanza 44.

76.   Stanzas 46 and 47.

77.   In Canto xi, Stanza 53:

> The which, more eath it were for mortall wight
> To tell the sands, or count the starres on hye,
> Or ought more hard, then thinke to reckon right.

The reference to Venus is in Canto xii, Stanza 2.

78.   In Catullus 61:

> ille pulueris Africi
> siderumque micantium
> subducat numerum prius,
> qui uestri numerare uolt
> multa milia ludi.

79.   Canto xii, Stanzas 1 and 2.

80.   Canto xi, Stanza 43. For Smith's comments see *Variorum,* IV, 333–334. See also pp. 311–312.

81.   Roche, pp. 167–184.

82.   *CCCHA,* lines 103–155. Book VII, Cantos 40–55.

83.   Lines 133–145. Also see lines 149–155.

84.   Stanza 42.

85.   Stanza 52.

86.   Lines 55–69.

87.   E. K., explaining that Rosalind is a feigned name, writes: "So doth Aruntius Stella every where call his Lady Asteris and Ianthis, albe it is wel knowen that her right name was Violantilla: as witnesseth Statius in his Epithalamium."

88.   Dan S. Norton in his unpublished dissertation (Princeton, 1940), "The Background of Spenser's *Prothalamion,*" pp. 124–127, describes the swans on the Thames. One writer of the time reported "three or four thousand tame swans. . . but I did not count them; I merely report what I heard." According to legend, Richard I brought the first swans to England from Cyprus, and they were always regarded as royal birds. *The Order for Swannes,* published about 1550, set forth the royal injunctions and common law concerning the birds. The Royal Swan-herd, supported by "the Kings Majesties Justices of Sessions of Swans," had jurisdiction over all the swans of the kingdom.

89.   *The Itinerary of John Leland,* ed. Thomas Hearne (Oxford, 1744–1745), IX, 1–108.

90.   Vallans' poem is printed by Hearne in Leland, *Itinerary,* V, v–xx.

91.   Lines 258–263.

92.   Leland, p. vi.

93.   Norton concludes: "When the *Prothalamion* is considered as a masque, all its elements seem integrated. Spenser's place in the poem becomes clear. Regarded as the dreamer of the vision, his position is justified so long as the poem follows the technique of the dream vision. Yet when that is abandoned, he remains as a character. It is necessary that he do so, for he is the presenter or 'truchman' of the masque. Like Ease in the *Maske of Cupid,* or Hymen and Reason in Jonson's *Hymenaei,* it is his function to introduce the masquers and interpret the action." I would add that this function is closely akin to the master-of-ceremonies role of epithalamists since Sappho and Catullus.

CHAPTER X

Chapman

1.   *The Poems of George Chapman,* ed. Phyllis B. Bartlett (Oxford, 1941), p. 8.

2.   See Robert H. Case, *English Epithalamies* (London and Chicago, 1896), pp. xxxv–xxxviii, for discussion of poems written for this wedding.

3.   Douglas Bush, *Mythology and the Renaissance Tradition in English Poetry* (New York, rev. 1963), p. 221.

4.   Bartlett, p. 11.

5.   *Ibid.,* p. 28.

6.   *Ibid.,* p. 161. The refrain is repeated in Stanzas 2, 3, and 4.

7.   See discussion of Catullus 62 in Chapter II.

8. Chapman's translation of Musaeus's *Hero and Leander* appears in *Homer's Batrachomyomachia, Hymns and Epigrams,* ed. Richard Hooper (London, 1858), pp. 207–235. It is reproduced from the 1616 edition and includes notes by the editor. The quoted passage is from p. 229, lines 388–394.

9. Bartlett, p. 137.

10. *Ibid.,* p. 154. This version follows the traditional tale of Hymen's winning of his bride as told by Servius and Boccaccio, but Chapman apparently used Cartari's account in *Imagines Deorum.* See Bush, p. 216.

11. Bartlett, p. 365.

12. Franck L. Schoell, *Etudes sur l'humanisme continental en Angleterre à la fin de la renaissance* (Paris, 1926). Quoted by Miss Bartlett, p. 10.

13. For an account of this marriage and its political ramifications, see S. R. Gardiner, *History of England, . . . 1603–1642,* II (London, 1883), 166–186, 304–363.

14. See lines 503–508, and 640–643 in Bartlett. For a brilliant clarification of Chapman's thesis in *Andromeda Liberata,* see Raymond B. Waddington's article, "Chapman's *Andromeda Liberta:* Mythology and Meaning," *PMLA,* LXXXI (March 1966), 34–44. Waddington argues that Perseus and Andromeda are to be considered types of Mars and Venus, thus indicating that Chapman wishes the story to be read as a *concordia discors* allegory. Certainly this is in keeping with the epithalamic tradition.

15. Bartlett, p. 327.

16.   See lines 501 ff.

17.   Lines 444 ff.

18.   Here are some of Chapman's variations:

> Haste ye that guide the web, haste spindles haste.
> Haste then who guide the web, haste spindles haste.
> Haste ye that rule the web, haste spindles haste.

19.   Lines 557–565.

20.   The last stanza of the "Parcarum" epithalamium, immediately preceding the "Apodosis," portrays the bridal couple's ascent to heaven to rule as stars:

> Starres ye are now, and overshine the earth:
> Starres shall ye be heerafter, and your birth
> In bodies rule heere, as your selves in heav'n,
> What heer Detraction steals, shall there be given:
> The bound that heer you freed shal triumph there
> The chaine that touch't her wrists shal be a starre
> Your beauties few can view, so bright they are:
> Like you shal be your birth, with grace disgrac't,
> Haste ye that rule the web, haste spindles haste.

Case, p. 83, remarking that Chapman is "well-nigh the obscurest of poets," paraphrases the stanza as follows:

Illustrious as ye are now, ye shall be stars in heaven hereafter, when your children ("your birth") shall rule here. Any scandal you suffer now will be compensated by glory there, where the bride's sufferance of a cruel tie, from which you freed her, shall be a glory to her. You are like stars in your beauty now; like them its light penetrates far. Your children will be like you; upon whose birth you must yet be prepared to find dishonourable imputations cast, though that birth is due to the noble course ye have taken.

CHAPTER XI

Jonson and Donne

1. All quotations from Ben Jonson are from the edition of his works ed. C. H. Herford, Percy and Evelyn Simpson (Oxford, 1925-1952). The comment here is from Jonson's notes to *Hymenaei.*

2. Stanzas 11, 12, 13 of the epithalamium in *Hymenaei.*

3. These lines are from the epithalamium concluding the masque for the marriage of Lord Ramsey, Viscount Haddington, and the Lady Elizabeth Radcliffe in 1608. Each of the seven stanzas has the same final line, "Shine, Hesperus, shine forth, thou wished star!" The final five lines of all the stanzas have the same motifs—Hymen's war, perfection, and Hesperus—and they are artfully varied from stanza to stanza.

4. From "Epithalamion made at Lincolnes Inne." See *Donne's Poetical Works,* ed. H. J. C. Grierson (London, 1938).

5. *Ibid.,* p. 136. From Stanza 2 of the song in Donne's *Ecclogue* for the marriage of the Earl of Somerset and the Countess of Essex.

6. Herford and Simpson, VII, 225.

7. The designations *Masque of Hymen* and *The Hue and Cry after Cupid,* given by W. Gifford, *The Works of Ben Jonson* (London, 1875, 1892) are used here although the masques were not thus titled in the first edition.

8. Herford and Simpson, VII, 210-229.

9. James A. S. McPeek, *Catullus in Strange and Distant*

Britain (Cambridge, 1939), pp. 191–207. McPeek remarks "No one who knows the original [meaning Catullus 61] can read the quasi-translation without impatience." The term "quasi-translation" does not seem to me to be accurate. Herford and Simpson call the poem: "a fine, sinewy adaption" of Catullus.

10. In Tasso's "Celebra le nozze del signor don Alfonso (d'Este) il giovine e de la signora donna Marfisa d'Este," 1578, line 93, the bride is described as "Sacra lieto trofeo . . . ."

11. In notes to the *Masque of Hymen*. See Herford and Simpson, VII, 226.

12. Herford and Simpson, VII, 220.

13. *Ibid.,* p. 226.

14. Lines 174–176.

15. Lines 116–119.

16. Lines 179–181.

17. Lines 130–132.

18. Herford and Simpson, VII, 210.

19. See Chapter X. We recall that in Chapman the goddess Ceremony leads Religion and is attended by Devotion, Order, State, Reverence, Society, Memory, Morality, *et al.*

20. Herford and Simpson, VII, 236–237.

21. *Ibid.,* VII, 240.

22. First printed in 1608 as *The Description of the Masque.*

23. The pun is on "maid-made": "Her, that would be a matron made."

24. *Ibid.,* VIII, 252–258.

25. Line 160.

26. Grierson, I, 127.

27. *Ibid.,* I, 141.

28. David Novarr, "Donne's 'Epithalamion Made at Lincoln's Inn': Context and Date," *RES,* VII, 250–263.

29. McPeek, p. 367.

30. Scaliger's section on the epithalamium includes a discussion of sacrificial rites. See *Poetices, libri septem* (Lyons, 1561), *Liber* III, *Caput ci,* 151–152.

31. See Chapter VI.

32. Donne's labels are not the same as those given by Ausonius, however.

33. J. B. Leishman, *The Metaphysical Poets* (Oxford, 1934).

34. Line 20.

35. In the St. Valentine's Day poem.

36. In the manner of Spenser's *Epithalamion.*

37. Lines 81–84.

38. See Herford and Simpson, p. 220.

39. Many critics have objected to the imagery here—Novarr sees it as more appropriate to the abatoir than the boudoir,

ignoring the fact that similar sacrificial imagery pervades Donne's sermons. I suspect the line would have been less offensive to Donne's contemporaries than to most modern readers. One modern critic who expresses approval of it is Adelheid Gaertner, in *Die englische Epithalamienliteratur im siebzehnten Jahrhundert und ihre vorbilder* (diss. Coburg, 1936). See pp. 10–15.

40.   Scaliger, III, *ci,* 150.

41.   Lines 25–30.

42.   The commonplace idea that the beauty of the bride blinds the onlookers appears in King James's fragmentary wedding masque of 1588. A soldier speaks:

>I whome no bloodie battells coulde effraye
>Am now become a simple womans praye,
>Bot what? no woman bot a Goddesse bright
>No shame to blinded be with such a light.

See *The Poems of James VI of Scotland,* ed. James Craigie (Edinburgh and London, 1958).

43.   Lines 91–96.

44.   Samuel Johnson, "Abraham Cowley," in *Lives of the English Poets* (Dublin, 1779–1781): "On reading the following lines, the reader may perhaps cry out—*Confusion worse confounded . . . .*" See p. 29.

45.   The doctrine of Erasmus's *De Conscribendis* echoes here.

46.   See *Claudian,* tr. Maurice Platnauer (London, 1922), p. 207.

47.   Donne does not call them shepherds.

48. Grierson, I, 131.

49. *Ibid.,* II, 94.

50. Lines 101–104.

51. Lines 204–207.

52.
> But, undiscerning Muse, which heart, which eyes
>   In this new couple dost thou prize,
>   When his eye as inflaming is
> As her's, and her heart loves as well as his?
>   Be tried by beauty, and then
> The bridegroom is a maid and not a man:
> If that by manly courage they be tried
> Which scorns unjust opinion, then the bride
> Becomes a man. Should chance or envy's art
> Divide these two, whom Nature scarce did part,
> Since both have the inflaming eye, and both the
>   loving heart?

53. Spenser's *Prothalamion,* Jonson's Weston epithalamium, and Donne's *Ecclogue.*

54. *The Sermons of John Donne,* ed. Evelyn M. Simpson and George R. Potter (Berkeley, 1953), VI, 316.

CHAPTER XII

Their Echoes Ring

1. See Thomas Dekker, *Satiro-mastix* (London, 1602), sig. B4. Dekker depicts Horace "sitting in a study behinde a Curtaine, a candle by him burning, bookes lying confusedly," muttering to himself:

To thee whose fore-head swels with roses,
Whose most haunted bower
Gives life and sent to every flower,
Whose most adored name incloses,
Things abstruse, deep and divine,
Whose yellow tresses shine,
Bright as Eoan fire.
O me thy Priest inspire.
For I to thee and thine immortall name,
In—in—golden tunes,
For I to thee and thine immortall name—
In—sacred raptures flowing, flowing, swimming,
                                    swimming:
In sacred raptures swimming,
Immortall name, game, dame, tame, lame, lame, lame. . . .

Asinius Bubo enters. Horace continues with his composition, and, eager for praise, reads a sample:

> Hor.   Marke now deare Asinius.
> Let these virgins quickly see thee,
> Leading out the Bride,
> Though theyr blushing cheekes they hide,
> Yet with kisses will they see thee,
> To untye theyre Virgin zone,
> They grieve to lye alone.
>
> Asini.   So doe I by Venus.

Asinius comments on the poem, and although his remark is a *double-entendre,* Horace is flattered, believing his poem is being praised as the best work he has yet done. Whereupon he asks, "You have seen my Acrosticks?"

Robert H. Case, in the introduction of *English Epithalamies* (London and Chicago, 1896), points out that Horace's "epithalamium" mocks a five-line ode in Jonson's *Poetaster,* Act III, scene i. In spite of his parody, Dekker himself may have had a hand in an epithalamium about this time, for one appears in a play on which he collaborated with Henry Chettle and William Haughton, *The Pleasant Comedy of Patient Grissil,* probably acted early in 1600. It is a brief "Hymeneus hymn," in the words of one of the characters, a tribute to Beauty and to the marriage-god—"Of wedlock, love, and youth is Hymen king." See *A Supplement to Dodsley's Old Plays* (London, 1853), printed for the Shakespeare Society, III, 83. The poem appears in Act V, ii.

2. See Robert Burton, *The Anatomy of Melancholy,* ed. the Rev. A. R. Shilleto, introd. by A. H. Bullen (London, 1893), III, 293–295.

3. For the principal university collections of epithalamia written for royal weddings of the period, see the Introduction and the Notes.

4. Burton, p. 293.

5. *Ibid.,* p. 294.

6. Case, pp. 54–64.

7. Henry, after the late prince, her brother. See Case, p. 59.

8. Lines 78–79.

9. Case, p. 65.

10. *Campion's Works,* ed. Percival Vivian (Oxford, 1909), p. 57. The poem is from the *Discription of a Maske, Presented before the Kinges Majestie at White-Hall, on Twelfth Night last (1607), in honour of the Lord Hayes and his bride . . . .*

11. James A. S. McPeek, *Catullus in Strange and Distant Britain* (Cambridge, 1939), p. 221.

12. See *The Complete Poetry of Robert Herrick,* ed. J. Max Patrick (Garden City, N. Y., 1963), pp. 76–81.

13.   *Ibid.,* Stanza 12.

14.   *Ibid.,* Stanza 14.

15.   Job, v. 26.

16.   Patrick, pp. 154–158.

17.   Stanza 5. The second pair of lines is from "The Entertainment: Or Porch-verse, at the Marriage of Master Henry Northly, and the most witty Mistresse Lettice Yard." See Patrick, p. 169.

18.   Edward Westermarck, *A Short History of Marriage* (New York, 1926), p. 195.

19.   Patrick, pp. 292–294.

20.   The last line is from Ovid, *Ars Amoris,* II, 152. See Patrick, 294.

21.   *Ibid.,* pp. 169–170.

22.   *Ibid.,* p. 287.

23.   Thomas Heywood, *A Marriage Triumph* (London, 1842, rep. for the Percy Society from 1613 edition). Heywood's work, in heroic verse, includes examples from mythology, St. Valentine as patron saint of the marriage day, and cherubim singing a nuptial hymn. A number of parallels with Ausonius are cited by Adelheid Gaertner, in *Die englische Epithalamienliteratur im siebzehnten Jahrhundert und ihre Vorbilder* (diss. Coburg, 1936), pp. 29–35. The following lines of Heywood are reminiscent of the description of the shield of Achilles in the *Iliad,* with the matrons standing in the doors admiring the bridal procession. (See Chapter I). Heywood describes the bride's coming forth:

> All eyes are fixed on her: the youthful fry
>   amazed stand at her majesty.

The nymphs and maids both envy and admire
Her matchless beauty, state and rich attire.
The graver matrons stand amazed with wonder.

24.   *A Marriage Hymne in Three Books* (1613). The author
says that at first he intended to make "only a short and
ordinary epithalamium but afterwards having considered
better of it . . . found it much fitter to divide it into three
bookes." Sample lines:

The gods of dancing, feasting, kissing, bedding,
Graces, and Muses came to make the wedding.

There is reference to union of rivers, Book II, p. 64.

25.   The complete title of the work (London, 1625) is *Epi-
thalamium   Gallo-Britannicum: or   Great-Britaines,
Frances, and the most parts of Europes unspeakable Joy
for the most happy Union, and blessed Contract of the
High and Mighty Prince Charles Prince of Wales, and the
Lady Henrette Maria, Daughter to Henry the fourth,
sirnamed the Great, late King of the French and Navarre,
and Sister to Lewis the thirteenth: Now King of the said
Dominions, Manifesting the royall Ancestors and famous
Progenitors of the Mighty Prince Charles, and the most illustrious Princesse, the Lady Henrette, Explaining the
sweete interchanges of Mariages, as have beene betweene
France and Greate Britaine. Presaging the destruction and
ruine of Antichrist, the establishment of the true Faith,
the propagation of the Gospell, the restitution of the Pala-
tinate, the overthrowing of the Enemies designes, the
erection of Peace, the increase of Plentie, and the generall
wellfare of all Christendome.*
         The dedication is "To the hope of his countrie, the
comfort of his father, the joy of his friends, the terrour
of his enemies, the most wise, valiant, and vertuous Prince;
the most high and mighty Charles, Prince of Wales, the
sole Sonne, and Chiefe solace of the most Potent, Prudent,
Pious, Learned, Peaceable, Warlick King James, King of
Great Britaine, France, and Ireland, &c." The poet apolo-

gizes for presuming to dedicate "such an indigested, immature embrio to your Highnesse . . . ." and refers to Charles as "the Conduit by which God conveys felicity not only to me, but millions of people." It is dedicated also to "George, Duke of Buckingham, Viscount Villers, Baron of Whaddon, Lord High Admirall of England, Justice in Eyre of all his Majesties Forests, Parkes, and Chases beyond Trent, Master of the Horse to his Majesty and one of the Gentlemen of his Majesties Bed Chamber . . . a chiefe instrument of hindring the mariage with Spaine, and furthering this with France, by which means you brought happinesse unto this Iland."

The wish for children is expressed in the language of Psalm 128, that "Shee being like a fruitfull Vine upon the wall-side, his children may bee like Olive branches round about his table," and the writer hopes that from Charles "shall spring princely sprigs." The bride is described as "a most excellent Virgin . . . likely to make a most blessed Yoake-fellow" and as "the Golden Chaine of Vertue . . . diamond . . . ornament of the world . . . Phoenix of her age."

The relation of man to wife is portrayed:

> She is but the vessell of which Hee is the Pilot; to be the Sun, when she is but the Moone, which must borrow light from his knowledge . . . . She knowes that She may be the crowne of the head, but She will not presume to be the head of the body . . . It is not hidden from Her, that Nature and Grace hath given man the superiority, that the strength of his body, the stoutnesse and courage of his minde, the stayednesse of his affections, the wisesome of his soul, the pregnancy of his wit, the dominion of his will, the soundnesse of his judgment, the ripenesse of his understanding, in a word, all the powers of his soule and the perfections of his body, doe pleade for and claime a Diadem of dominion and government over women, which are the weaker sex; She desires but to rest in his bosome, to be his heart, and not his head.

The author follows the rhetoricians' advice that equal space should be devoted to praise of the families of bride and bridegroom; he devotes six pages to the genealogy of the kings of England, and six pages to the ancestors of the queen. He expresses confidence that the bride will "open her brest to entertaine the truth, and unfold Her arms to embrace affectionately this our ancient Catholicke, Apostolicke, and reformed Religion." The main motif of the poem, apart from panegyric, is the "great hope, nay almost assurance, that not onely She, but millions will be brought and wrought to embrace the Christian faith, to favor and follow the true Religion, by the means of this happy union and blessed contract."

26. Andrew Willet, *A Treatise of Solomon's Marriage* (London, 1612).

27. *The Works of George Peele,* ed. A. H. Bullen (London, 1888, rep. 1599 edition *The Love of King David and Fair Bethsabe*).

28. Lily B. Campbell, *Divine Poetry and Drama in 16th Century England* (Berkeley, 1959), describes the development of literature based on the Bible as having three phases: (1) translation of the Bible into prose, and the poetic parts into English verse; (2) adaptation of Bible story to the various literary genres as they become current in secular literature; and (3) use of Bible story as foundation, ornament, or atmosphere in original creations. The development of the Biblical aspect of the epithalamium in English illustrates all the three phases Miss Campbell mentions. She calls attention to Peele's play as an example of a divine play in the tradition of divine poetry in which the epithalamium is treated as an ornament.

For other uses of the Salmacis motif in epithalamia, see *FQ,* Book VIII, Canto 46, and *Poésies Diverses Tirées de La Muse Chrestienne de Pierre Poupo,* ed. Ernest Roy (Paris, 1886), the *Epithalame de S. Bruneau et Nic. Le Bey,* p. 108.

29. George Wither, *Epithalamia, or Nuptiall Poems* . . . (London, 1612). The first edition is dated 1612, as the mar-

riage took place on Feb. 14, 1612–13. The preceding
winter had been very severe; see Frank Sidgwick's edition
of Wither's poems, I, p. 199. The poet describes the tempestuous and windy weather and asks his Muse the reason
for it. She explains that the thunder was Jove summoning
his legions, and the winds were the Tritons "sounding in the
deep" to warn the rivers and streams of "A match concluded, 'twixt great Thame and Rhine." Descriptions of
the preparations for the wedding, the shows and triumphs,
the sea fight and fireworks, and "what meditations the
mind may be occupied about when we behold them" occupy nine pages in the first edition, followed by the ten-
page nuptial song, two pages of comment by the poet on
his own role, and three pages of epigrams on marriage.
The poems, with notes, appear in Sidgwick's edition (London, 1902), I, 153–182, and 199–201, and also in editions
of the *Juvenilia* (London, 1626 and 1633), II, 451–483.

Francis Beaumont's work for the same occasion, *The
Masque of the Inner-Temple and Gray's Inn,* also has as
its central motif the marriage of the rivers, Thamesis and
Rhine. The "Device or Argument" begins: "Jupiter and
Juno, willing to do honour to the marriage of the two famous rivers, Thamesis and Rhine, employ their messengers
severally, Mercury and Iris, for that purpose. They meet
and contend: Then Mercury, for his part, brings forth an
anti-masque all of spirits or divine natures. . . ." The masque is reprinted from the original quarto (n.d.) in *The
Works of Beaumont and Fletcher,* ed. Henry Weber
(Edinburgh, 1812), pp. 324–343.

For Drayton's epithalamium of rivers, see his *Poly-
Olbion* (London, 1622), pp. 236–244, and the folding plate
which precedes it. On a map of the area, human figures
are pictured at the junction of the Thame and Isis, with
bride and bridegroom joining hands and being crowned, as
nymphs strew flowers and musicians play. An account of
the wedding of the Isis and the Thame, the poem may have
been suggested by Spenser's Thames-Medway canto of
FQ, but it is more closely related to Camden's Latin
poem; as in Camden, the union of rivers in Drayton's song
is a prelude to reference to the site as the home of Eng-

land's kings. See Chapter IX of the present study and the notes to the poem provided by J. William Hebel in his edition reprinted from that of 1622, *The Works of Michael Drayton* (Oxford, 1931–1941). In Hebel's edition the poem appears in IV, 302–311, and the notes in V, 238.

30.   *The Muses Elizium* (London, 1630), p. 69.

31.   *MND*, V, ii.

32.   *Tempest*, IV, i.

33.   *AYLI*, V, iv.

34.   *R & J*, III, ii.

35.   John Webster, *The Tragedy of the Dutchesse of Malfy* (London, 1623), Act IV, scene ii, sig. I4.

36.   Westermarck, p. 203, discusses the ritualistic "feet-washing."

37.   See Chapter III.

38.   Case, xii, see *Seneca His Tenne Tragedies Translated into English* (London, 1581), pp. 119–140.

39.   *Medea, A Tragedie,* Englished by E. S. (London, 1648).

40.   See McPeek, p. 376.

41.   See Miss Gaertner's comments on this group, pp. 36–50.

42.   Case, p. 51.

43.   Besides his elaborate *Marriage Triumphe,* Heywood wrote three short marriage poems which appeared in *Pleasant Dialogs and Dramas* (London, 1637). Two are acrostics on the names of the bride. Sylvester's acrostic

on the name of Martha Nicolson appeared among other original poems with his translation of Du Bartas, 1621.

44.   *Poems of Thomas Carew,* ed. Rhodes Dunlap (Oxford, 1949), p. 79. Carew's poem is a prolonged conceit on the effect of the storm on the wedding day. The usual conventions are altered, with the Sun hiding his face so that his beams will not compete with the shining face of the bride, which outshines him. He dares only to spy on her, peeping between the clouds, like a masquer going to a feast. The winds proclaim that all sighs and tears have been assigned to them by the cheerful bridegroom. There are tempests in the air, but eternal calm in the marriage.

45.   Louis L. Martz in *The Poetry of Meditation* (New Haven and London, rev. 1962), p. 140, points to the use of the procedure for a "contemplation of our state in our death-bed" by John Donne in his *Second Anniversary:* "Thinke thy selfe labouring now with broken breath," "Thinke thee laid on thy death-bed, loose and slacke," "Thinke thy selfe parch'd with fevers violence," "Thinke that thou hear'st thy knell," "Thinke Satans Sergeants round about thee bee," "Thinke thy friends weeping round," etc. Carew uses the technique as a contemplation of the nuptial bed:

> But ere thou feed, that thou may'st better taste
> Thy present joyes, think on thy torments past:
> Think on the mercy freed thee, think upon
> Her vertues, graces, beauties, one by one.
> So shalt thou relish all, enjoy the whole
> Delight of her fair body, and pure soul.

The Platonic exchange-of-souls motif of Chapman and Donne appears also in Carew's "An Hymeneal Dialogue," echoing Castiglione's doctrine in *The Courtier* that "the spirits meet together and in that sweet encounter the one taketh the other's nature and quality." See the chorus in Carew's poem, p. 66, in Dunlap's edition:

> O blest dis-union that doth so
> Our bodies from our souls divide
> As two do one, and one four grow
> Each by contraction multiplied. . . .

46. See Francis Quarles, *Argalus and Parthenia* (London [1632]), Book III, 106.

47. Miss Gaertner notes this, p. 83, and attributes it to the fact that Quarles is a Christian poet.

48. The "Epithalame . . ." appears in *Divine Poems* (London, 1643), pp. 388–430. Poetic versions of parts of the Canticle appear throughout the *Emblemes*. In this connection, Christopher Harvey's translation of the 45th Psalm, entitled "The Rhetorick of the Heart," is also of interest. See *The School of the Heart* (London, 1676), pp. 193–194.

49. Vaughan's Works, ed. L. C. Martin (Oxford, 1914). "To the Best and Most Accomplished Couple . . ." is marked by his characteristic images of brilliance and light, and the "peculiar quiet power" which Bush has noted:

> Blessings as rich and fragrant crown your heads
>   As the mild heaven on roses sheds. . . .
> Fresh as the hours may all your pleasures be,
>   And healthful as eternity!
>   Sweet as the flowers' first breath, and close
>   As th' unseen spreadings of the rose. . . .
> Like the day's warmth may all your comforts be,
>   Untoiled for, and serene as he;
>   Yet free and full as is that sheaf
>   Of sunbeams gilding every leaf. . . .

50. *The Poems English, Latin, and Greek of Richard Crashaw,* ed. L. C. Martin (Oxford, 1927), p. 406. Crashaw's epithalamium begins as a burlesque elegy for "a matchlesse maydenhead that now is dead," with the poet summoning as mourners a row of "virgin Tapers of pure waxe made in

the Hive of Love," as yet unlighted by Hymen's flame. The maidenhead is described:

> A fine thinn negative thing it was,
> a nothing with a dainty name.

Like a vain woman admiring herself in the glass, it preens its feathers, and regards itself as "a selfe crownd King: a froward flower," filled with pride. It is really, however, the Phoenix, whose greatest nobility is in death. Despite the fantastic themes, the poem is delicate, and meticulously constructed. See the comments of Mary Ellen Rickey, *Rhyme and Meaning in Richard Crashaw* (Lexington, Ky., 1961), p. 30.

51. *Marvell's Poems and Letters,* ed. H. N. Margoliouth (Oxford, 1927), I, 119–123.

52. See *Domiduca Oxoniensis* (Oxford, 1662) for sixteen English poems illustrating these motifs. The collection also includes about a hundred poems in other languages, including Latin, Greek, Hebrew, and Persian.

53. *The Poems of John Oldham,* ed. Bonamy Dobree (So. Ill. Uni. Press, 1960), pp. 244–247.

54. For excerpt from Dryden's translation of Theocritus 18, see p. 367.
    Matthew Prior's first published work, according to H. Bunker Wright and Monroe K. Spears, *The Literary Works of Matthew Prior* (Oxford, 1959), was a Latin epithalamium appearing in *Hymenaeus Cantabrigiensis* in 1683. His four epithalamia in English are more indebted to Virgil, Chaucer, Spenser, and Milton than to Catullus, Statius, Claudian, or the rhetoricians. His first and best is the eighty-four-line poem for the marriage in 1685 of his patron, Charles Sackville, sixth Earl of Dorset, a pastoral singing match between Damon and Lycidas, with alternating symmetrical stanzas. Although the poem at first portrays Venus as queen of harmony and love, who

brought order out of chaos, her power gives way to that of the Christian God, "Thou Almighty King of Heav'n and Love." The Venus motif appears also in his epithalamium written in 1690, "A Hymn to Venus, upon a Marriage," which declares the power of love to bring order out of chaos, and faith that marriage may "defeat the conquest of the Grave." The main theme of his epithalamium in 1688 for the marriage of Charles Montagu (who had collaborated with him in *The Hind and the Panther Transvers'd)* is the poet's distress at losing his friend, an idea which appeared earlier in the epithalamium of Areodatus Seba, French Latinist of the sixteenth century. (See Chapter IV.) His shortest and last nuptial poem, appearing in 1704, wishes that the couple's wedding night may be like the night when Jove disguised himself as Amphitryon, husband of Alcmena, seduced her, and made Nature prolong the darkness to cover the space of three nights.

55.   Settle apparently began in the eighties and continued for many years to write eulogistic poems for important occasions in the lives of distinguished persons—funerals, births, returns from travel, recoveries from sickness, and weddings. A typical binding, that for the wedding poem of Edmund Morris in 1721, is of red morocco, the cover displaying a large coat of arms with elaborate border of gold, flowers, Cupid's heads, and flying angels blowing trumpets. Samuel Johnson pointed out (in *Idler,* No. 12) that Settle had a standing epithalamium "of which only the first and last leaves were varied occasionally, and the intermediate pages were, by general terms, left applicable alike to every character." In his bibliography of Settle's works, F. C. Brown lists five epithalamia which are identical (except for title page and the page which treats of the couple's illustrious ancestry). The five are for the weddings of Westfield, Ironmonger, Drake, Watts, and Green. I have compared the Drake poem with three others which Brown does not list —Cobham, Littleton, and Morris—and find it identical with them also except for the pages cited and an occasional word which may have been altered by the printer.

56.   Quoted from the Edmund Morris epithalamium (London, 1721).

57.   More than a hundred epithalamia, including these from the twentieth century, appear in my anthology, *High Wedlock Then Be Honoured* (The Viking Press, Inc., New York, 1970).

Index